Public Service Improvement

Public Service Improvement

Theories and Evidence

Edited by

Rachel Ashworth, George Boyne, and Tom Entwistle

OXFORD
UNIVERSITY PRESS

OXFORD
UNIVERSITY PRESS

Great Clarendon Street, Oxford OX2 6DP

Oxford University Press is a department of the University of Oxford.
It furthers the University's objective of excellence in research, scholarship,
and education by publishing worldwide in

Oxford New York

Auckland Cape Town Dar es Salaam Hong Kong Karachi
Kuala Lumpur Madrid Melbourne Mexico City Nairobi
New Delhi Shanghai Taipei Toronto

With offices in

Argentina Austria Brazil Chile Czech Republic France Greece
Guatemala Hungary Italy Japan Poland Portugal Singapore
South Korea Switzerland Thailand Turkey Ukraine Vietnam

Oxford is a registered trade mark of Oxford University Press
in the UK and in certain other countries

Published in the United States
by Oxford University Press Inc., New York

© Oxford University Press, 2010

The moral rights of the authors have been asserted
Database right Oxford University Press (maker)

First published 2010

British Library Cataloguing in Publication Data
Data available

Library of Congress Cataloging in Publication Data
Data available

Typeset by SPI Publisher Services, Pondicherry, India
Printed in Great Britain
on acid-free paper by
MPG Books Group, Bodmin and King's Lynn

ISBN 978–0–19–954547–6 (Hbk.)
      978–0–19–954548–3 (Pbk.)

1 3 5 7 9 10 8 6 4 2

CONTENTS

LIST OF CONTRIBUTORS

Rhys Andrews is a Research Fellow in Cardiff Business School, Cardiff University. His primary research interests are in strategic management, organizational environments, and public service performance. He contributed to *Public Service Performance: Measurement and Management* (Cambridge University Press, 2006). He has also published articles in *Journal of Public Administration Research and Theory, Public Administration, Public Administration Review,* and other journals.

Rachel Ashworth is a Reader in Public Services Management based at Cardiff Business School. Her research interests include performance improvement and public services, organizational accountability across the public sector and the application of institutional theory to public service reform. She has published in a number of refereed journals including: *Public Administration, Journal of Public Administration Research and Theory, Journal of Management Studies, Policy and Politics, Government and Policy,* and *Public Management Review.*

George A. Boyne is Professor of Public Sector Management at Cardiff Business School. His books include *Evaluating Public Management Reforms* (Open University Press, 2003) and *Perspectives on Public Service Performance: Measurement and Management* (Cambridge University Press, 2006). He has also published over 110 articles in academic journals such as *Administration and Society, Journal of Management Studies, Journal of Public Administration Research and Theory, Public Administration,* and *Public Administration Review.* He has obtained, as principal or co-applicant, research funding of over £6 million from bodies including the Economic and Social Research Council, the Leverhulme Trust, the Joseph Rowntree Foundation, and UK central government departments. He is an Associate Editor of the *British Journal of Management* and the *Journal of Public Administration Research and Theory,* and President-Elect of the US Public Management Research Association. He has acted as an adviser to UK bodies such as the Audit Commission, the National Audit Office, and the Local Government Association, and is a member of the UK Economic and Social Research Council Grants Board.

James Downe is a Senior Research Fellow at Cardiff Business School. Current research interests include issues relating to the local government modernisation agenda including organizational learning, inspection, political leadership, and service improvement. He is currently working on an evaluation of local government policy for the Welsh Assembly Government and a project assessing the impact and effectiveness of the ethical framework in English local government. James has a background in researching electoral issues in local government and recently published a co-authored book entitled *One Vote, One Value: electoral re-districting in English local government.* He has had papers published in a number of refereed journals including: *Public Administration, Environment and Planning C: Government and Policy, Policy and Politics* and *Public Management Review.*

Tom Entwistle is a Senior Lecturer in Public Policy and Management and Director of Cardiff's Masters in Public Administration programme. His research interests lie in the areas of partnership, local governance, central-local relations, and the policy process. He is currently working on an evaluation of local government policy for the Welsh Assembly Government, having previously worked on a number of studies for UK central government. He has been published in a number of refereed journals including: *Public Administration, Environment and Planning, Policy* and *Politics* and *Urban Studies.*

Julian Gould-Williams is a Senior Lecturer in Human Resource Management at Cardiff Business School. His research interests focus on exploring the relationship between HRM practice and individual and organisational performance outcomes in the public sector. His earlier work focused on the effects of management practice on employee outcomes and customer satisfaction in the service sector. He has published in *Public Administration, Public Administration Review, Public Management Review, Administration and Society, International Journal of Human Resource Management, British Journal of Industrial Relations,* and the *British Journal of Management.*

Nicolai Petrovsky is a Research Fellow at Cardiff Business School. His main research interests are the performance of bureaucracies in new and established democracies. He has published articles in *Journal of Politics, Public Administration, Public Money and Management,* and *Defence and Peace Economics.*

Steve Martin is Professor of Public Policy and Management at Cardiff Business School and the Director of the Centre for Local and Regional Government Research. His research interests are in the evaluation of public policy and public service improvement. He has directed a series of major research projects for EU, UK, and other governments attracting more than £10 million in external research funding. He has published widely in leading academic journals including *Public Administration, Policy and Politics, Government and Policy,* the *British Journal of Management,* and *Public Management Review.* He is a member of the Editorial Board of *Public Money and Management* and *Local Government Studies.* His latest book *Public Services Inspection in the* UK was published in 2008.

Richard M. Walker is a Professor of Public Management and Policy at Cardiff University (School of City and Regional Planning). He is also Professor at the Centre of Urban Planning and Environmental Management at the University of Hong Kong. Richard's research interests are in the determinants of performance in public organizations, with particular reference to strategy and innovation. He has raised over £4 million in research grants as principle or co-investigator from bodies including the ESRC, JRF, British Academy, and government departments. He was awarded a Fellowship by the Advanced Institute for Management Research in 2003. His books include *Public Service Performance* (2007), *The New Managerialism and Public Service Professions* (2005) and *Evaluating Public Management Reforms* (2003). Research articles have been published in *Administration and Society*, *Journal of Public Administration Research and Theory*, *Public Administration*, and *Public Administration Review*. Richard has also acted as an advisor to bodies including the Audit Commission and the OECD.

1 Theories of Public Service Improvement: An Introduction

George Boyne, Tom Entwistle, and Rachel Ashworth

Introduction

It is commonplace for public management scholarship to point to waves of reform reshaping public service delivery across the globe (Hood 2000; Pollitt and Bouck-aert 2004). In such a way the tools of the 'new public management' have been widely described as challenging the assumptions and practices of traditional public administration (Hood 1991). The move from government to 'governance' is used to chart the 'hollowing out' of the state and the rise of increasingly fragmented networks of public service delivery organizations (Rhodes 1996; Stoker 1998). More recently, scholars have sought to combine these descriptive endeavours by pointing variously to a 'new public service', 'public value management', or 'new public governance' as heralding the next chapter in the history of public management reform (Denhardt and Denhardt 2000; Stoker 2006; Osborne 2006).

While scholars rightly question the suitability of these labels—considering, for example, whether the new public management really was new and in turn whether it has been replaced or changed—the prominence of the individual ingredients which make up these reforms is undeniable (Entwistle, Marinetto, and Ashworth 2007; O'Flynn 2007). The public management journals contain many detailed studies of competition, regulation, leadership, partnership, in-novation, and so forth. The reasoning behind the introduction of these reforms is as debated as the labels given to them. Some identify the very global character of these changes as rooted in neo-liberal hegemony of the last three decades or so (Geddes 2000). Others point to policy advocacy, lesson drawing, and imitation between countries (Common 1998). Still others consider the indi-vidual incentives as perceived by senior policy-makers (Dunleavy 1986).

The suggestion that these reforms might genuinely have been introduced to deliver public service improvement has received rather less attention in the literature. This is surprising because it is this rationale that very often provides the official justification for the introduction of these radical changes. There are, indeed, good instrumental reasons to think that policy-makers might be sincerely committed to the improvement agenda. Improved public services promise, for example, to enhance public welfare, reduce public expenditure, promote economic growth, and, of course not the least, boost the electoral prospects of political incumbents.

When viewed, however, from the service improvement perspective the public management reform agenda has moved faster than academic theory and evidence. Despite calls for evidence-based policy and practice (Boaz et al. 2006, 2008), few of the policies that have been adopted have been underpinned by a clear causal logic or a body of supportive empirical results. Similarly, although perhaps surprisingly, little of the academic work focused on these reforms has sought to test claims that particular reforms have actually delivered service improvement (Pollitt 2000). The vast majority of public management scholarship considers the improvement question only implicitly, focusing instead on the political and organizational implications of particular policy initiatives.

The purpose of this book is to take a step back from the very detailed debates about particular policies which prevail in different sectors and consider the theoretical and empirical underpinning of public management reforms as improvement mechanisms. What is their theoretical basis? Do predictions of 'improvement' flow directly from those assumptions? Is the expectation that the reforms will lead to better services supported by empirical evidence? We consider these questions by identifying and unpacking the theoretical basis of a range of strategies for service improvement. We review the results of empirical evaluations of public service reforms from the developed world, drawing in addition, on a range of evaluations conducted by the authors of this book, both individually and collectively over the last ten years. These 'Cardiff studies of public service improvement' provide a unique basis for evaluating the theoretical and empirical validity of public management reforms.

In this introductory chapter we deal with three main issues. First, we consider the meaning of the term 'public service improvement'. We identify a variety of interpretations of improvement and suggest that individual reforms may have contradictory effects and that whole programmes of reform are almost certain to do so. Second, what does a 'good' theory of public service improvement look like? We argue that a valid theory should have clear assumptions and a consistent causal logic, an explicit description of the mechanisms of improvement, and specific predictions not only about the consequences that will be produced, but also about the circumstances under which these are likely to occur. Third, we describe the 'Cardiff studies of public service improvement' which, together with a review of evidence from research conducted across the developed world, provide us with our evidence base. Finally, we summarize the reform mechanisms that we focus upon in this book, and provide an overview of its structure and content.

What is public service improvement?

Public service improvement can be defined relatively easily in conceptual terms. Boyne describes it as 'a closer correspondence between perceptions of actual and desired standards of public services' (Boyne 2003*a*, p. 223). Unfortunately the measurement of 'actual and desired standards' is far from straightforward. It is possible, though, to identify three approaches to the measurement of standards in the literature.

The outcome or 'goal attainment model' is premised on the assumption that all public services might reasonably be expected to fulfil policy goals of one form or another (Amirkhanyan, Kim, and Lambright 2008, p. 328). Health services are provided to sections of society who would not otherwise purchase them on the assumption that a healthier population will benefit us all both socially and economically. The outcome-focused approach to service improvement suggests that changing performance, and with it the possibility of improvement, should be judged in terms of the realization of outcomes framed in specific policy interventions. In such a way the goal or purpose of a health service might be to raise the standards of the population's physical well-being, suggesting that improvement could be assessed by examining indicators of morbidity and mortality. Certainly the literature on organizational effectiveness in the public sector draws heavily on this model. Rainey and Steinbauer (1999, p. 13), for example, argue that a public agency is more effective if it 'achieves the mission as conceived by the organization and its stakeholders, or pursues achievement of it in an evidently successful way'.

There are however at least two significant difficulties with the outcome-focused approach to defining and measuring service improvement. First, some policies and services may not have explicitly articulated formal goals. Indeed goal ambiguity is often identified as one of the defining features of public sector organizations (Rainey 1989, 1993). Reflecting the compromises of the political process, formal goals are likely to constitute generic mission statements such as to 'increase the health of the nation' rather than concrete objectives. However, even where desired outcomes can be defined in measurable terms the outcome-focused approach is presented by further perhaps more significant problems of attribution and time lags (Boyne 2003, p. 216; Pollitt 1995). There is, for example, very good evidence that stopping smoking improves health and reduces mortality. But while improvements in the mortality rate may reasonably be regarded as the final outcome of a smoking cessation service, outcomes of this sort do not provide a very good measure of the performance of such a service, for the simple reason that smoking is only one of a huge number of determinants of mortality, many of which operate over very lengthy timescales. Even if studies can be framed over a sufficient time period to capture the health benefits of smoking cessation, smokers may have stopped smoking without recourse to the cessation service or indeed have continued to smoke but nonetheless become healthier in other ways.

Difficulties with the timescales, measurement, and attribution of changes in final outcomes explain recourse to the second approach apparent in the literature of using service outputs as a measure of performance. Output measures may focus on the quantity, quality, or efficiency of a service. The performance of school education may, for example, be judged by the test scores of those leaving school. Critics of these measures point to two likely problems. First, in many cases the relationship between the output (the test score in this case) and the final outcome (the competencies of the students) may be contested. Some commentators have suggested, for example, that improving tests scores might be explained by slippage in grade standards (Coe 2007). Others argue that measures of this kind distort the behaviour of public servants who resort to a series of game playing tactics to meet targets (Bevan and Hood 2006; Hood 2006). The quality of teaching, and with it the final outcome of an educated population, may be sacrificed for narrow revision exercises designed to maximize test scores (Alexander and Flutter 2009).

In place of particular outputs, the final approach to measuring performance is focused on the processes and practices used to deliver those services. The introduction of new processes or structures of service delivery may provide an early marker of improved outputs and outcomes. Boyne and Law refer to these as a 'step on the way to a final outcome' (2005, p. 254). Service managers often define improvement in these terms. Herman and Renz observe that public service managers 'do not rely on bottomline outcomes as meaningful indicators of organizational effectiveness preferring instead evidence of following correct procedures or doing things right' (1997, p. 200).

Governments across the world have established regulatory agencies with the job of measuring this dimension of performance. Their efforts are premised on the presumption that there is a right way of doing things; and that the adoption of best practice will lead to the improvement of outputs and outcomes. Regulators may, for example, visit schools and grade them on the quality of their classroom teaching or leadership. Judgements of this kind may be less open to manipulation and gaming—although this of course is debated—but performance measures of this kind are even further removed from the final outcomes expected of public policy. More troubling still, it is not always the case that the efficacy of the management practices, promoted or required by regulatory bodies, have been properly evidenced before their dissemination. In these cases, as Boyne explains, 'the potential antecedents of service improvement are being confused with the improvement itself' (2003a, p. 219).

Aside from debates about which dimensions of performance are most appropriate for the measurement of service improvement, we need to recognize that services are judged by a variety of internal and external groups (Connolly, Conlon, and Deutsch 1980). The perceptions of performance will vary on the basis of who is being asked to respond, how they are asked, and under what conditions (Connolly, Conlon, and Deutsch 1980). The multiple constituencies served by public services use different criteria to assess performance or, alternatively, attach different weights to the same criteria. Performance is not then best seen as a single statement or measure but rather as a set of several statements reflecting alternative criteria. As power alters between groups over time so do performance criteria change correspondingly. From this perspective, a service has improved so long as multiple constituencies perceive it as having done so (Zammuto 1984).

Different measures of performance together with the varied perspectives of different stakeholders allow for fundamental disagreements in the identification of service improvement. The current debate in the UK media about refuse services provides a case in point. England's percentage rate of municipal waste recycling has quadrupled in the last decade. While for some this output measure provides clear evidence of service improvement, others claim that it has been achieved by process changes (like a move from weekly to fortnightly refuse collection) which amount to a clear service deterioration. Others still, focused on the final outcome of sustainable waste management, question whether the environmental costs of some municipal recycling activities outweigh the benefits (for a review of the arguments, see Hickman [2009]).

In such a way it is perfectly possible that a particular public service could be regarded as worsening in terms of government inspection and performance indicators while local citizens maintain that it is improving. Public service improvement must then be viewed as an arena for political struggle and conflict as alternative stakeholders impose their criteria for success and failure on public services. The more prominent the service improvement agenda becomes, the more political is the definition and measurement of improvement. The implication of this, as Boaz et al. explain, is that in place of the '"What works?" questions that have been considered to be appropriate to medicine', students of public service improvement must ask: 'What works, for whom, in what circumstances?' (Boaz et al. 2008, p. 244).

Although the concept of public service improvement is 'inherently political and contestable' (Boyne 2003*a*, p. 368) we maintain that the attempt to define, measure, and explain it is a legitimate and important area of inquiry. That is not to say, of course, that it is the only way of analysing the management reforms which have swept across the globe over recent decades. Policies may be introduced, and organizations changed, for reasons other than service improvement. An important vein of the policy and management literature provides an account of policy and organizational change which is entirely devoid of these considerations (Edelman 1964; Fairclough 2000; Fischer

2003). For Edelman, the policy process—and by implication the resultant nuts and bolts of service delivery—is best captured in terms of the identification and resolution of symbolic problems (1964). Indeed as the literature reviews reported in this book indicate, much of the work to date focused on policy or management interventions has considered the improvement question only implicitly if at all. Rather than looking for evidence of improvement, scholars have chosen to study the political and organizational implications of new processes and structures. As a consequence we often know rather more about the politics of a particular reform than we do about its effectiveness.

What does a good theory of public service improvement look like?

A good theory of public service improvement should be capable of explaining shifts in service standards over time, and explaining why some organizations provide better services than others. If the theory works, then a change in the explanatory variables that are assumed to be important (e.g. organizational culture, leadership, or strategy processes) should in turn produce a change in service performance.

We take the view, however, that no theory can be proved conclusively right or wrong—an approach which has been described as 'temperate rationalism' (Newton-Smith 1981) or 'sophisticated falsificationism' (Lakatos 1970; Caldwell 1982). The validity of a theory can be accepted only provisionally, because it may be undermined by further quantitative or qualitative tests. Similarly, even a theory which appears to be empirically invalid may be retained, because the fault may lie not in the theory but the evidence. Nevertheless, theories which are supported by empirical evidence can generally be deemed more valid than those lacking such support. As Lakatos puts it, this approach 'shifts the problem of how to appraise theories to the problem of how to appraise series of theories' (1970, p. 119). 'There is', as he explains, 'no falsification before the emergence of a better theory' (1970, p. 119).

Consistency with empirical evidence is not, however, the only characteristic of a good theory of service improvement. A theory should be clear about the causal mechanisms hypothesized to drive improvement explaining, for example, why and how rational planning might impact on performance. Further, it should also have clear and plausible assumptions about the motives and behaviour of the actors (policy-makers, managers, service consumers) who are believed to make a difference to service performance.

A good theory of service improvement is unlikely to work equally well in all circumstances. Even if, for example, external regulation of service providers always has some positive effect on performance, the *strength* of this effect is unlikely to be uniform. Theories of service improvement should specify the other variables that are likely to modify their validity. We assume, in other words, that all good theories are contingency theories. This does not mean that we believe that each public service organization is unique and that generalizations about service improvement are impossible. Rather, a good theory should stipulate the limits of generalization, without simply degenerating into a description of the characteristics of specific cases and thereby losing all theoretical value.

An appreciation of the likely contingencies affecting a theory of service improvement underlines the importance of the distinction between public and private management. Put simply, important differences between the sectors—from goal clarity to red tape—mean that improvement theories which seem to work well in private management will not necessarily produce the same results in the public realm (Boyne 2002). Although important, the line between the sectors is not, however, easily drawn. Margaret Thatcher's privatization programme in the United Kingdom transferred the ownership of whole industries from the public to the private sector but could not, of course, shake the presumption of many that the provision of basic infrastructure—like water and sewage services—remained a public service. Indeed Keynes argued that the distinction between public and private institutions lay in motive and not ownership. Public institutions are, according to Keynes, those which work for the public good (Skidelsky 1989). Bozeman captures the fuzziness of the distinction between the sectors in his identification of degrees of publicness (1987).

Where public services are increasingly delivered by public, private, and voluntary sector organizations it would clearly be a mistake to assert that public service management is either entirely the same or entirely different from private management (Rainey and Bozeman 2000). While in some areas there are good reasons to think that the mechanisms of improvement will work similarly for public and private services, in others there is a need for a distinctively public service take on the theories and evidence of service improvement. The question as to whether a good theory of public service improvement is different from a private service theory of improvement is considered more fully in a number of the chapters in this book.

Evidence base

The chapters in this book draw on two main sources of evidence. First, each chapter presents the results of a 'systematic review' of the empirical studies of the different theories of public service improvement. Chapter 3, for example, asks: Is there any evidence that the regulation of public services actually improves their performance? In considering this question we conducted comprehensive searches of Thomson Reuters' *Web of Knowledge* embracing a number of search criteria. Chapter 9, for example, combined the criteria of performance, effectiveness, evidence, outcomes, and evaluation with different descriptions of alliance-activity like networks, partnerships, and collaboration. The products of these searches, together with the references contained in them, were further sorted to identify studies which provided empirical evidence on the links between the key variable and public service performance.

While the outcome of these searches varied considerably—from relatively large literatures in the case of partnership and culture, to very few studies in the case of innovation and leadership—none of our themes generated an unmanageably large number of studies. Indeed, in some areas (innovation and planning) the reverse is true; there was a dearth of rigorous studies of performance. Of course even on the home turf of medical science the notion of a systematic review is not without complications. It is particularly difficult, for example, to weigh qualitative against quantitative evidence (Dixon-Woods et al. 2001). These difficulties are even more pronounced in the social sciences (Tranfield, Denys, and Smart 2003; Boaz et al. 2006). Fundamental differences between disciplines suggest that reviews of the management literature cannot hope to be as systematic as those in medicine (Learmonth 2008; Morrell 2008). That said, systematic reviews, or as close as we can get to them in the social sciences, provide a good starting point for an inquiry of the type considered in this book.

The second leg of each chapter is provided by theories and evidence which emerged from series of research studies conducted by the Public Management Research Group at Cardiff University between 1997 and 2008. The main projects, which are identified in Table 1.1 below, are large and longitudinal, and provide a valuable set of data for evaluating the validity of theories of public service improvement. The projects cover the wide range of external (e.g. socio-economic environment, regulation) and internal (e.g. leadership, culture) influences on public service improvement that we analyse in subsequent chapters. In this book, we draw together the main lessons from these projects for the first time and synthesize our findings with concepts and evidence from studies conducted in other nations.

Plan of the book

The chapters which follow consider three different sets of influences on performance, distinguishing between those which are external to the organization and which therefore form its environment, those which are intrinsic to

Table 1.1. Cardiff studies of service improvement

Project	Dates	Funder[a]	Cardiff researchers contributing to this book	Cited in chapters:
Evaluation of the Wales Best Value Pilot Programme	1998–2000	WAG	Boyne, Gould-Williams, and Walker	4
Devolution and regulation: Political control of public agencies in Scotland and Wales	1999–2000	ESRC	Ashworth, Boyne, and Walker	2
Impact of inspection on local government	1999–2004	JRF	Downe and Martin	2
Long-term evaluation of best value	2001–2006	DCLG	Ashworth, Boyne, Entwistle, Martin, and Walker	1, 2, 4, 6, 8
Strategy and service improvement	2002–2006	ESRC	Andrews, Boyne, and Walker	1, 4, 9
Partnerships between the public, private, and voluntary sectors	2002–2003	WAG	Entwistle and Martin	9
Local government modernization agenda	2003–2009	DCLG	Ashworth, Downe, Entwistle, and Martin	2
Long-term evaluation of local public service agreements	2004–2007	DCLG	Boyne	4
HRM and performance in the public sector	2006–2008	ESRC	Gould-Williams	7
AIM Fellowship on Public Service Failure and turnaround	2003–2005	ESRC	Boyne	4
AIM Fellowship on Innovation and Public Service performance	2003–2005	ESRC	Walker	8
Performance improvement regimes in local government	2006–2009	ESRC	Downe and Martin	2
Leadership change and public services	2006–2008	ESRC	Boyne and Petrovsky	5
How public management matters	2006–2010	ESRC	Andrews, Boyne, and Walker	4, 9, 10

[a] DCLG: Department for Communities and Local Government; ESRC: Economic and Social Research Council; JRF: Joseph Rowntree Foundation; NAfW: National Assembly for Wales; WAG Welsh Assembly Government.

it—like its structure, culture, processes, and leadership—and those which are adopted by it in the form of strategies that might improve performance (see Fig. 1.1). While no distinction of this type is watertight—organizational learning, for example, embraces a range of activities plausibly contained under all three headings—it has the merit of ordering the chapters in something approaching a logical manner.

Interventions intended to prompt service improvement are apparent at all three of these levels. Some—like tighter regulation—seek to change the environment in which public service organizations operate. Others are intended to act more immediately. New processes, cultures, or forms of management are often prescribed or adopted in the belief that they will improve organizational effectiveness. More effective organizations will, it is presumed, produce improved public services. Other mechanisms are envisaged as acting more directly still. It is often assumed, for example, that innovation, either in the service itself or the way in which it is delivered, is synonymous with improvement. Similarly, collaborative forms of service delivery are believed by many to offer a direct way of adding value to service delivery. That is to say, certain strategies, as distinct from the wider characteristics of the organizations which adopt them, are believed to be effective in their own right.

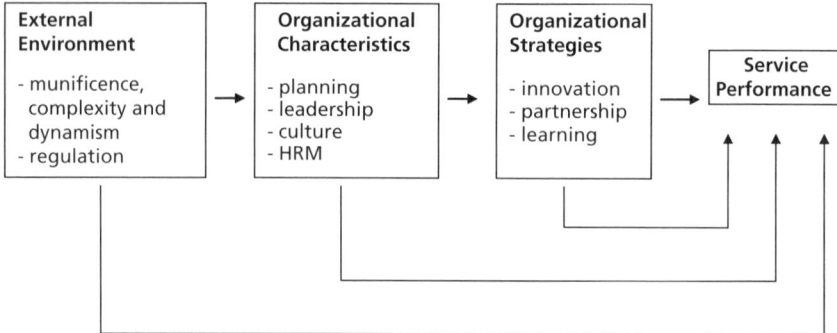

Figure 1.1. Connections between theories of public service performance

Chapters 2 and 3 are focused on the external environment in which public service organizations operate. In Chapter 2, Rhys Andrews considers the different ways in which organizational environments are described in the management literature. Andrews suggests that Dess and Beard's (1984) focus on munificence, complexity, and dynamism has clear applicability to the public service environment. He takes munificence to describe the availability of critical resources like community or political support, complexity is defined as the diversity and dispersion of a population, while dynamism is used to capture the rate of change in external circumstances and the relative unpredictability of that change. While few have attempted to analyse all three of these, Andrews finds a number of studies of the interaction of individual components of the environment and public service performance.

In Chapter 3, Steve Martin considers the performance effects of external regulation or inspection, one of the staples of the new public management. Regulation might have an improvement effect to the extent that it inclines public service organizations to make changes that would not otherwise be considered. Organizations may, for example, change their priorities or put in place new processes or structures in an effort to respond to inspection. Although a number of studies suggest regulation has exactly this effect, Martin also finds considerable evidence of unintended consequences in the form of gaming activities, depressed morale, and increased staff turnover. Much less work, however, has sought to track the consequences of these changes in processes and structures into the final outputs and outcomes of public service delivery. Regulation may prompt organizations to change, but does it deliver service improvement?

Chapters 2–5 move from an external to an internal perspective to consider some of the ingredients which define public service organizations. In Chapter 4, George Boyne considers the impact of strategic planning. Against the backdrop of the well-rehearsed argument between rational planners and incrementalists, Boyne asks whether organizations that analyse their environments, set clear goals, and put in place formal plans for implementation produce better results than those which 'muddle through'. Although Boyne finds a number of studies of the performance effects of goal clarity and target setting, little work has been done on the analysis and formalization aspects of planning.

In Chapter 5, Nicolai Petrovsky looks at the improvement effect of changes in, and different approaches to, the leadership of public service organizations. Although the performance effects of leadership are well-documented in the private management literature, little work has been done in the public sector. There are, however, as Petrovsky explains, good reasons to think that the 'lessons' from private management cannot simply be read across to the public sector. First, public organizations are typically led by both elected politicians and appointed officials; second, they often have multiple, ambiguous, even conflicting goals, and finally they operate under rules which specify what they are allowed to do, rather than what they cannot do. Differences between the sectors call for a distinctive body of public management research into the relationship between leadership and performance.

Rachel Ashworth considers organizational culture in Chapter 6—variously defined as the 'shared basic assumptions', practices, and values of an organiza- tion—asking whether particular types of culture are positively associated with improvement. Warning of the acute methodological difficulties of researching such deeply held and often taken-for-granted phenomena, Ashworth finds a number of studies that point in general terms to the importance of culture as a determinant of public service effectiveness. However, those studies which have, in her words, 'taken greater care in the interpretation, construction, and measurement of culture' suggest a need for considerable caution in hypothe- sizing a simple relationship between organizational culture and performance.

Julian Gould-Williams asks similar questions of human resource manage- ment in Chapter 7: Do best practice approaches to HRM translate into improved public service delivery? Surveying the search for what has been described as the subject's 'Holy Grail', Gould-Williams finds uncertainty in the identification of the key ingredients of best practice. But even when those ingredients are stipulated in advance—'high-commitment' approaches to HRM, for example, usually embrace training, careful recruitment, reward, and performance management—the association with organizational per- formance remains contested. Partly this might be explained by the fact that one size is unlikely to fit all. Because different organizations may need to fit their HR practices to the challenges confronting them, the link between HR and performance may then be contingent.

Chapters 9–11 consider the strategies or policies adopted by individual organizations. In Chapter 8, Richard Walker examines the effects of innov- ation, the process 'through which new ideas, objects and practices are created, developed or reinvented.' Although a vast literature distinguishes between different types of innovation and the causes or prompts which lead to the adoption of new approaches, Walker finds very few studies of the relationship between innovation and performance in the public services. The deficiency is important because we already know that innovation in the public services is likely to take a different form to that seen in private management.

In Chapter 9, Tom Entwistle considers the merits of collaborating in inter-organizational partnerships designed to access resources, join up different programmes, or engage different stakeholders. The vast majority of this work investigates three sets of contingencies believed to influence effectiveness. The behavioural school points to the importance of agreed goals, trust, and devolved forms of leadership; those focused on collaborative structures consider the degree of centralization and the density of interactions; while what might be regarded as the environmental school considers, amongst other factors, life-cycles and relationships with higher levels of government. Very few studies, however, have compared collaboration to other forms of organization like merger, working alone, or competition.

In Chapter 10, James Downe looks at the evidence that inter-organizational learning leads to service improvement. With one or two exceptions, Downe reports that commentators have focused more on the processes of learning than the outcomes in terms of service improvement. The question as to whether or not an organization has learnt is itself profoundly difficult to answer. As with collaboration, commentators have focused more on different manifestations of learning and the contingencies that seem to effect it—like receptive cultures, explicit knowledge, communities of practice, and active leadership—than they have the downstream effects of any organizational changes adopted.

Chapter 11 draws together our analysis to consider, within the constraints of our existing knowledge, which of the influences seem to matter most to service improvement. If a reforming government, or a public service organization itself, wished to broach just one or two reforms, where would their energies be best spent? Building on this analysis we conclude by identifying some of the key gaps in our understanding of public service improvement and pointing to the most pressing agendas for future research.

REFERENCES

Alexander, R. J. and Flutter, J. (2009). *Towards a New Primary Curriculum.* Cambridge: University of Cambridge Faculty of Education.

Amirkhanyan, A. A., Kim, H. J. and Lambright, K. T. (2008). Does the Public Sector Outperform the Nonprofit and For-Profit Sectors? Evidence from a National Panel Study on Nursing Home Quality and Access. *Journal of Policy Analysis and Management* 27(2), 326–53.

Andrews, R., Boyne, G. A. and Enticott, G. (2006). Performance Failure in the Public Sector: Misfortune or Mismanagement? *Public Management Review* 8(2), 273–96.

Bevan, G. and Hood, C. (2006). 'What's measured is what matters: Targets and gaming in the English public health care system'. *Public Administration*, 84(3), 517–538.

Boaz, A., Ashby, D., Denyer, D., Egan, M., Harden, A., Jones, D. R., Pawson, R. and Tranfield, D. (2006). A Multitude of Syntheses: A Comparison of Five Approaches from Diverse Policy Fields. *Evidence and Policy* 2(4), 479–502.

—— Grayson, L., Levitt, R. and Solesbury, W. (2008). Does Evidence-Based Policy Work? *Evidence and Policy* 4(2), 233–53.

Boyne, G. A. (2002). Public and Private Management: What's the Difference. *Journal of Management Studies* 39(1), 97–122.

—— (2003*a*). What is Public Service Improvement? *Public Administration* 81(2), 211–27.

—— (2003*b*). Sources of Public Service Improvement: A Critical Review and Research Agenda. *Journal of Public Administration Research and Theory* 13(3), 367–94.

—— and Law, J. (2005). Setting Public Service Outcome Targets: Lessons from Local Public Service Agreements. *Public Money and Management* 25(4), 253–60.

Caldwell, B. (1982). *Beyond Positivism: Economic Methodology in the Twentieth Century.* London: Allen & Unwin.

Coe, R. (2007). *Changes in Standards at GCSE and A Level: Evidence from ALIS and YELLIS.* Durham, UK: Durham University, Centre for Curriculum Evaluation and Management.

Common, R. K. (1998). Convergence and Transfer: A Review of the Globalization of the New Public Management. *International Journal of Public Sector Management* 11(6), 440–50.

Connolly, T., Conlon, E. J. and Deutsch, S. J. (1980). Organizational Effectiveness: A Multiple Constituency Approach. *Academy of Management Review* 5(2), 211–17.

Denhardt, R. B. and Denhardt, J. V. (2000). The New Public Service: Serving Rather than Steering. *Public Administration Review* 60(6), 549–59.

Dess, G. G. and Beard, D. W. (1984). Dimensions of Organizational Task Environments. *Administrative Science Quarterly* 29(1), 52–73.

Dunleavy, P. (1986). Explaining the Privatization Boom: Public Choice Versus Radical Approaches. *Public Administration* 64(1), 13–34.

Edelman, M. (1964). *The Symbolic Uses of Politics.* Urbana, IL: University of Illinois Press.

Entwistle, T., Marinetto, M. and Ashworth, R. (2007). New Labour, the New Public Management and Changing forms of Human Resource Management. *International Journal of Human Resource Management* 18(9), 1569–74.

Fairclough, N. (2000). *New Labour, New Language.* London: Routledge.

Fischer, F. (2003). *Reframing Public Policy: Discursive Politics and Deliberative Practices.* Oxford: Oxford University Press.

Geddes, M. (2000). 'Tackling Social Exclusion in the European Union? The Limits to the New Orthodoxy of Local Partnership'. *International Journal of Urban and Regional Research*, 24(4), 782–800.

Hickman, L. (2009). The Truth about Recycling. *The Guardian*, 26 February 2009.

Hood, C. (1991). 'A Public Management for All Seasons'. *Public Administration*, 69(1), 3–19.

Hood, C. (2006). 'Gaming in Targetworld: The Targets Approach to Managing British Public Services'. *Public Administration Review* 66(4), 515–521.

Hood, Christopher (2000). *The Art of the State: Culture, Rhetoric and Public Management.* Oxford: Oxford University Press.

Lakatos, I. (1970). Falsification and the Methodology of Scientific Research Programmes, in I. Lakatos and A. Musgrave (eds.), *Criticism and the Growth of Knowledge,* Cambridge: Cambridge University Press, pp. 91–196.

Learmonth, M. (2008). Evidence-Based Management: A Backlash Against Pluralism in Organizational Studies. *Organization* 15(2), 283–91.

Morrell, K. (2008). The Narrative of Evidence Based Management: A Polemic. *Journal of Management Studies* 43(3), 613–35.

Newton-Smith, W. (1981). *The Rationality of Science.* London: Routledge.

O'Flynn, J. (2007). From New Public Management to Public Value: Paradigmatic Change and Implications. *Australian Journal of Public Administration* 66(3), 353–66.

Osborne, S. P. (2006). 'The New Public Governance'. *Public Management Review,* 8(3), 377–387.

Pollitt, C. (1995). 'Justification by Works or by Faith'. *Evaluation,* 1(2), 133–154.

Pollitt, C. (2000). Is the Emperor in His Underwear? An Analysis of the Impacts of Public Management Reform. *Public Management* 2(1), 181–99.

—— and Bouckaert, H. (2004). *Public Management Reform: A Comparative Analysis.* Oxford: Oxford University Press.

Rainey, H. G. (1989). Public Management—Recent Research on the Political Context and Managerial roles, Structures and Behaviors. *Journal of Management* 15(2), 229–50.

—— (1993). A Theory of Goal Ambiguity in Public Organizations, in J. L. Perry (ed.), *Research in Public Administration,* Volume 2. Greenwich, CT: JAI Press, pp. 121–66.

—— and Bozeman, B. (2000). Comparing Public and Private Organizations: Empirical Research and the Power of the a priori. *Journal of Public Administration Research and Theory* 10(2), 447–69.

—— and Steinbauer, P. (1999). Galloping Elephants: Developing Elements of a Theory of Effective Government Organizations. *Journal of Public Administration Research and Theory* 9(1), 1–32.

Rhodes, R. A. W. (1996). The New Governance: Governing Without Government. *Political Studies* 44(4), 652–67.

Skidelsky, R. (1989). Keynes and the State, in D. Helm (ed.), *The Economic Borders of the State.* Oxford: Oxford University Press.

Stoker, G. (1998). Governance as Theory. *International Social Science Journal* 50(155), 17–28.

—— (2006). Public Value Management: A New Narrative for Networked Governance? *American Review of Public Administration* 36(1), 41–57.

Tranfield, D., Denys, D. and Smart, P. (2003). Towards a Methodology for Developing Evidence Informed Management Knowledge by Means of Systematic Review. *British Journal of Management* 14(3), 207–22.

Zammuto, R. F. (1984). A Comparison of Multiple Constituency Models of Organizational Effectiveness. *Academy of Management Review* 9(4), 606–16.

2 Organizational Environments

Rhys Andrews

Introduction

Organizational environments are a key issue in management research (e.g. Boyd and Gove 2006; Dess and Beard 1984; Harris 2004). However, despite widespread acknowledgement of the unique circumstances that public organizations confront (e.g. Boyne 2002; Hoggett 2006; Rainey, Backoff, and Levine 1976) and a wide evidence base on spatial variations in the broader context that they face, a surprisingly small number of studies have systematically conceptualized organizational environments in the public sector and investigated their relationship with service improvement. This chapter explores the impact of environments on public organizations. Is performance linked to external environmental circumstances? Do some dimensions of the environment matter more than others? To explore these questions, the chapter draws on empirical research which has focused explicitly on the independent impact of the organizational environment on public service performance. While a number of studies of the determinants of public service improvement include environmental measures alongside managerial or political variables (e.g. Andrews, Boyne, and Enticott [2006]; Champagne et al. [1993]; Meier and O'Toole [2008]), the objective of this chapter is to provide an assessment of the evidence isolating the effects of key dimensions of the environment on the achievements of public organizations. Each of the following chapters in the book examines whether the adoption of certain managerial and organizational characteristics enables public organizations to perform well within their specific contexts. Here, however, our concern is solely with the constraining effects of environments on public service providers. In addition, the chapter concentrates on technical aspects of the environment faced by public organizations, such as the sheer quantity and diversity of client needs, rather than institutional aspects of the environment, such as regulation and inspection. The impact of these latter constraints is considered in subsequent chapters.

In the first part of the chapter, theories of the organizational environment are outlined and hypotheses on the potential impact of different dimensions of the environment on performance are presented. The findings from, and limitations of, existing evidence on the impact of environments on organizational performance in the public sector are then reviewed, before conclusions are drawn for theories of public service improvement.

What is the organizational environment?

The conceptualization and measurement of organizational environments is a vital issue within organizational theory. According to Boulding (1978), environments can be crudely characterized as 'everything else' outside an organization that might influence its behaviour. Research on the effects of external circumstances on organizations began with the work of contingency theorists. They claimed that managers made strategic choices based on the assessment of the environmental conditions faced by their organization (Chandler 1962; Child 1972). This argument was later refined by scholars, such as Miles and Snow (1978), to suggest that organizational performance was dependent on the adoption of a consistent strategy for aligning an organization with its environment. In its most extreme form, this position implies that organizations failing to achieve environmental fit will cease to exist (see Hannan and Freeman [1977]).

A concern with the environment has also been a central feature of other important theoretical perspectives within organizational studies. For example, the work of resource-dependency theorists, such as Pfeffer and Salancik (1978), emphasizing the impact of external sources of financial and political support on organizations serves as a useful corrective to the focus on managerial perceptions of complexity and change found in contingency theory. However, resource-dependency theories are not well equipped to accommodate the 'simple-complex' and 'static–dynamic' dimensions of the environment that are key external determinants of managerial decision-making (Duncan 1972). Nonetheless, a variety of alternative methods for conceptualizing and evaluating the multiple elements of change and continuity with organizational environments have been developed. Some of these, such as Porter's 'Five Forces' model (1980) are of little relevance to public organizations as they primarily focus on market structure and competition. Others, such as Political Economic Social Technological Environmental and Legal (PESTEL) analysis (Johnson and Scholes 2002), are classification schema that restrict the derivation of directional hypotheses suitable for empirical testing. However, it is possible to identify two key perspectives on the environment which have underpinned empirical analysis of organizational performance during the past decade or so: Dess and Beard's model (1984) of organizational task environments and the insights of institutional theory.

Building on the previous work of contingency theorists, Dess and Beard (1984) identify three key dimensions of the organizational environment that are likely to influence organizational behaviour and outcomes: *munificence* (resource capacity), *complexity* (homogeneity–heterogeneity, concentration–dispersion), and *dynamism* (stability–instability, turbulence). The broad generalizability of these analytical categories makes them applicable to public as well as private organizations. Moreover, they are susceptible to measurement using 'objective' variables drawn from archival sources, and 'subjective' measures gauging managerial perceptions of the environment.

Within this short chapter on organizational environments, it is not possible to examine each of the many varieties of institutional theory. For the sake of brevity and clarity, the chapter therefore focuses on the work of Richard Scott. According to Scott (2001), there are three institutional pillars that reflect the varying but overlapping ways in which external forces affect organizational populations: the regulative pillar, the normative pillar, and the cultural–cognitive pillar. The regulative pillar pertains to 'explicit regulatory processes' within an organizational field, which encompass 'rule-setting, monitoring, and sanctioning activities' (Scott 2001, 52). These processes typically entail the exertion of isomorphic pressures towards legitimacy on organizations through more or less formal social and political structures (DiMaggio and Powell 1983). By contrast, the normative pillar refers directly to those prescriptive expectations that are embedded within an organizational field. These expectations determine appropriate goals for different actors and how they should be achieved. They are therefore especially potent determinants of the behaviour of public organizations, as the rights and responsibilities incumbent upon these organizations is arguably a defining characteristic of their 'publicness' (Boyne 2002). The cultural–cognitive pillar relates to the relative salience of the subjective interpretations of social life that are shared by actors within a given area. Such interpretations can influence organizational choices, by providing them with more or less coherent ways of symbolizing their organizational mission (Meyer and Rowan 1977).

Although it is possible to utilize institutionalist approaches to examine the determinants of public service performance (see, e.g., Andrews [2008]), Dess and Beard's model more readily meets Harris' criteria (2004) for the successful conceptualization of the organizational environment: empirical testability, temporal validity, international generalizability, and predictive validity (see Boyd and Gove [2006]). Moreover, key institutional constraints on public organizations are covered in later chapters within the book (see especially Martin's chapter (Chapter 3, this volume) on inspection). This chapter therefore focuses on the potential effects of environmental munificence, complexity, and dynamism on public service organizations.

Environmental munificence is constituted by 'the scarcity or abundance of critical resources' available within an organization's operating context, but over which they typically have relatively little direct control (Castrogiovanni 1991, p. 542). Munificence can buffer organizations from environmental pressures by generating financial slack (Cyert and March 1963). It can also facilitate 'organizational growth and stability' (Dess and Beard 1984, p. 55). Although budgetary processes in the public sector militate against the accrual of significant slack, there are several ways in which public organizations operating in a munificent environment can develop a greater fund of residual resources. For instance, community-based organizations can meet local needs, thereby generating increased capacity for the delivery of services. A further important aspect of munificence is the political support organizations are able to mobilize, especially in times of crisis (Hirschman 1970). Environmental munificence therefore relates to the relative impact of external social, economic, and political circumstances on the discretionary resources available to public organizations. The 'resource publicness' of public services makes them especially sensitive to changes in such levels of munificence, as their finances and institutional legitimacy are largely dependent on non-market sources (Bozeman 1987).

Environmental complexity comprises the heterogeneity and the dispersion of an organization's domain. In a heterogeneous environment, an organization provides services to many diverse groups of customers and clients (Dess and Beard 1984). These circumstances require higher levels of information-processing skills and systems to cope with complex customer requirements, increasing the strain on the resource capacity of an organization (Dutton, Fahey, and Narayanan 1983). Environmental dispersion is present where organizations provide services across a broad geographical domain (Dess and Beard 1984). This increases the need for strategic management and complex partnership arrangements with suppliers, customers, and other stakeholders, thereby generating additional costs (Aldrich 1979). By contrast, where services are concentrated in a narrow domain, benefits from interdependence (such as multi-output production) are likely to accrue (Starbuck 1976). Public organizations are typically required by law to serve heterogeneous and often widely dispersed groups of service users. They may also have to balance the demands of myriad external stakeholders, such as voters, regulators, and the media. Complexity in the public sector is therefore likely to reflect the relative heterogeneity and geographical dispersion of citizens, stakeholders, and service users.

Environmental dynamism comprises the rate of change in external circumstances (instability), and the relative unpredictability (or turbulence) of that change (Emery and Trist 1965). Organizations typically seek to cope with turbulence and instability in the environment through the introduction of strategic management and vertical integration (Dess and Beard 1984). Many commentators argue that organizational environments in the public sector are exceptionally dynamic (Ginter, Swayne, and Duncan 2002). Although major shifts in the social and economic environment of public organizations are often known in advance (e.g. demographic change), and play a role in central and local government planning and decision-making, perceived deviations from expected environmental changes are still likely to affect the performance of public service providers.

Theories of organizational environments and performance

ENVIRONMENTAL MUNIFICENCE

Variations in performance are likely where some public organizations have more economic resources than others. Prosperous organizations can afford to deliver more and better provisions, whereas poor organizations face a material restriction on their responsiveness and effectiveness, and the range of discretionary services they can offer (Boaden and Alford 1969). Beyond central government compensation to equalize levels of funding per unit of service need (Bennett 1982), the economic resources available to support public services are likely to be influenced by the relative prosperity of service users.

Disadvantaged individuals and families are less able to 'co-produce' services (Williams 2003). For example, poor parents cannot afford to subsidize state schools (e.g. through donations or unpaid help) or pay for home tuition to raise the level of their children's school examination performance. They are also less able to reduce resource pressures by substituting public with private services. Similarly, performance may be adversely affected by the lack of local neighbourhood support needed to assist vulnerable people in less-advantaged areas (Wilson 1991). Moreover, attempts to provide a standard level of service regardless of the socio-economic circumstances of different areas may produce worse outcomes in disadvantaged areas. For instance, in deprived areas in England, primary care teams have to work harder to provide the same level of care than their counterparts in more affluent areas (Carlisle, Avery, and Marsh 2002).

Differences in resource availability may also stem from variations in the size of the clientele served by public organizations. Scale economies may be reaped by spreading fixed costs over more units of output and from having greater capacity to provide services across large client groups (see Boyne [1996]). The relative magnitude of the environment of public organizations is typically determined by the statutory territorial boundaries of the population they serve. Hence the size of the client population is a further aspect of munificence that is beyond managerial control.

Public organizations require the support of a wide range of external stakeholders, including central government, citizens, and service users (Hirschman 1970). Baum and Oliver's analysis (1991) of failing child nurseries in Toronto indicates that interactions between service providers and key stakeholders were conducive to organizational survival if they were 'endorsed by the wider institutional environment' (p. 215). High levels of social capital amongst the users of public service users may also lead to improved organizational performance by enabling them to overcome collective action problems associated with influencing policy-makers (Putnam 2000). Indeed, the presence of a strong civic culture within an area may dictate agenda-setting or constrain the range of alternatives available to public organizations (Elkins and Simeon 1979).

Managers' perceptions of environmental munificence are also an important potential determinant of performance, as they often influence decisions on resource allocation (see Begun and Kaissi [2004]). For public organizations, perceptions of munificence are likely to reflect the extent to which managers believe the overall 'degree of difficulty' in the circumstances they face constrains their ability to deliver services. For example, in deprived areas with a tradition of community engagement, managers may perceive it to be easier to implement new service initiatives (Middleton, Murie, and Groves 2005).

ENVIRONMENTAL COMPLEXITY

The environmental complexity faced by public organizations is likely to be, in part, a product of the demographic characteristics of their users and stakeholders. In particular, if their service clientele is relatively homogeneous (e.g. mostly white middle class), it may be comparatively straightforward to elicit their preferences and provide a 'standardized' service that addresses their needs. By contrast, for a heterogeneous population (e.g. many different ethnic groups), greater effort may be required to identify their divergent preferences, and it may be necessary to provide a wider range of services to meet their requirements (Boaden and Alford 1969). It is common for schools in areas of high ethnic diversity to struggle to address more varied learning problems (see Jencks and Phillips [1998]), especially those experienced by disadvantaged pupils (Jasinski 2000). Areas with a wider spread of age groups also have more complex housing (Withers 1997) and health care (Birch and Maynard 1986) needs than those which are less fragmented. Moreover, high levels of community heterogeneity can damage stocks of social capital within local communities (Putnam 2007). Public organizations operating in socially heterogeneous areas may have to devote substantial resources of time and money to building, developing, and maintaining good community relations (Office of the Deputy Prime Minister 2004). This is all likely to make effectiveness and equity more difficult to achieve where environmental heterogeneity is high.

At any given population level, task complexity will also increase when service users are dispersed across a wide geographical area. For example, it may be necessary to provide additional schools, day-care centres, and supplementary 'outreach' programmes. By contrast, the provision of services within a narrow geographical area could generate scope economies (Grosskopf and Yaisawamg 1990). Static facilities in urban areas may be able to offer a wide range of services from the same site. The cost of a standard unit of service output could also rise with sparsity—for instance, in rural areas, refuse vehicles need to travel further between premises.

Public organizations require greater sensitivity to an array of diverse interests and constituencies than their private sector counterparts (see Hoggett [2006]; Rainey, Backoff, and Levine [1976]). Public managers' perceptions of the heterogeneity of the needs and dispersion of clients may therefore be much more nuanced than the relative levels of task complexity revealed by objective measures. For example, managers' views on the complex circumstances they face may manifest an especially deep understanding of how the needs of similar social groups widely differ across the various geographical areas that they serve (Docherty, Goodlad, and Paddison 2001). Perceptions of task complexity could therefore reflect an especially strong awareness of the multiple and potentially conflicting organizational goals that public managers are expected to meet. In public organizations, the 'goal ambiguity' associated with perceptions of high levels of goal complexity has been shown to result in poor performance as managers struggle to satisfy myriad competing objectives (Chun and Rainey 2005).

ENVIRONMENTAL DYNAMISM

Environmental stability is a prerequisite for organizational decision-makers to direct and plan the use of resources effectively. Large or unexpected shifts in the circumstances that they face may lead public managers to be increasingly cautious about developing new services, and to become progressively less willing or able to adapt to environmental change, potentially resulting in 'threat-rigidity' (Staw et al. 1981). 'Objective' levels of environmental dynamism are therefore likely to reflect conditions which hamper public managers' efforts to coordinate and plan effective responses to existing and future service needs. D'Aveni (1998) suggests that changes in consumer expectations create dynamism in an organization's environment. As the rate of change in client and stakeholder diversity rises, the need to accumulate new knowledge about their expectations places ever-greater burdens on service providers, requiring, in particular, the devotion of additional resources to environmental scanning (Boyd and Fulk 1996). The added investment that environmental dynamism is likely to require may therefore make it harder for public organizations to continue to perform at a consistent level. Indeed, in a dynamic environment, some public organizations could be willing to allow service quality to deteriorate during the short term to protect their long-term financial plans (Ladd 1992).

In the public sector, the increasing interconnectedness of demographic diversity and change, and the growth of multi-organizational and multi-governmental networks, places ever greater burdens on public managers to perceive and manage a dynamic environment (O'Toole 1997). Downey and Slocum (1975) argue that cognitive biases associated with low tolerance of ambiguity can cause underestimation of the effects of environmental dynamism, which in turn can result in poor decision-making. Pressure to deliver customer-led services in what are perceived to be unstable or unpredictable circumstances could therefore lead to inertia or an absence of strategic behaviour altogether. This may render public managers excessively dependent on cues from external stakeholders, especially those given by their political principals (Rainey 1997). In such circumstances, performance is likely to suffer.

Empirical evidence on organizational environments and performance

EMPIRICAL STUDIES AND THEIR CHARACTERISTICS

A wide array of studies asses the effects of difficult environmental circumstances at the individual level, especially for health (e.g. Shah and Cook [2008]; Wilkinson [1997]), and educational outcomes (e.g. Jasinski [2000]; Tam and Bassett [2004]), or on levels of public service expenditure (see Boyne [2003] for a review). However, rather less is known about their impact on organizational performance. Moreover, most research on public organizations does not utilize a comprehensive theoretical model of the environment. Rather than adopt the kind of conceptual framework proposed by Dess and Beard, it focuses on the relationship between specific contextual variables, such as deprivation (e.g. Croll [2002]) or neighbourhood segregation (e.g. Gordon and Monastiriotis [2006]), and public service outcomes. As a result, a thorough review of the available evidence requires the adaptation of additional search terms for relative environmental munificence (e.g. deprivation, poverty, resources), complexity (e.g. diversity, sparsity), and dynamism (e.g. change, growth), in conjunction with those for performance (e.g. achievement, effectiveness). This expanded search revealed fifteen example studies

Table 2.1 Evidence of impact of environment on public service performance

Study	Dimension of environment	Type of measure	Country and sector	Sample and time period	Measure of performance	Finding
Andrews (2004)	Munificence (socio-economic)	Objective	England, local government	144 local governments, 2000/1	Best Value Performance Indicators	Low munificence associated with worse performance
Andrews (2007)	Munificence (socio-economic and political) Complexity	Objective	England, local government, education, health trusts, police, fire, prisons	148 local government areas, 2002–4	Failure judgements made by regulatory agencies	High munificence associated with less failure and high complexity with more
Andrews (2009)	Munificence Complexity Dynamism (socio-economic)	Objective and subjective	Wales, UK, local government	59 service departments, 2002–3	National Assembly for Wales Performance Indicators	High munificence associated with better performance, high complexity and dynamism with worse
Andrews and Boyne (2008)	Munificence Complexity Dynamism (socio-economic and political)	Objective	England, local government, education, health trusts, police, fire, prisons	148 local government areas, 2002–4	Failure judgements made by regulatory agencies	High munificence associated with less failure, high complexity and dynamism with more
Andrews et al. (2005)	Munificence (socio-economic and political) Complexity (socio-economic)	Objective	England, local government	147 local governments, 2002	Comprehensive Performance Assessments	High munificence associated with better performance, high complexity with worse
Coffe and Geys (2005)	Munificence (socio-economic and political) Complexity (political)	Objective	Belgium, local government	305 local governments, 2000	Budget surplus	Mixed: social munificence associated with better performance, economic munificence with worse; political complexity associated with worse performance

(continued)

Table 2.1 Continued

Study	Dimension of environment	Type of measure	Country and sector	Sample and time period	Measure of performance	Finding
Croll (2002)	Munificence (socio-economic)	Objective	England, education	40 primary schools, 1997	Standard Assessment Tests	Low munificence associated with worse performance
Gordon and Monastiriotis (2006)	Munificence (socio-economic)	Objective	England, education	779 secondary schools, 1999	5 GCSEs A*–C	Low munificence associated with worse performance
Gutierrez-Romero, Haubrich, and McLean (2008)	Munificence (socio-economic and political) Complexity (socio-economic)	Objective	England, local government	148 local governments, 2002–4	Comprehensive Performance Assessments	High munificence associated with better performance, high complexity with worse.
Lynch (1995)	Munificence	Objective	Scotland, health	208 general practices, 1991–2	Child immunizations	Low munificence associated with worse performance
Meier and Bohte (2003)	Complexity (socio-economic heterogeneity)	Objective	Texas, US, education	1,043 School districts, 1995–8	Absenteeism, student retention, class dropout	High complexity associated with more failure
Odeck and Alkadi (2004)	Complexity (dispersion)	Objective	Norway, local government	47 bus operators, 1994	Efficiency	Low dispersion associated with scale efficiency
Rice (2001)	Munificence (socio-economic) Complexity (socio-economic)	Objective and subjective	Iowa, US, local government	114 local governments, 1994/7	Perceptions of government responsiveness and effectiveness	High munificence associated with better performance
West et al. (2001)	Munificence	Objective	England, education	96 local service departments, 1996	KS1 target met 5 GCSEs A*–G 5 GCSEs A*–C	Low munificence associated with poor performance
Xu (2006)	Munificence Complexity (socio-economic)	Objective	US, state governments	50 state governments, 2001	Health Achievement Index	High munificence associated with better performance, high complexity with worse

that focus specifically on the link between organizational environments and public service performance. Despite the appropriateness of their content, these studies, which are summarized in Table 2.1, are problematic in at least two ways.

First, the available evidence invariably focuses on only one (e.g. munificence in Croll [2002]) or two (e.g. munificence and complexity in Gordon and Monastiriotis [2006]) dimensions of the environment, and only two studies provide evidence on the independent impact of environmental dynamism on performance (Andrews 2009; Andrews and Boyne 2008), even though this is arguably a defining characteristic of the 'publicness' of public organizations (see Boyne [2002]). To develop and fully test theoretical models of organizational environments, it is necessary to investigate the effects of all three dimensions of the environment identified by Dess and Beard.

Second, most empirical studies have focused on objective quantifiable measures, such as aggregated demographic data (e.g. Andrews et al. [2005]), rather than subjective measures directly assessing how key organizational stakeholders perceive their organizational environments. If the aim is to 'explain similarities and differences between individual organizations', then perceptions of the environment are important explanatory variables (Castrogiovanni 1991, p. 546). However, only one of the studies identified in Table 2.1 considers the impact of perceived environments on public service performance (Andrews 2009).

Despite their limitations, the studies examined below provide a strong platform for developing an understanding of the relationship between organizational environments and performance. The evidence covers a wide range of public services ranging from single purpose organizations, such as schools, to multipurpose organizations, such as local governments. Each of the studies typically draws on a large sample of organizations and utilizes different dependent variables, including measures of organizational failure as well as performance, thereby increasing the generalizeability of the findings. They all use formal tests of statistical significance, and most implement multivariate techniques to control for the potential effects of other relevant contextual variables.

EVIDENCE FROM THE STUDIES

Environmental munificence

A number of studies in the education sector have examined the effects of munificence alone on performance. For example, West et al. (2001) focus on levels of poverty and educational attainment in ninety-six English local government education departments. In this study, the quantity of need, taken as an indicator of low munificence, is measured using a variety of indicators, such as the proportion of children dependent on income support recipients; the proportion of children in lone-parent families; and the proportion of children with special educational needs. All of the measures of poverty were found to have separate and combined negative effects on education performance. These findings are confirmed in Croll's analysis (2002) of the academic achievement of pupils in forty English primary schools, which finds a very strong negative correlation (−0.70) between free school meal eligibility and achievement in the Standard Assessment Tests.

Studies in other areas of the public sector have also revealed a similar relationship between munificence and performance. For instance, Andrews (2004) examines the impact of socio-economic munificence on 144 English local governments, finding a series of negative correlations between socio-economic deprivation and a wide range of performance indicators. In particular, three-quarters of the education indicators, half of the housing and waste management indicators, and a third of those for benefits and revenues were negatively correlated with deprivation. Lynch (1995) assesses differences between child immunization rates in 208 general practices in deprived and prosperous areas in Greater Glasgow. Deprivation was measured using the Jarman index, which comprises items of particular relevance for health-care provision: elderly living alone, single-parent households, under-fives, overcrowded households, unskilled workers, house-movers, unemployed, and residents in ethnic minorities. Performance was measured as the achievement of high-target payments for childhood immunization uptake rates of 90 per cent or more during the four quarters of 1991/2. Lynch finds a statistically significant relationship between deprivation and non-achievement of the performance target by general practices.

Several studies furnish evidence on size and local government performance. Travers et al. (1993) present a series of bivariate correlations between population size and measures of local government efficiency and effectiveness in England, including housing costs, fire service expenditure, and school examination results. They find relationships between size and performance that are inconsistent in both direction and degree of statistical significance, leading them to claim that no firm conclusions can be drawn on the presence of size effects. Boyne (1996) tests for linear and non-linear scale effects, measured in terms of service outputs and needs, on multiple performance indicators in six local authority service areas in 1993/4 across England and Wales. He finds strong evidence of non-linear U-shaped scale effects when controlling for local government structure, concluding that 'there is no one optimum scale of service provision' (Boyne 1996, p. 824). However, evidence from a number of European studies provides firmer evidence on the relationship between size and community-orientated outcomes. For example, Mouritzen (1989) finds a negative correlation between city size and citizen satisfaction with Danish municipal governments, while cross-European studies of attitudes towards local government at an individual level provide further confirmation of this finding (e.g. Denters [2002]).

Environmental complexity

Public organizations arguably face an inherently more complex environment than their private sector counterparts, due to the contested nature of the public sphere and their mandated role in responding to multiple dimensions of market failure (Hoggett 2006). However, few studies have focused exclusively on the effects of environmental heterogeneity on public service performance, and almost none have considered the isolated impact of dispersion.

Meier and Bohte (2003) examine the relationship between various measures of task heterogeneity and organizational 'micro-failures' in over 1,000 Texas school districts during a four-year period (1995–8). They find that school districts are more likely to suffer high absenteeism if they have a higher percentage of black and Latino students and that the class dropout rate is influenced by numbers of low-income students. High levels of class retention are principally associated with the percentage of low-income students, and also with the percentage of black students. Odeck and Alkadi (2004) assess whether the performance of forty-seven Norwegian public transport services is harmed by the presence of scale and scope diseconomies in rural areas. They find that the increased complexity associated with delivering services in rural areas is significantly associated with scale diseconomies, but not scope diseconomies. Thus, geographical aspects of rural areas, such as the terrain, rather than multi-output production appear to be making it harder to deliver value for money in the dispersed environment faced by some bus operators.

Despite the absence of evidence specifically on the effects of complexity, a growing number of studies have explored its impact alongside aspects of environmental munificence. Andrews et al. (2005) assess the influence of socio-economic and political munificence, and socio-economic complexity on the core service performance of 147 English local governments. They find that socio-economic munificence measured in terms of population growth and fewer lone-parent households is conducive to better service performance in English local governments, but that socio-economic heterogeneity makes high standards more difficult to achieve. The findings of Andrews et al. (2005) are corroborated and extended in a subsequent analysis of the performance of English local governments carried out by Gutiérrez-Romero, Haubrich, and McLean (2008). On the basis of panel data analysis they find that different dimensions of multiple deprivation have varying effects on performance, with poor skills, high crime, and poor living-environment having a statistically significant negative effect, but poor housing and low income no significant effect.

Broadly similar findings to those uncovered by studies of English local government have been presented in research within specific areas of public service delivery. For example, Xu (2006) assesses the impact of demographic and economic characteristics on health achievement across the US states. High levels of poverty and unemployment were associated with poorer health achievement. Higher proportions of females, older individuals, and minorities in the population were also associated with lower health achievement, while a large urban population was associated with better achievement. The impact of socio-economic munificence and complexity on educational outcomes is also considered in Gordon and Monastiriotis' study (2006) of 779 secondary schools in Greater London. The results of their statistical analysis suggest that low munificence, in the form of a high proportion of lone-parent families and high unemployment, is associated with worse school examination performance. However, schools serving larger middle-class and Asian feeder populations performed better, indicating that some dimensions of heterogeneity may have a positive relationship with public service improvement.

In recent years, studies of size effects on local government performance have grown in methodological sophistication. For example, Andrews, Chen, and Martin (2006) carried out almost 700 tests of the relationship between size and performance in English local government, controlling for external constraints shown to be important determinants of performance. Although they find that the relationship between population size and performance is a complex mosaic of insignificant, positive, negative, and non-linear effects, the balance of their evidence tends to support the assumption that large governments perform better than small ones.

The influence of Robert Putnam's work on social capital has been matched by greater efforts to model its impact on public service performance at the organizational level. For instance, Rice (2001) and Coffe and Geys (2005) assess the relationship between levels of social capital within municipalities and local government performance in Iowa and Belgium, finding consistently positive effects, even when controlling for other measures of munificence and measures of complexity. Similarly, Andrews (2007) finds that high levels of political participation, a 'collectivist' political culture, strong interpersonal trust, and vibrant associational life reduce the risk of public service failure, when controlling for other environmental constraints.

Environmental dynamism

Although dynamism is arguably characteristic of environments in the public sector (Boyne 2002; Ginter, Swayne, and Duncan 2002), there is currently little research investigating its influence on public service performance. Nevertheless, two 'Cardiff studies' furnish evidence on its impact when controlling for munificence and complexity. Indeed, these studies provide comprehensive analyses of the Dess and Beard model of the organizational environment, and the second of them provides a systematic exploration of perceived environmental circumstances.

Andrews and Boyne (2008) examine the effects of objective measures of socio-economic and political *munificence, complexity, and dynamism* on the likelihood of public organizations operating within 148 local government administrative areas being classified as failing by central government regulatory agencies. The statistical results provide general support for the hypotheses that organizations are more likely to fail if they are confronted by an environment that is low in economic and political munificence, complex (in both the diversity and distribution of client groups), and dynamic (especially if changes in munificence are unpredictable). Andrews (2009) explores the effects of objective and subjective socio-economic environments on the performance of fifty-nine Welsh local authority service departments. The results from this analysis suggest that variations in performance are positively related to objective and subjective measures of environmental munificence, but negatively to objective and subjective measures of dynamism. However, while delivering services in conditions of high recorded complexity are likely to lead to lower performance, managers' perceptions of greater complexity are not associated with worse performance.

The handful of studies that examine the impact of environmental *dynamism* on public services assume that environmental change is continuous, typically following a pattern of linear equilibrium. However, dramatic and unexpected environmental transformations may have more serious short-term implications for performance than processes of change wrought over the course of months, years, or decades. Such environmental 'jolts' are sudden 'perturbations whose occurrences are difficult to foresee and whose impacts are disruptive and potentially inimical' (Meyer 1982, p. 515). For example, worker strikes or viral outbreaks can cause profound upheavals across organizational fields. Although there are currently no studies of the independent effects of such sudden environmental shifts on public service performance, researchers have begun to investigate the extent to which managers have been able to reduce the impact of natural disasters on performance (e.g. Meier, O'Toole, and Hicklin [forthcoming]).

Unresolved research issues

The studies reviewed in this chapter furnish wide-ranging evidence on the extent to which organizational environments constrain public organizations. However, very little is known about whether the relative tractability of the environment may influence public service achievements. While Meier and O'Toole (2008) provide evidence of the environmental buffering activities undertaken by public organizations to protect core routines and processes, there have been almost no systematic attempts to examine the relative 'malleability' of environments.

Arguably, all circumstances within the purview of public organizations may be at least partially malleable rather than fixed—for example, local government performance may influence the size and composition of the local population through fiscal migration (John, Dowding, and Biggs 1995). Thus, the extent to which environments are susceptible to the proactive influence of organizations would reveal much about the nature of public service improvement.

Within the broader management literature, evidence on deliberate attempts to reshape the context in which organizations operate (aside from entering new markets or exiting existing ones) draw largely on the concept of environmental enactment. According to Weick (1969), when managers construct, rearrange, or eradicate certain elements of their task environment in order to achieve desired goals, they 'enact' the external circumstances faced by their organization. For public organizations this might entail devising strategies to improve the capacity of clients to co-produce services or the proactive management of relationships with key external stakeholders. For example, Johnson and Fauske (2000) show how school principals in a sample of US schools frequently pre-empt potential environmental threats and seize opportunities associated with potentially favourable external events. This, in turn, enables them to accumulate greater personal and organizational legitimacy in the eyes of staff, students, parents, and legislators. Nevertheless, to fully explore the tractability of public sector environments it is also necessary to consider managerial actions at lower levels of the organizational hierarchy. For instance, the *ad hoc* interventions made by street-level bureaucrats, such as police officers, social workers, and teachers, are premised on their knowledge 'about what works as a result of daily interactions with clients' (Maynard-Moody, Musheno, and Palumbo 1990). Given that the existing empirical evidence confirms that organizational environments matter, public management researchers would therefore do well to investigate the capacity of organizations to enact environments that are more conducive to service improvement.

Conclusion

This chapter has explored organizational environments and public service improvement. The evidence reviewed here illustrates that variations in the performance of public organizations are, as expected, influenced by measures of the environmental munificence, complexity, and dynamism confronted by organizations. Organizations operating in a munificent, simple, stable, and predictable context appear to perform better than their counterparts in less favourable circumstances. Indeed, each of the dimensions of the environment identified by Dess and Beard (1984) seems to have an important impact on the prospects of service improvement. This illustrates that it is essential for researchers, policy-makers, and practitioners to acknowledge the impact of environments on organizational outcomes. In addition, more work is required to supplement and extend the extremely limited evidence on the influence of managers' perceptions of the environment on performance, especially in terms of the processes of environmental enactment to which they give rise.

Although the evidence surveyed here largely confirms the hypothesized effects of environmental munificence, complexity, and dynamism, it suffers from limitations that should be addressed in future studies. In particular, the reported findings may simply be a product of where and when the empirical studies were conducted. The evidence base to date is largely restricted to Anglophone countries. To what extent are the environments in these countries comparable with those faced by public organizations in other developed countries with contrasting welfare state regimes? Moreover, to what extent, and in what ways, do public sector organizational environments differ in developing countries? In addition, the existing studies do not typically examine the ways in which public managers and organizations seek to change the environments in which they operate and the resulting effects on performance. Despite these challenges for public management research, the evidence presented in this chapter highlights that organizational environments place important constraints on managers and organizations in the public sector, and that this must be acknowledged in the theory and practice of public service improvement.

REFERENCES

Aldrich, H. E. (1979). *Organizations and Environment.* Englewood Cliffs, NJ: Prentice-Hall.

Andrews, R. (2004). Analysing Deprivation and Local Authority Performance: The Implications for CPA. *Public Money & Management* 24, 19–26.

—— (2007). Civic Culture and Public Service Failure: An Empirical Exploration. *Urban Studies* 44, 845–64.

—— (2008). An Institutionalist Approach to Spatial Variations in Public Service Failure: Evidence from England. *European Urban and Regional Studies* 15, 349–62.

—— (2009). Organizational Task Environments and Performance: An Empirical Analysis. *International Public Management Journal* 12, 1–23.

—— and Boyne, G. A. (2008). Organizational Environments and Public Service Failure: An Empirical Analysis. *Environment and Planning C—Government and Policy* 26, 788–807.

Andrews, R., Boyne, G. A., Chen, A. and Martin, S. (2006). *Population Size and Local Authority Performance.* London: Office of the Deputy Prime Minister.

—— —— and Enticott, G. (2006). Performance Failure in the Public Sector: Misfortune or Mismanagement? *Public Management Review* 8, 273–96.

—— —— Law, J. and Walker, R. M. (2005). External Constraints and Local Service Standards: The Case of Comprehensive Performance Assessment in English Local Government. *Public Administration* 83, 639–56.

Baum, J. A. C. and Oliver, C. (1991). Institutional Linkages and Organizational Mortality. *Administrative Science Quarterly* 36, 187–218.

Begun, J. W. and Kaissi, A. A. (2004). Uncertainty in Health Care Environments: Myth or Reality? *Health Care Management Review* 29, 31–9.

Bennett, R. (1982). *Central Grants to Local Governments.* Cambridge: Cambridge University Press.

Birch, S. and Maynard, A. (1986). Performance Indicators and Performance Assessment in the UK National Health Service: Implications for Management and Planning. *International Journal of Health Planning and Management* 1, 287–306.

Boaden, N. T. and Alford, R. R. (1969). Sources of Diversity in English Local Government Decisions. *Public Administration* 47, 203–23.

Boulding, K. E. (1978). *Ecodynamics.* Beverly Hills, CA: Sage.

Boyd, B. and Fulk, J. (1996). Executive Scanning and Perceived Environmental Uncertainty: A Multidimensional Model. *Journal of Management* 22, 1–21.

—— and Gove, S. (2006). Managerial Constraint: The Intersection between Organizational Task Environment and Discretion, in D. Ketchen and D. Bergh (eds.), *Research Methodology in Strategy and Management,* Volume 3. Oxford: JAI Press, pp. 57–96.

Boyne, G. A. (1996). Scale, Performance and the New Public Management: An Empirical Analysis of Local Authority Services. *Journal of Management Studies* 33, 809–26.

—— (2002). Public and Private Management: What's the Difference? *Journal of Management Studies* 39, 97–122.

—— (2003). Sources of Public Service Improvement: A Critical Review and Research Agenda. *Journal of Public Administration Research and Theory* 13, 367–94.

Bozeman, B. (1987). *All Organizations Are Public: Bridging Public and Private Organization Theory.* San Francisco, CA: Jossey-Bass.

Carlisle, R., Avery, A. J. and Marsh, P. (2002). Primary Care Teams Work Harder in Deprived Areas. *Journal of Public Health Medicine* 24, 43–8.

Castrogiovanni, G. J. (1991). Environmental Munificence: A Theoretical Assessment. *Academy of Management Review* 16, 542–65.

Champagne, F., Leduc, N., Denis, J-L. and Pineault, R. (1993). Organizational and Environmental Determinants of the Performance of Public Health Units. *Social Science & Medicine* 37, 85–95.

Chandler, A. (1962). *Strategy and Structure: Chapters in the History of the Industrial Enterprise.* Cambridge, MA: MIT Press.

Child, J. (1972). Organizational Environment, Structure and Performance: The Role of Strategic Choice. *Sociology* 6, 1–22.

Chun, Y. H. and Rainey, H. G. (2005). Goal Ambiguity and Organizational Performance in US Federal Agencies. *Journal of Public Administration Research and Theory* 15, 529–57.

Coffe, H. and Geys, B. (2005). Institutional Performance and Social Capital: An Application to the Local Government Level. *Journal of Urban Affairs* 27, 485–502.

Croll, P. (2002). Social Deprivation, School-Level Achievement and Special Educational Needs. *Educational Research* 44, 43–53.

Cyert, R. M. and March, J. G. (1963). *A Behavioral Theory of the Firm.* Englewood Cliffs, NJ: Prentice-Hall.

D'Aveni, R. (1998). Waking up to the New Era of Hypercompetition. *Washington Quarterly* 21, 183–96.

Denters, B. (2002). Size and Political Trust: Evidence from Denmark, the Netherlands, Norway and the United Kingdom. *Government and Policy* 20, 793–812.

Dess, G. G. and Beard, D. W. (1984). Dimensions of Organizational Task Environments. *Administrative Science Quarterly* 29, 52–73.

DiMaggio, P. J. and Powell, W. W. (1983). The Iron Cage Revisited: Institutional Isomorphism and Collective Rationality in Organizational Fields. *American Sociological Review* 48, 147–60.

Docherty, I., Goodlad, R. and Paddison, R. (2001). Civic Culture, Community and Citizen Participation in Contrasting Neighbourhoods. *Urban Studies* 38, 2225–50.

Downey, H. K. and Slocum, J. W. (1975). Uncertainty: Measures, Research, and Sources of Variation. *Academy of Management Journal* 18, 562–78.

Duncan, R. (1972). Characteristics of Organizational Environments and Perceived Uncertainty. *Administrative Science Quarterly* 17, 313–27.

Dutton, J. M., Fahey, L. and Narayanan, V. K. (1983). Toward Understanding Strategic Issue Diagnosis. *Strategic Management Journal* 4, 307–23.

Elkins, D. J. and Simeon, E. B. (1979). A Cause in Search of Its Effect, or What Does Political Culture Explain? *Comparative Politics* 11, 127–45.

Emery, F. E. and Trist, E. L. (1965). The Causal Texture of Organizational Environments. *Human Relations* 18, 21–32.

Ginter, P. M., Swayne, L. E. and Duncan, W. J. (2002). *Strategic Management of Health Care Organizations*, Fourth edition. Oxford: Blackwell.

Gordon, I. and Monastiriotis, V. (2006). Urban Size, Spatial Segregation and Inequality in Education Outcomes. *Urban Studies* 43, 213–36.

Grosskopf, S. and Yaisawamg, S. (1990). Economies of Scope in the Provision of Local Public Services. *National Tax Journal* 43, 61–74.

Gutiérrez Romero, R., Haubrich, D. and McLean, I. (2008). The Limits of Performance Assessments of Public Bodies: External Constraints in English Local Government. *Environment and Planning C: Government and Policy* 26, 767–87.

Hannan, M. T. and Freeman, J. (1977). The Population Ecology of Organizations. *American Journal of Sociology* 82, 929–64.

Harris, R. D. (2004). Organizational Task Environments: An Evaluation of Convergent and Discriminant Validity. *Journal of Management Studies* 41, 857–82.

Hirschman, A. O. (1970). *Exit, Voice and Loyalty: Responses to Decline in Firms, Organizations and States.* Cambridge, MA: Harvard University Press.

Hoggett, P. (2006). Conflict, Ambivalence, and the Contested Purpose of Public Organizations. *Human Relations* 59, 175–94.

Jasinski, J. L. (2000). Beyond High School: An Examination of Hispanic Educational Attainment. *Social Science Quarterly* 81, 276–90.

Jencks, C. and Phillips, M. (eds.) (1998). *The Black—White Test Score Gap.* Washington, DC: The Brookings Institution.

John, P., Dowding, K. and Biggs, S. (1995). Residential Mobility in London: A Micro-level Test of the Behavioural Assumptions of the Tiebout Model. *British Journal of Political Science* 25, 379–97.

Johnson, B. L. Jr. and Fauske, J. R. (2000). Principals and the Political Economy of Environmental Enactment. *Educational Administration Quarterly* 36, 159–85.

Johnson, G. and Scholes, K. (2002). *Exploring Corporate Strategy,* Sixth edition. Harlow: Prentice-Hall.

Ladd, H. F. (1992). Population Growth, Density and the Costs of Providing Public Services. *Urban Studies* 29, 273–95.

Lynch, M. (1995). Effect of Practice and Patient Population Characteristics on the Uptake of Childhood Immunizations. *British Journal of General Practice* 45, 205–8.

Maynard-Moody, S., Musheno, M. and Palumbo, D. (1990). Street-wise Social Policy: Resolving the Dilemma of Street-level Influence and Successful Implementation. *Western Political Quarterly* 43, 833–48.

Meier, K. J. and Bohte, J. (2003). Not with a Bang but a Whimper: Explaining Organizational Failures. *Administration and Society* 35, 104–21.

—— and O'Toole, L. J., Jr. (2008). Management Theory and Occam's Razor: How Public Organizations Buffer the Environment. *Administration and Society* 39, 931–58.

———— Hicklin, A. (Forthcoming). I've Seen Fire and I've Seen Rain: Public Management and Performance After a Natural Disaster. *Administration & Society.*

Meyer, A. D. (1982). Adapting to Environmental Jolts. *Administrative Science Quarterly* 27, 515–37.

—— and Rowan, B. (1977). Institutionalized Organizations: Formal Structure as Myth and Ceremony. *American Journal of Sociology* 83, 340–63.

Middleton, A., Murie, A. and Groves, R. (2005). Social Capital and Neighbourhoods that Work. *Urban Studies* 42, 1711–38.

Miles, R. and Snow, C. (1978). *Organizational Strategy, Structure and Process.* London: McGraw Hill.

Mouritzen, P. E. (1989). City Size and Citizens' Satisfaction: Two Competing Theories Revisited. *European Journal of Political Research* 17, 661–88.

O'Toole L. J., Jr. (1997). Treating Networks Seriously: Practical and Research-Based Agendas in Public Administration. *Public Administration Review* 57, 45–52.

Odeck, J. and Alkadi, A. (2004). The Performance of Subsidized Urban and Rural Public Bus Operators: Empirical Evidence from Norway. *Annals of Regional Science* 38, 413–31.

Office of the Deputy Prime Minister (2004). *Learning from the Experience of Recovery.* London: Office of the Deputy Prime Minister.

Pfeffer, J. and Salancik, G. R. (1978). *The External Control of Organizations.* New York: Harper & Row.

Porter, M. (1980). *Competitive Strategy: Techniques for Analyzing Industries and Competitors.* New York: Free Press.

Putnam, R. (2000). *Bowling Alone: The Collapse and Revival of American Community.* New York: Simon & Schuster.

Putnam, R. (2007). *E Pluribus Unum:* Diversity and Community in the Twenty-first Century. *Scandinavian Political Studies* 30, 137–74.

Rainey, H. G. (1997). *Understanding and Managing Public Organizations*, Second edition. San Francisco, CA: Jossey-Bass.

—— Backoff, R. W. and Levine, C. H. (1976). Comparing Public and Private Organizations. *Public Administration Review* 36, 233–44.

Rice, T. W. (2001). Social Capital and Government Performance in Iowa Communities. *Journal of Urban Affairs* 23, 375–89.

Scott, W. R. (2001). *Institutions and Organizations*, Second edition. London: Sage.

Shah, S. M. and Cook, D. G. (2008). Socio-economic Determinants of Casualty and NHS Direct Use. *Journal of Public Health* 30, 75–81.

Starbuck, W. H. (1976). Organizations and Their Environments, in M. D. Dunnette (ed.), *Handbook of Industrial and Organizational Psychology*. Chicago, IL: Rand McNally.

Staw, B., Sandelands, L. and Dutton, J. (1981). Threat-Rigidity Cycles in Organizational Behavior: A Multi-Level Analysis. *Administrative Science Quarterly* 26, 501–24.

Tam, M. Y. S. and Bassett, G. W. (2004). Does Diversity Matter? Measuring the Impact of High School Diversity on Freshman GPA. *Policy Studies Journal* 32, 129–43.

Travers, T., Jones, G. and Burnham, J. (1993). *The Impact of Population Size on Local Authority Costs and Effectiveness*. York: Joseph Rowntree Foundation.

Weick, K. E. (1969). *The Social Psychology of Organizing*. Reading, MA: Addison-Wesley.

West, A., Pennell, H., Travers, T. and West, R. (2001). Financing School-Based Education in England: Poverty, Examination Results, and Expenditure. *Environment and Planning C: Government and Policy* 19, 461–71.

Wilkinson, R. G. (1997). Socioeconomic Determinants of Health—Health Inequalities: Relative or Absolute Material Standards? *British Medical Journal* 314, 591–5.

Williams, C. (2003). Harnessing Social Capital: Some Lessons from Rural England. *Local Government Studies* 29, 75–90.

Wilson, W. J. (1991). Studying Inner-City Social Dislocations: The Challenge of Public Agenda Research. *American Sociological Review* 56, 1–14.

Withers, S. D. (1997). Demographic Polarization of Housing Affordability *in situ* Major United States Metropolitan Areas. *Urban Geography* 18, 296–323.

Xu, K. T. (2006). State-level Variations in Income-related Inequality in Health and Health Achievement in the US. *Social Science & Medicine* 63, 457–64.

3 Regulation

Steve Martin

Introduction

One of the distinguishing features of the public sector is the scale, scope, and extent of regulation (Boyne 2003*a*; Hood et al. 1998). Unlike their commercial counterparts, managers of public services are not free to choose what goods and services they will provide or which customers they want to serve. They work within fairly tightly drawn parameters set by legal duties and powers and a range of other regulatory controls. Traditionally regulation has been associated with safeguards designed to ensure financial propriety and the delivery of minimum service standards. However, in recent years it has also been seen as a 'driver' of improvement with an increasingly important role to play in public services management. Whilst these developments have perhaps been most marked and best documented in the United Kingdom, the growth of performance auditing and public services inspection has been a cross-national phenomenon involving 'the transformation of existing, and the emergence of new, formal institutions of monitoring' (Power 2003, p. 188) in continental Europe, North America, and Australia.

These developments have been intimately bound up with the emergence of the 'regulatory state' as an alternative form of governance to the traditional welfare state. The latter is characterized by integration between policy-making and service delivery and direct provision of services by government. By contrast, the regulatory state involves the separation of policy and delivery through privatization, contracting out, and the creation of arm's-length operational units. Public services are freed from traditional bureaucratic controls but become subject to new forms of steering by regulatory bodies which set standards, monitor performance, and specify contracts on behalf of governments (Scott 2004).

This chapter first examines the main types of regulation which apply to public services, highlighting in particular the growing importance of public services audit and inspection. Next it examines the theoretical links between regulation and improvement. It then assesses empirical evidence about this relationship. Finally it explores the implications for future research.

Definitions

In its broadest sense, regulation is concerned with the attempt by a government or a government agency to shape the behaviour of individuals, professions, organizations, or institutions. Baldwin and Cave (1999, p. 2) define it as 'sustained and focused control exercised by a public agency over activities that are valued by a community', whilst James (2000, p. 327) describes it as 'achieving public goals using rules or standards of behaviour backed up by sanctions or rewards of the state'.

National and local governments regulate the activities of public sector agencies in a variety of ways. Regulation is often underpinned by legal obligations and sanctions (including financial penalties and in extreme cases imprisonment), as for example in the case of health and safety, trading standards, and environmental protection. In general, the threat of punishments is more effective in regulation than the offer of rewards (Braithwaite 2000), but the latter can nevertheless play an important role. Ayres and Braithwaite (1992) write of an 'enforcement pyramid' at the apex of which is the regulators' powers to prevent activities. Examples include competition laws which control entry to a market, the sale of permits, the granting of licensing to trade, and restrictions on physical developments through spatial planning controls. Moving further down this 'pyramid', regulators provide incentives such as tax breaks and public subsidies and non-financial rewards such as awards which are designed to induce certain kinds of organizational and individual behaviours that are thought to be associated with desired outcomes (or to desist from behaviours associated with unwanted outcomes). Towards the bottom of the pyramid, regulators exert influence through persuasion (education, information, and advice) and voluntary codes of self-regulation. Ideally, the choice of regulatory instruments should be responsive to the nature of the perceived risks, and in general it is in the interests of both the regulators and those who they regulate to operate at the base of the pyramid (Ayres and Braithwaite 1992).

Government regulation of private organizations is typically motivated by the absence of market pressures or by market failure. Windfall taxes and price controls are designed to prevent monopolies or oligopolies exploiting their position in ways which penalize consumers. Regulators may also seek to reduce the power of monopoly producers by encouraging new entrants to supply markets in order to increase competition. A second reason for imposing regulation is to secure continuity of supply of vital public goods and/or to protect the needs of particularly vulnerable consumers (such as the elderly and those on low incomes). A third function of regulators is to ensure that service users have the information they need to make informed decisions. Fourth, it is often designed to ensure that providers and consumers take account of externalities which are not reflected adequately in unregulated exchanges.

All of these rationales also apply to the regulation of public services. Many public service providers enjoy monopoly status and therefore lack competitive pressures to maximize their efficiency and the quality of their services. They frequently provide services upon which the most vulnerable members of society are highly dependent. And it is often the case that clients, pupils, patients, and taxpayers lack sufficient information to hold public services to account. It is not therefore surprising that public services find themselves subject to a range of different forms of regulation. Hood and Scott (1996, p. 321) define the regulation of public sector bodies as 'processes by which standards are set, monitored and/or enforced in some way, by bureaucratic actors who are somewhat separate from units or bodies that have direct operational or service delivery responsibilities'. Hood et al. (2000, p. 284) introduce the concept of 'regulation inside government' which they define as 'oversight of bureaucracies by other public agencies operating at arm's-length from the direct line of command, the overseers being endowed with some sort of official authority over their charges'. They identify three distinctive features of this form of regulation. First, regulators have official authority over the body (or bodies) which they regulate. This may for example be through control over resources, the laying down of procedures that they must follow, or the setting of service standards which they must achieve. Second, there is an organizational separation between the regulator and the regulated body. Third, the regulator monitors performance and uses persuasion and/or direction to modify the actions of the regulated body.

According to Hood and his colleagues, there are five main forms of activity which fulfil these criteria: adjudication, authorization, certification, audit, and inspection. Adjudication includes complaints handling systems and a variety of different forms of scrutiny by individuals and/or organizations set up specifically for this purpose—for example, inquiries undertaken by public services ombudsmen. Authorization and certification include the formal and informal regulations by which central government departments influence other government agencies (such as executive agencies) and local service providers such as hospitals, schools, police services, and local authorities. They include the imposition of constraints on activities (e.g. restrictions on UK local government's powers to trade); enabling powers (e.g. the power to promote well-being granted to local councils in England and Wales); and mandatory requirements (e.g. the duty of Best Value and a duty to collaborate). Audit focuses on the stewardship of public money and the financial viability of public bodies, and usually involves regular checking of an organization's accounts and financial management systems by accounting professionals. Inspection focuses on service quality and outcomes, and normally consists of selective, episodic checks that organizations are meeting minimum standards or conforming to agreed standards of 'good practice'. Inspectors come from a more diverse range of backgrounds than auditors. Teams often include people with experience of general management and lay assessors.

Adjudication, authorization, and certification all have an important role to play in quality assurance. However, public services audit and inspection in recent years have been seen as most likely to contribute to efforts to improve performance. This chapter therefore focuses primarily on these two forms of regulation. With the increasing use of performance auditing around the globe, and particularly in the United States and Europe (Barzelay 1997; English and Skaerbaek 2007; Pollitt 2003), the distinction between audit and inspection has become increasingly blurred. Inspectors and auditors have sought to 'blend their respective concerns with quality and efficiency' (Midwinter and McGarvey 2001, p. 843) with the result that there has been a 'homogenization and standardization of audit and inspection processes' (Power 2003, p. 189), with audit 'pushed towards a more inspectorial style of approach' (Bowerman et al. 2000, p. 83). Auditors have taken an increasing interest in performance and both inspection and audit have become more concerned with aspects of corporate capacity such as leadership and the use of resources. However, Power (1997) maintains that, in spite of the convergence between them, the two activities remain distinct. Inspection is, he argues, more likely to create a dialogue because standards are less clear cut and judgements may therefore be negotiated with inspected bodies.

Theories of regulation and improvement

It is helpful to distinguish between three theoretical perspectives on the possible links between regulation and public services improvement. The traditional view of regulation of public services sees it as a means of ensuring that services meet minimum standards. Regulation is regarded as a means of providing public assurance. As such it has links to the concepts of risk assessment and total quality management. A second perspective conceptualizes regulation as a response to absence of competition and contestability which drive improvement in private goods markets. It echoes the rationale for regulation of privatized former state monopolies in sectors such as telecommunications, water, electricity, and gas supply and draws on economic theory. The third perspective views regulation as an 'agent of improvement'. It borrows (implicitly at least) from the business management literature and in particular draws on theories of leadership, motivation, and organizational learning.

REGULATION FOR ASSURANCE

A number of scholars have linked the development of the 'regulatory state' (Majone 1994) to a loss of faith in traditional forms of bureaucratic control and professional expertise (Newman 1998, 2001). Theories which see the role of regulation as offering assurance therefore provide a persuasive account of its growth in recent years. It is argued that high profile failures in areas such as child protection, combined with less deferential attitudes on the part of service users and increasing risk aversion in the wider population, mean that citizens and their elected representatives are now unwilling to rely on teachers, clinicians, social workers, and other experts to safeguard the interests of pupils, patients, and clients (Davies 2000). The result has been a shift away from relations based on trust in status to a much greater reliance on explicit, codified standards and practices (Hughes et al. 1997).

According to this view, regulation serves a powerful socio-political function, providing policy-makers with a way of being able to exert 'control at a distance' (Hoggett 1996) over increasingly decentralized and dispersed forms of service delivery to which functions traditionally provided directly by the state have been hived off (Clarke et al. 2000). The data generated by audit, inspection, and other forms of regulation have proved useful to governments wishing to monitor the performance of these semi-autonomous delivery organizations, and provided chief executives and non-executive board members of these organizations with the information they need to exert control over 'frontline' services (Humphrey 2003).

The concept of 'risk regulation regimes' offers a useful theoretical framework which helps in the identification of the possible impacts of regulatory mechanisms on performance. Drawing on cybernetic theory, Hood et al. (2001) distinguish three components which they suggest form the basis of any regulatory regime: ways of gathering information; ways of setting standards, goals, or targets; and ways of changing behaviour to meet standards or targets. Boyne et al. (2002) extend this framework to suggest that the effectiveness of regulation will be related to the expertise of the regulators and levels of resistance, ritual compliance, regulatory capture, performance ambiguity, and the extent of information gaps.

A number of authors highlight the importance of the 'relational distance' between inspectors and those whom they inspect. They suggest that by avoiding regulatory capture and maintaining their independence (or 'distance'), regulators are able to highlight service failings without fear or favour. But a number of researchers have suggested that this may be counterproductive because inspected bodies are likely to resist recommendations made by regulators whom they regard as remote and unsympathetic, and 'punitive' regimes may therefore be more likely to encourage gaming (Day and Klein 1990; Hughes et al. 1997).

Hughes et al. (1997) suggest that the nature of the regulatory regime which develops in any given situation is determined by the public standing of those whose activities are being regulated, their ability to lay claim to specialist knowledge or expertise, their capacity to act collectively to resist inspection, and the level of concern about their current performance. Hood et al. (1999) echo this view. They found that the more distant regulators were from those whom they were regulating (in terms of their professional training and social background), the more formal and rule-bound was the approach to inspection.

REGULATION AS CONTESTABILITY

A second theoretical perspective on the regulation of public services sees it as compensating for the absence of effective competition in supply markets. According to this view, because dissatisfied service users are unable to go elsewhere and taxpayers cannot act like shareholders to keep inefficient providers in check, the role of the regulator is to manage supply markets to safeguard their interests.

This perspective on regulation of services has been influential in shaping policy in the United Kingdom and elsewhere. It has, for example, underpinned the work of the UK Treasury's Better Regulation Executive which oversees the regulation of both public and private sector markets. And it is increasingly being seen in the way in which regulators of public services account for their activities. The former chair of the UK Audit Commission, for example, has stated that 'the regulator's challenge has been to create a substitute form of pressure' (Strachan 2005 quoted in Grace 2005, p. 558), and social care inspectorates in Britain also explicitly define their role as regulating the mixed market of provision of care for vulnerable adults (Platt 2005). Seen from this perspective, regulation acts as a counterweight to producer interests in order to safeguard the needs of users and taxpayers. Price controls limit the scope for budget maximization and bureau shaping by providers, thus helping to ensure efficient service provision. The setting of minimum standards exerts pressure on providers to safeguard service quality, especially where service users have access to some form of redress or financial compensation.

In many countries the public sector organizations are not monopoly suppliers of major public services such as health, education, and training. They operate in quasi-markets in which they face competition—from other public agencies and/or from the private and not-for-profit sectors. As noted above, regulators can play a role in creating and nurturing these markets. They may also help to ensure that they operate effectively. In particular they often have a role in alleviating measurement problems and information asymmetries. Definitions of performance in the public sector are often ambiguous or contested.

Outcomes can be difficult to quantify and compare. And providers invariably have access to more accurate, up-to-date, and comprehensive information about costs and quality than the commissioners or users of services. In these circumstances regulators may assist the functioning of supply markets by generating and disseminating comparative performance data which enable both commissioners and service users to make informed choices about which providers to access.

REGULATION AS AN AGENT OF IMPROVEMENT

In recent years governments around the world have been urgently seeking ways to secure improvement in their public services (Boyne 2003*b*). The third view of regulation identified above sees it as a means of achieving this. This perspective has been particularly influential in the United Kingdom where performance auditing and external inspection have been seen explicitly as a way of 'driving through' public services reform (Downe and Martin 2007). But it is also reflected in the activities of supreme audit institutions in many other countries (including, e.g., the United States General Accounting Office, the *Bundes* and *Landesrechnungshoefe* in Germany, and the National Audit Office in Australia) and at local level. In the Netherlands, Sweden, and France, for example, local authority associations have negotiated with the central government for the introduction of national benchmarking schemes to facilitate performance comparisons (Fouchet and Guenoun 2007; Hendriks and Tops 2003; Smith 2007). In Germany, where there is tradition of voluntary performance management by the local government (Reichard 2003), the Länder have started to scrutinize the accountancy and budgeting processes of the municipalities in much more detail and recently imposed a new requirement that they operate a system of output-oriented performance management known as 'Produktorientierte Haushalt' (Bloomfield 2006). In Ontario, a Municipal Performance Measurement Program incorporating measures of effectiveness and efficiency has been adopted by municipalities (Findlay 2007).

Many inspectorates now explicitly define their purpose as 'agents of improvement'. Audit Scotland (2008), for example, describes itself as 'holding to account and helping to improve'. Its aim is to 'provide assurance to elected officials, board members, and the public at large about how public money is used, while at the same time helping public bodies improve they way they are managed and the services they deliver'. The Audit Commission in England goes further. It states: 'Our mission is to be a driving force in the improvement of public services. We promote good practice and help those responsible for public services to achieve better outcomes for citizens, with a focus on those people who need public services most'. And the Wales Audit Office is currently switching resources away from its traditional audit function in favour of disseminating good practice. Researchers have found that this view of the role of regulation is also echoed by local inspection teams. Humphrey (2002, p. 470) reports that the social services Joint Review Team which she shadowed 'conceptualised itself primarily as an improvement agency, as it aspires to work hand-in-hand with senior managers to the benefit of all stakeholders, and reviewers make frequent references to their "free consultancy services"'.

Negative impacts on performance

Set against these explanations of how regulation is in theory linked to public service improvement, there are a number of critiques which suggest that it may in fact have no significant impact or even lead to negative effects on performance.

Power (1997, 2003) argues that regulation consists of self-serving 'rituals of verification' which promote the interests of regulators and their political masters and mistresses rather than performance improvement. Regulators need to make organizations 'auditable'. As a result, performance 'is not so much verified as constructed around the audit process itself' (Power 1997, p. 51). According to this view, regulators find it easier to observe deficiencies in procedural characteristics than to measure substantive outcomes. As a result, regulation may provide false reassurance and introduce perverse in-centives which distort organizational priorities and individual behaviours (Clarke 2008; Humphrey 2001, 2002). Jones (2000, p. 29), for example, notes that in education 'there is considerable concern about the introduction of systems of service measurement and quality assessment which are elec-tronically sophisticated but theoretically elementary and imperfect'. And the recent introduction of composite performance measures in UK public ser-vices has come in for particular criticism because of their vulnerability to categorization errors and gaming and their disregard of important external influences on performance (see Andrews [2004]; Andrews et al. [2005]; Jacobs and Goddard [2007]; McLean et al. [2007]; Palmer and Kenway [2004]).

A second important critique of regulation of public services argues that sustainable improvement cannot be forced from the outside but depends on organizations' capacity for reflection and self-improvement (Fink 1999; Jones 2005; Newman 2001). Inspection can in fact make it more difficult for poor-performing organizations to improve because the stigma associated with bad inspection reports leads to defensiveness and makes it difficult for them to retain and recruit good staff (Davis and Martin 2008).

A third area of concern is the cost of regulation. Inspectorates need staff and finance and inspected bodies may incur significant compliance costs. Performance monitoring is likely to 'distract middle- and upper-level officials, create massive paperwork, and produce major unintended effects' (Hood and Peters 2004, p. 278). Studies also suggest that inspection takes a toll on staff (see Brimblecombe et al. [1996]; Grubb [1999]; Weiner [2002]) and can cause widespread disruption to the service delivery (Earley 1998). In a study of twenty-four school inspections, Wilcox and Gray (1996) found evidence of persistent teacher anxiety even in schools which received good reports. Critics also argue that regulation stifles innovation by rewarding conformity rather than risk-taking (van Thiel and Leeuw 2002).

Theoretical perspectives on the potential impact of regulation on public services therefore offer a range of sometimes contradictory propositions. Its alleged benefits include public assurance, better functioning of supply markets for public services, and direct improvements through the identification of organizations which are underperforming. But the literature also demonstrates the existence of significant concern about the financial, opportunity, and human costs associated with regulation. It is noticeable that regulators frequently justify their activities in terms of instrumental gains including cost savings and performance improvements—what Pollitt and Summa (1997) call a 'managerialist' rather than a 'constitutional' rationale. And yet, as a number of scholars have noted, there is very little rigorous evidence about the real costs and benefits of regulation or its impact on improvement (Boyne et al. 2002; Byatt and Lyons 2001; Davis et al. 2004; Hood et al. 1999, 2000).

Evidence of regulation and improvement

The remainder of this chapter seeks to begin to fill this gap by examining empirical studies of the impact of inspection on the performance of public services. A literature search revealed that most studies that have explored this relationship share a number of features. They focus on the direct impacts of inspection and are therefore aligned with the third of the rationales for regulation outlined above. They have little to say about indirect effects on performance—either through improving the operation of supply markets or increasing accountability. Most focused on just one sector (usually schools or local government services) and assessed impacts in terms of senior managers' perceptions of the performance of their organizations and/or government performance indicators. Studies have also focused on UK public services, perhaps because of the availability of performance data and (as described earlier) also because British policy-makers have emphasized the role of regulation in driving improvement. (A study of summaries reviewed is given in Table 3.1.)

The largest single body of empirical research on the impacts of inspection focuses on school effectiveness. Much of this concludes that inspections have led to changes in management systems and teaching practice but that the relationship with improvements in educational attainment is complex and contingent.

Ousten et al. (1997) surveyed head teachers in 683 English secondary schools immediately before and two years after they were inspected. They report that inspections were widely credited with having helped to clarify the responsibilities of the senior management team and with improvements in personal and social education, tutorial programmes, and provision for those with special needs. They also led to the development of stronger links between schools' development plans and their budget planning processes. Kogan and Maden (1999) report similar effects. They found that 58 per cent of the schools had made changes to teaching styles and curriculum organization following inspections. Four in ten had increased pupil monitoring and testing. More than a quarter had changed management structures and a fifth had increased staff development. Furthermore, an evaluation of revised Ofsted inspection processes after September 2005 (known as 'Section 5 inspections') reached similar conclusions. Nearly two-thirds of survey respondents and just over half of those interviewed considered that the inspection had helped them prioritize and clarify areas for improvement but had not highlighted wholly new issues or areas of concern (McCrone et al. 2007).

But Kogan and Maden (1999) found that inspection had little impact on performance. Two-thirds of teachers believed that it had not improved students' test scores. Case et al. (2000), who studied the lead up to inspections, the inspection process, and its impact one year later in three schools, are similarly sceptical about the impact on improvement. They conclude that 'despite the intensity of the OFSTED experience, teachers in our study indicate that, 1 year after inspection, it has no lasting impact on what they do in the classroom'. They argue that teachers stage-manage inspections through nominal compliance with formal procedures, but that the process is of no lasting value in terms of increasing accountability or supporting improvement. Like other researchers, they point to significant negative impacts. They found that inspections increased levels of stress and anxiety among teachers who are often left feeling humiliated and undervalued. Kogan and Maden (1999) point to similar effects—a quarter of the schools which they surveyed reported that staff sickness had gone up following inspections and a fifth had experienced an increase in early retirements.

A small number of studies have analysed the impacts of inspection on educational attainment using performance data rather than perceptions. Cullingford and Daniels (1999, p. 66) analysed GCSE results in 426 English

Table 3.1. Summary of empirical evidence

Study	Type of inspection	Country and sector	Sample and time period	Measures of performance	Findings
Andrews and Martin (2007, 2010)	Performance frameworks	England, Scotland, and Wales health service; local government; police; fire and rescue services	All unitary local authority areas 2000/1 to 2004/5	Statutory performance indicators	Intensive inspection is associated with more rapid performance improvement
Andrews et al. (2008)	Service inspections	Welsh local government services	51 local authority departments 2000 to 2002	Statutory performance indicators	No significant differences between performance of services which had been inspected and those which had not
Brown and Lilford (2006)	Star ratings	English health service	303 English Primary Care Trusts 2004/5	Star ratings, Aggregated Quality and Outcomes Framework scores, Dr Foster mortality index; Dr Foster equity index, NHS Litigation Authority Risk Management standards	Star ratings lack sufficient construct validity to measure the underlying concept of quality
Case et al. (2000)	School inspections	English primary schools	3 schools mid and late 1990s (precise date not specified)	Non-participant observation; interviews and focus groups with teachers	Inspections led to intensification of control over teachers and increased levels of stress and illness but no lasting impacts on classroom practice
Chapman (2001)	School inspections	English schools	5 English secondary schools 1999/2000	Teachers' perceptions of impacts of inspection on their practice	22% of teachers reported that they intended to change their practice as a result of the inspection. The culture of schools played a key role in determining how teachers responded to inspection
Cullingford and Daniels (1999)	School inspections	English secondary schools	426 schools 1994–97	Percentage of pupils attaining grades of A* to C in GCSE examinations	Results improved less in the year in which schools were inspected than in those which were not inspected
Downe and Martin (2007)	Best value inspection	English local government	2,387 inspection reports 5 case study inspections 2001–5	Games–Howell test of mean inspection scores critical incident analysis Managers' perceptions of improvements in quality of services	Inspection scores are unreliable basis on which to judge performance because of inconsistencies in the application of inspection methods

Study	Program	Context	Data	Outcome measures	Findings
Downe et al. (2008)	Best Value Audit	Scottish local government	Surveys of managers in 16 councils Interviews in 7 councils 2007	Managers', politicians', and other local stakeholders' perceptions of improvements in service quality	There are few examples of a direct link between inspection and specific improvements. But inspection encourages awareness of performance and makes it more difficult for authorities to ignore poor performance. Best value audits are seen by managers as a catalyst for improvement in managerial processes and a means of increasing local capacity for self-evaluation and learning. There is little evidence of direct improvements in service outcomes
Given (2005)	Star ratings	English-health care	Cross-sectional analysis of 17 NHS trusts	Managers' perceptions of improvements in performance of HR functions	Poor data quality and inconsistent incentives mean that star ratings are of limited relevance in evaluating or driving the performance of hospitals' HR function
Humphrey (2003)	Joint reviews	English-social-services departments	3 case study authorities 1999–2001	Managers' perceptions of service quality	The impact of inspection is contingent on the capacity of inspected authorities to respond effectively to them. It tends to widen rather than narrow the gap between good and poor performers
Kogan and Maden (1999)	School inspections	English schools	Surveys of teachers, school governors, and parents 1996/1997	Teachers', governors', and parents' perceptions of improvements in teaching practices and students' test scores	Inspections followed by changes in teaching styles, curriculum organization, and management structures, and by increases in pupil monitoring and testing, staff sickness, early retirement, and staff development. Two-thirds of schools report no impact on pupils' test scores. Parents more likely than teachers to attribute changes to inspection

(continued)

Table 3.1. Continued

Study	Type of inspection	Country and sector	Sample and time period	Measures of performance	Findings
Martin et al. (2003, 2006)	Best value inspections	English local government	Surveys of senior managers in a stratified sample of approximately 100 councils In-depth case studies of 42 services which had undergone significant improvement 2001 to 2004	Managers' perceptions of service quality performance indicators	25% of survey respondents believed that the benefits of best value inspections outweighed the costs But inspection had been instrumental in encouraging improvement in 10 out of 42 in-depth case studies
McCrone et al. (2007)	Schools inspection	Schools England	Survey of 1,597 schools. Interviews with 169 head teachers, senior managers, governors, parents, and 243 pupils in 336 schools Analysis of key case-study school documents and test and examination results 2005/2006	Perceptions of effectiveness of teaching and improvements in students' test scores and test results	Nearly two-thirds of survey respondents and more than half of interviewees believed inspection had contributed to improvement Some evidence of a link between inspection recommendations and improvement in exam results at key stage 2 and key stage 4 in high-performing secondary schools
Ofsted (2007)	Childcare, education and skills training for young people	Schools, local government, training agencies England	Synthesis studies bringing together results of evaluations based on surveys, case studies, and document analysis 2006	Perceptions of students' attainment Inspection reports	Regulation acts as a catalyst for improvement but its impact varies between organizations Organizations judged to be inadequate usually make fastest progress in improving management practices. Inspection has had a significant impact on education policy and spending priorities
Ousten et al. (1997)	School inspections	English secondary schools	Before and after surveys of head teachers of 683 schools 1993–96	Senior managers' perceptions of changes in teaching practices and improvements in students' attainment levels	Inspections linked to improvements in internal processes and some evidence of improvements in outcomes

| Shaw et al. (2003) | School inspections | English secondary schools | Multivariate modelling of examination scores 1992–97 | GCSE scores A* to C grades | Inspection was associated with improvement in high-performing schools but had a negative impact on those where students had relatively low levels of attainment |
| Thomas et al. (2000) | School inspections | Special needs schools, England | Comparisons of school action plans rated as 'successful' and 'unsuccessful' by inspectors. Interviews with senior management team and governors in 14 schools. Late 1990s (precise dates unspecified) | 'Index of progress'; Senior teachers' and boards of governors' perceptions of management and teaching practices | Schools were traumatized by being placed in special measures, but the process led to improvements in terms of greater clarity of purpose and strategic direction, school leadership, and performance monitoring. Follow-up inspections seen as providing valuable advice and support |

secondary schools over a four-year period using logistic regression to model changes to results in the year in which they were inspected. They found that the percentage of students achieving five or more A* to C passes at GCSE (public examinations taken at age 16) improved more slowly than in those schools that were not inspected. They therefore concluded that inspection had a negative impact on performance. However, McCrone et al. (2007) found some evidence that specific recommendations relating to particular subjects led to improvements in examination results at key stage two (primary school) and at key stage 4 in those secondary schools where the majority of pupils were already achieving good grades. Shaw et al. (2003) reach a similar conclusion. They modelled the impact of inspection on the percentage of pupils attaining five or more A* to C grades in GCSE examinations in 3,047 schools (which is almost all state-funded schools in England). They controlled for other influences on results and analysed scores before and after inspections over the first full cycle of Ofsted inspections (which covered the period from 1992 to 1997). They found that performance in selective schools, which comprised about 5 per cent of state schools in England and where 80 to 90 per cent of pupils achieved five or more A* to C grades, increased by an average of 1 per cent per year following inspections, whereas in mixed comprehensive schools (which constituted about two-thirds of the population and where on average just 30% of pupils achieved five or more A* to C grades) results declined by 0.5 per cent in each of the years following inspections. In the case of single-sex comprehensive schools for boys, where around 35 percent of pupils achieved five or more A* to C grades, performance neither improved nor declined. But in single-sex girls' comprehensive schools and in grant-maintained schools, where 50 per cent and 45 per cent of students attained five or more A* to C grades respectively, performance improved by 2 per cent per annum post inspection.

Interestingly, studies based on teachers' perceptions of performance also suggest that impacts of inspection may be contingent on a school's prior performance. Chapman (2001) found marked variations among schools in the numbers of teachers who expected to change their teaching practices as a result of recent inspection reports. Those working in schools which already had a focus on improvement had the most positive interactions with inspectors and were most likely to report that inspection reports would change the ways in which they taught. Perceptions of impact also seem to vary widely among different types of informants. Kogan and Maden (1999) found that parents took a far more positive view of the effects of inspection on educational quality, standards, and financial management than teachers and head teachers (three-quarters of whom claimed that changes which followed inspections would have occurred in any case). School governors took a more positive view of inspection than teachers but were more sceptical than parents. Of course, teachers are not impartial informants. Their perceptions of inspection may be coloured by a degree of resentment about the burdens which inspections impose on them. However, they have a much more detailed knowledge of what actually happens in the classroom than parents and are therefore better placed to judge whether inspection is linked with improvement in teaching practices and student attainment. The fact that parents' perceptions are more positive reflects the fact that the public is reassured by the knowledge that schools are subject to external scrutiny.

Research on the impact of inspections in local government services suggests that its impacts are similarly contingent in this sector. Humphrey (2003) analysed the impacts of joint reviews of local authority of social services departments through interviews with managers and social workers in three councils—one of which was judged by the review team to be 'excellent', one of which was middle ranking, and one of which narrowly escaped being referred for ministerial intervention. She found that managers and staff in the best-performing authority had found the inspection beneficial and believed that it had led to improvements. But their counterparts in the other two authorities were more sceptical. Interviewees in the middle-ranking authority reported that the review team's conclusions and recommendations had been valid and had led to improvements in internal processes, particularly performance management systems' but that 'this was offset by the absence of tangible improvements for staff or service users at the grass roots' (p. 732). In the poorest-performing authority the review was seen as having made things worse because it damaged staff morale leading increasing numbers of staff to 'jump ship'. Humphrey concludes that the impact of joint reviews on performance improvement varies according to the capacity of the inspected bodies to respond positively to findings. As a result, inspections almost certainly exacerbate the overall inequalities between authorities, with a notable polarization between 'the best' and the 'the worst' (p. 731).

There is also evidence that different inspection methodologies have differential impacts, with some approaches perceived to be more effective than others in encouraging improvement. Research suggests that Comprehensive Performance Assessments (CPAs), which measured the overall performance of councils in England, were seen by local authority managers as being more effective in driving improvement than inspections which focused on individual local government services (Downe and Martin 2006). A survey in 2001 found that only 36 per cent of senior managers believed that service inspections had helped to encourage significant performance improvement in their authority; two-thirds reported that they focused unduly on management processes and neglected outcomes; 70 per cent believed that the costs of inspection associated with them were too high; and just 25 per cent believed that these costs were outweighed by the benefits (Martin et al. 2003). A follow-up survey three years later found an increase in the proportion of respondents who believed that costs outweighed benefits. However, a series of in-depth case studies of services in English local authorities found that inspection had been a significant factor in ten of forty-two cases. In some instances it had highlighted problems of which authorities had been unaware. In others, managers had known that services were underperforming but had been unwilling or unable to address difficulties until they were highlighted by inspectors (Martin et al. 2006).

An evaluation of Best Value Audits (BVAs) in Scotland, which are analogous to CPAs, found that three-quarters of the senior managers believed that they had acted as a catalyst for improvement and more than two-thirds reported that they had increased their authority's capacity for self-evaluation (Downe et al. 2008). But interviews suggested that most of the improvements had been in managerial processes rather than service outcomes, and managers complained that inspectors failed to offer sufficient practical advice on how to improve.

Andrews et al. (2008) examined the impacts of inspection on the performance of fifty-one local government departments including education, social services, housing, highways, public protection, and benefits and revenues. They compared the performance of services which had been inspected with those which had not over a two-year period using government performance indicators and controlling for external influences such as levels of spending and deprivation. The analysis found no relationship between inspection and performance, and the authors therefore concluded that the value of inspection lies in enhancing the accountability of public organizations rather than driving performance improvement. However, research by Andrews and Martin (2007, 2010) suggests that over a longer time period the intensity of inspection may influence rates of improvement. Their analysis found that government performance indicators showed that services had improved more rapidly in those parts of the United Kingdom which had the most intensive forms of inspection. They conclude that this may be indicative of a positive association between certain kinds of inspection and performance.

Evaluations of inspection in the British National Health Service (Benson et al. 2004, 2006; Day and Klein 2001, 2004; NHS Confederation 2003; Walshe et al. 2001) echo those findings of research on education and local government services. Walshe (2008) provides an overview of the research in this field. He reports that studies have concluded that inspection of health services has tended to focus on internal processes and structures rather than service outcomes. It has contributed to some significant structural changes, particularly to senior management teams. And whilst reviews rarely generated entirely new knowledge about organizational performance and weaknesses, they have brought these issues to the fore, making it more difficult for organizations to ignore weaknesses and failings. However, it is difficult to identify measurable improvements in performance associated with inspection and, as in other sectors, there are concerns about the costs of inspection and the validity of criteria used by inspectors.

However, studies of the impact of aggregate measures (known at the time as 'star ratings') in the National Health Service cast doubt on their validity. Brown and Lilford (2006) undertook a cross-sectional analysis of primary care trusts in England and found no correlation between star ratings and other overall methods of performance assessment including Quality and Outcomes Framework, Litigation Authority Standards, and hospital mortality. Similarly, Givan (2005), who examined the impact of star ratings in driving improvement in hospital HR departments, concluded that 'poor data quality and inconsistent incentives make the ratings of limited relevance in either evaluating or driving the performance of the hospital HR function' (p. 634).

Conclusions

Evaluating the impacts of regulation is difficult. Policy-makers and inspection bodies are reticent about independent analyses, preferring to assert rather than having to prove the importance of inspection and other forms of regulation. Any attempt to assess its impacts faces formidable methodological challenges. The costs of public services inspection are not easily quantified. Few inspected bodies keep systematic records of the amounts of staff time that is given over to preparing for, and responding to, inspection visits, and it is difficult accurately to gauge indirect and opportunity costs. The negative impacts of inspection on innovation, staff sickness, motivation, retention, and recruitment remain largely unknown.

The benefits of public services inspection are similarly elusive. Given that regulation regimes are for the most part mandatory and applied comprehensively, there is rarely a 'counterfactual' against which to measure progress in its absence. Moreover, because the concept of 'performance' in public services is multi-dimensional, what constitutes improvement is invariably ambiguous and can be contested. Inspection may, for example, drive up quality as organizations invest in additional staff or new capital to secure the improvements demanded by the inspectors. But this may increase taxes and demoralize staff who are required to work more intensively. To complicate matters further, in the case of services such as education it may take several years for the impact of inspection to influence outcomes by which time it may be impossible to isolate its effects from other variables. This is a particular problem where governments intentionally pursue a range of different policies and initiatives in tandem.

In light of these complexities, it is not surprising that Hood et al. (2000, p. 298) identify 'a continuing "evidence vacuum" about the marginal effects (positive or negative) of increasing or reducing investment in the regulation of government'. The empirical studies reviewed in this chapter are limited—most focus on the United Kingdom and are concerned with health, local government, or schools—there is far less evidence about the impact of regulation on the police, probation services, prisons, the courts, fire and rescue services, and a host of other services. But even this admittedly narrow evidence base provides some useful insights. Four conclusions stand out.

First, there are persistent and widespread concerns, particularly among those at the receiving end of regulation, about its costs and its unintended consequences. Second, in spite of this, there is evidence of a link between inspection and improvements in internal structures and processes in a range of different service sectors. Inspection seems to be associated in particular with changes in management and leadership and the ability of organizations to prioritize. Third, these changes in internal processes may lead to improvement in service outcomes but this is far from guaranteed. Fourth, the impact of inspection is highly contingent. It varies between sectors and between organizations within the same sector. Different methodologies may have different effects, and some activities are more 'auditable' than others. In some services there are obvious ways of achieving improvement which can be implemented relatively easily. Moreover, there is clear evidence that the effectiveness of inspection is associated with an organization's ability to respond to recommendations, which in turn seems to depend on its leadership and managerial capacity and prior performance.

These findings have potentially important implications for policy. For example, recent policy in England (and to some extent other parts of the United Kingdom) has been predicated on the concept of 'earned autonomy'. The assumption is that inspection is of particular benefit to poor performers but that once they have achieved a basic level of competence they can be given greater freedom to act independently and regulate their own performance. As Power (1994) notes, one of the outcomes of this kind of thinking is that where organizations fail to improve there are inevitably calls for yet more audit and inspection, rather than an examination of its effectiveness, and several of the studies described above suggest that this model may be flawed since, contrary to the policy-makers' expectations, it seems that it is often the top performers which benefit most from inspection. This finding highlights the importance of using regulation in combination with other measures to support improvement. As a recent study of the impacts of school inspection in seven OECD countries concluded:

Without follow-up advice and monitoring to help a school to improve, a sound programme of teacher development which takes the morale of the teachers into account, a real understanding of how institutions work and how to manage change, and more willingness on the part of the authorities to put resources into schools with problems, post-evaluation improvement in many schools is likely to be short-term and limited. (OECS/CERI 1995, pp. 24–5)

There is then a challenging research agenda to be pursued on the subject of regulation and improvement in public services. The fragmentary evidence that is currently available is sufficient to show that this is an intellectually challenging field of enquiry with considerable potential for policy relevance. The need in the future is for empirical studies which cover a much broader range of services, and for more research from outside the United Kingdom. There is also a need for research which uses measures other than the perceptions of those who are subject to regulation. Existing studies draw heavily on surveys and interviews with teachers, local government managers, clinicians, and so forth. Their views are important but unlikely to tell the whole story. These groups might perhaps be expected to play down the benefits of regulation (e.g. by claiming that changes 'would have happened in any case') and to be concerned about the associated costs and disruption to their activities. Future research might therefore make more use of the perceptions of other actors (such as inspectors and service users) and of performance measures to shed light on why and how it is that regulation is associated with improvement in outcomes in some situations but not others. This will help to advance general theory about the determinants of performance. It should also inform policy by indicating those situations in which regulation is likely to be most effective and those where it is unlikely to work, and other policy instruments must therefore be used to support improvement.

REFERENCES

Andrews, R. (2004). Analysing deprivation and local authority performance: the implications for CPA. *Public Money and Management* 24(1), 19–26.

—— and Martin, S.J. (2007). Has devolution improved public services? An analysis of the comparative performance of local public services in England and Wales? *Public Money and Management* 27(2), 149–56.

—— —— (2010). Regional variations in public service outcomes: the impact of policy divergence in England, Scotland and Wales. *Regional Studies* 43 forthcoming.

—— Boyne, G., Law, J. and Walker, R. (2005). External constraints on local service standards: the case of Comprehensive Performance Assessment in English local government. *Public Administration* 83(3), 639–56.

—— —— —— —— (2008). Organizational strategy, external regulation and public service performance. *Public Administration* 86(1), 185–203.

Audit Scotland (2008). *Priorities and Risks Framework: 2008/9—2010/11 National Audit Planning Tool for Local Government.* Edinburgh: Audit Scotland.

Ayres, I. and Braithwaite, J. (1992). *Responsive Regulation: Transcending the Deregulation Debate.* Oxford: Oxford University Press.

Baldwin, R. and Cave, M. (1999). *Understanding Regulation: Theory, Strategy and Practice.* Oxford: Oxford University Press.

Barzelay, M. (1997). Central Audit Institutions and Performance Auditing: A Comparative Analysis of Organizational Strategies in the OECD. *Governance* 10(3), 235–60.

Benson, L.A., Boyd, A. and Walshe, K. (2004). *Learning from CHI: The Impact of Healthcare Regulation.* Manchester: MCHM.

—— —— —— (2006). Learning from regulatory interventions in healthcare: The Commission for Health Improvement and its clinical governance review process. *Clinical Governance: An International Journal* 11(3), 213–24.

Bloomfield, J. (2006). *Central Governments' Policy Approaches Towards Local Government on the Issues of Performance and Cost-Effectiveness.* Brussels: Council of European Municipalities.

Bowerman, M., Raby, H. and Humphrey C. (2000). In search of the audit society: some evidence from health care, police and schools. *International Auditing of Journal* 4, 71–100.

Boyne, G. (2003a). What is public service improvement? *Public Administration* 81, 211–27.

—— (2003b). Sources of public service improvement: a critical review and research agenda. *Journal of Public Administration Research and Theory* 13(3), 367–94.

—— Day, P. and Walker R.M. (2002). The evaluation of public service inspection: a theoretical framework. *Urban Studies* 39(7), 1197–212.

Braithwaite, J. (2000). Rewards and regulation. *Journal of Law and Society* 29(1), 12–26.

Brimblecombe, N., Ormston, M. and Shaw, M. (1996). Teachers' perceptions of inspection, in P. Earley, B. Fidler, and J. Ousten (eds.), *Improvement Through Inspection: Complementary Approaches to School Development.* London: David Fulton.

Brown, C. and Lilford, R. (2006). Cross sectional study of performance indicators for English Primary Care Trusts: testing construct validity and identifying explanatory variables. *BNC Health Services Research* 6(81).

Byatt, I. and Lyons, M. (2001). *Role of External Regulation in Improving Performance.* London: H. M. Treasury.

Case, P., Case, S. and Catling, S. (2000). Please show you're working: a critical assessment of the impact of OFSTED inspection on primary teachers. *British Journal of Sociology of Education* 21(4), 605–21.

Chapman, C. (2001). Changing classrooms through inspection. *School Leadership and Management* 21(1), 59–73.

Clarke, J. (2008). Performance paradoxes: the politics of evaluation in public services, in H. Davis and S.J. Martin (eds.), *Public Services Inspection.* London: Jessica Kingsley.

—— Gewirtz, S., Hughes, G. and Humphrey, J. (2000). Guarding the public interest? Auditing public services, in J. Clarke, S. Gerwitz, and E. McLaughlin (eds.), *New Managerialism, New Welfare?* London: Sage.

Cullingford, C. and Daniels, S. (1999). Effects of Ofsted inspections on school performance. In C. Cullingford (ed.), *An Inspector Calls—OFSTED and Its Effect on School Standards* pp. 59–96. London: Kogan Page.

Davies, C. (2000). The demise of professional self-regulation: a moment to mourn?, in J. Clarke, S. Gerwitz, and E. McLaughlin (eds.), *New Managerialism, New Welfare?* London: Sage.

Davis H. and Martin, S.J. (eds.) (2008). *Public Services Inspection*. London: Jessica Kingsley.

——Downe, J. and Martin, S.J. (2004). *The Changing Role of Audit Commission Inspection of Local Government*. York: Joseph Rowntree Foundation.

Day, P. and Klein, R. (2001). *Auditing the Auditors: Audit in the National Health Service*. London: The Stationery Office/Nuffield Trust.

——(1990). *Inspecting the Inspectorates*. York: Joseph Rowntree Foundation.

Downe, J. and Martin, S.J. (2006). Joined up policy in practice? the coherence and impacts of the local government modernisation agenda. *Local Government Studies* 32(4), 465–88.

—— —— (2007). Regulation inside government: processes and impacts of inspection of local public services. *Policy and Politics* 35(2), 215–32.

——Grace, C., Martin, S.J. and Nutley, S. (2008). Best value audits in Scotland: winning without scoring? *Public Money and Management* 28(1), 77–84.

Earley, P. (1998). *School Improvement After Inspection?* London: Paul Chapman.

English, L. and Skaerbaek, P. (2007). Performance auditing and the modernization of the public sector. *Financial Accountability & Management* 23(3), 239–41.

Findlay, S. (2007). Ontario's performance improvement regimes, in *Solace Foundation Imprint*. London: Solace Foundation, July, pp. 72–4.

Fink, D. (1999). Deadwood didn't kill itself: a pathology of failing schools. *Education Management and Administration* 27(2), 131–41.

Fouchet, R. and Guenoun, M. (2007). Performance management in intermunicipal authorities. *International Journal of Public Sector Performance Management* 1(1), 62–82.

Givan, R. (2005). Seeing stars: human resources performance indicators in the National Health Service. *Personnel Review* 34(6), 634–47.

Grace, C. (2005). Change and improvement in audit and inspection: a strategic approach for the 21st century. *Local Government Studies* 31(5), 575–96.

Grubb, W. N. (1999). Improvement or control? A US view of English inspection, in C. Cullingford (ed.), *An Inspector Calls—OFSTED and Its Effect on School Standards*. London: Kogan Page.

Hendriks, F. and Tops, P. (2003). Local public management reforms in the Netherlands: fads, fashions and winds of change. *Public Administration* 81(2), 301–23.

Hoggett, P. (1996). New modes of control in the public service. *Public Administration* 74(1), 9–32.

Hood, C. and Peters, G. (2004). The middle aging of new public management: into the age of paradox. *Journal of Public Administration Research and Theory* 14(3), 267–82.

——and Scott, C. (1996). Bureaucratic regulation and the new public management in the UK: mirror image developments? *Journal of Law and Society* 23(3), 321–45.

——Peters, G., James, O., Jones, G., Scott, C. and Travers, T. (1998). Regulation inside government: where the new public management meets the audit explosion. *Public Money & Management* 18(2), 61–8.

Hood, C., Scott, C., James, O., Jones, G. and Travers, T. (1999). *Regulation Inside Government*. Oxford: Oxford University Press.

—— James, O. and Scott, C. (2000). Regulation inside government: has it increased, it is increasing, should it be diminished? *Public Administration* 78(2), 283–304.

—— Rothstein, H. and Baldwin, R. (2001). *The Government of Risk: Understanding Risk Regulation Regimes*. Oxford: Oxford University Press.

Hughes, G., Mears, R. and Winch, C. (1997). An inspector calls? Regulation and accountability in three public services. *Policy and Politics* 25(3), 299–313.

Humphrey, J. (2001). Bewitched or bewildered? 'Facts' and 'values' in audit commission texts. *Local Government Studies* 27(2), 19–43.

Humphrey, J. (2002). A scientific approach to politics? On the trial of the Audit Commission. *Critical Perspectives on Accounting* 13, 39–62.

—— (2003). New labour and the regulatory reform of social care. *Critical Social Policy* 23(1), 5–24.

Jacobs, R. and Goddard, M. (2007). How do performance indicators add up? An examination of composite indicators in public services. *Public Money and Management* 27(2), 95–102.

James, O. (2000). Regulation inside government: public interest justifications and regulatory failures, *Public Administration* 78(2), 327–43.

Jones, K. (2000). *The Making of Social Policy*. London: Athlone Press.

Jones, S. (2005). Five faults and a submission: the case of the Local Government Improvement Programme. *Local Government Studies* 31(5), 655–76.

Kogan, M. and Maden, M. (1999). An evaluation of the evaluators: the OFSTED system of school inspection, in C. Cullingford (eds.), *An Inspector Calls—OFSTED and Its Effect on School Standards*. London: Kogan Page, pp. 9–31.

Majone, G. (1994). The rise of the regulatory state in Europe, in W.C. Müller and V. Wright (eds.), *The State in Western Europe: Retreat or Redefinition?* Ilford: Frank Cass. pp. 77–101.

Martin, S.J., Walker, R.M., Enticott, G., Ashworth, R., Boyne, G.A., Dowson, L., Entwistle, T., Law, J. and Sanderson, I. (2003). *Evaluation of the Long-Term Impact of the Best Value Regime: Baseline Report*. London: Office of the Deputy Prime Minister.

—— Entwistle, T., Ashworth, R., Boyne, G.A., Chen, A., Dowson, L., Enticott, G., Law, J. and Walker, R.M. (2006). *The Long-Term Evaluation of the Best Value Regime: Final Report*. London: Department for Communities and Local Government.

McCrone, T., Rudd, P., Blenkinsop, S., Wade, P., Rutt, S. and Yeshanew, T. (2007). *Evaluation of the Impact of Section 5 Inspections*. London: NFER.

McLean, I., Haubrich, D. and Gutierrez-Romero, R. (2007). The perils and pitfalls of performance measurement: The CPA regime for local authorities in England. *Public Money & Management* 27(2), 111–17.

Midwinter, A. and McGarvey, N. (2001). In search of the regulatory state: evidence from Scotland, *public administration* 79(4), 825–49.

Newman, J. (1998). Mangerialism and social welfare, in G. Huges and G. Lewis (eds), in *Unsettling Welfare: The Reconstruction of Social policy*. London: Routledge.

Newman, J. (2001). *Modernising Governance*. London: Sage Publications.

NHS Confederation (2003). *Re-reviewing the Reviewers: A Second Survey of NHS Trust Experience of CHI Clinical Governance Reviews.* London: NHS Confederation.

OECS/CERI (1995). *Schools Under Scrutiny.* Paris: OECD.

Ofsted (2007). *Review of the Impact of Inspection.* London: Ofsted.

Ousten, J., Fidler, B. and Earley, P. (1997). What do schools do after OFSTED school inspections—and before? *School Leadership and Management* 17(1), 95–104.

Palmer, G. and Kenway, P. (2004). *Comprehensive Performance Assessment and Deprivation: A Review by the New Policy Institute, a Report Commissioned by the Audit Commission.* London: New Policy Institute.

Platt, D. (2005). 'The Role of Social Care Inspection', Paper presented to the ESRC Seminar Series on *The Development of Scrutiny Across the U.K.* Cardiff: Cardiff University.

Pollitt, C. (2003). Performance auditing in Western Europe: trends and choices. *Critical Perspectives in Accounting* 14, 157–70.

—— and Summa, H. (1997). Reflexive watchdogs? How supreme audit bodies account for themselves. *Public Administration* 75, 313–36.

Power, M. (1994). *The Audit Explosion.* London: Demos.

—— (1997). *The Audit Society: Rituals of Verification.* Oxford: Oxford University Press.

—— (2003). Evaluating the audit explosion. *Law and Policy* 25(3), 185–202.

Reichard, C. (2003). Local public management reforms in Germany. *Public Administration* 81(2), 345–63.

Scott, C. (2004). Regulation in the age of governance: the rise of the post-regulatory state, in J. Jordana and D. Levi Faur (eds.), *The Politics of Regulation*, Cheltenham: Edward Elgar.

Shaw, I., Newton, D.P., Aitkin, M. and Darnell, R. (2003). Do OFSTED inspections of secondary schools make a difference to GCSE results? *British Educational Research Journal* 29(1), 63–75.

Smith, J. (2007). Improving performance—a European perspective, in *Solace Foundation Imprint.* London: Solace Foundation, July, pp. 65–7.

Thomas, G., Yee, W.C. and Lee, J. (2000). 'Failing' special schools—action planning and recovery from special measures assessments. *Research Papers in Education* 15(1), 3–24.

van Thiel, S. and Leeuw, F.L. (2002). The performance paradox in the public sector. *Public Performance and Management Review* 25(3), 267–82.

Walshe, K. (2008). 'Regulation and inspection of health services' in H. Davis and S.J. Martin (eds.), *Public Services Inspection*, London: Jessica Kingsley, pp. 71–89.

—— Wallace, L., Latham, L., Freeman, T. and Spurgeon, P. (2001). The external review of quality improvement in healthcare organisations: a qualitative study. *International Journal of Quality in Health Care* 13(5), 367–74.

Weiner, G. (2002). Auditing failure: moral competence and school effectiveness. *British Educational Research Journal* 28(6), 789–804.

Wilcox, B. and Gray, J. (1996). *Inspecting Schools: Holding Schools to Account and Helping Schools to Improve.* Buckingham: Oxford University Press.

4 Strategic Planning

George Boyne

Introduction

A recurring theme in attempts to improve public service performance is the need for organizations to adopt strategic planning. The idea that clear goals, targets, data analysis, and formal plans can enhance performance seems to appeal to governments across the globe (Downs and Larkey 1986; Poister and Streib 2005; Pollitt and Bouckaert 2004; Verheijen and Dobrolyubova 2007). This has led to one of the enduring debates in the public management literature: What are the relative merits of rationalism and incrementalism as alternative styles of organizational policy-making? (Dror 1973; Lindblom 1959, 1979; Simon 1961; Weiss and Woodhouse 1992; Wildavsky 1973). Is organizational performance likely to be improved by setting unambiguous goals and targets, formally analysing the feasibility of policy options and making detailed plans, or by leaving goals vague and adapting incrementally to new political circumstances? The aim of this chapter is to address this question by evaluating theories and evidence on the links between planning and the performance of public organizations. Depending on the assumptions that are made, and the arguments that are built upon them, planning can be hypothesized to have either a positive or negative effect on performance. Although planning has many advocates, in both academic and policy circles, it is also widely criticized as difficult, expensive, and counterproductive. In the first part of the chapter, the theoretical bases of these opposing views are considered in more detail. Next, the empirical evidence on the impact of planning on performance is summarized and critically reviewed. The validity of alternative theories of planning is then reassessed, and it is argued that its effects on performance may be contingent not only on technical and political aspects of the planning process but also on the institutional context in which it is attempted.

Theories of planning

WHAT IS PLANNING?

Planning can be defined broadly as an attempt to enhance performance by forecasting changes in the organization and its environment, setting objectives, and developing strategies for the achievement of these objectives (Capon et al. 1987; Wildavsky 1973). To some extent, all organizations engage in planning, even if only loosely and intuitively. By contrast, strategic planning is intended to be explicit, rational, rigorous, and systematic, and it involves the application of scientific methods to policy problems (Friedman 1987; van Gunsteren 1976). Organizational strategies are based not on incremental drift or leaps in the dark, but on 'logical' techniques and processes (Mintzberg 1994). At the core of planning theory is the belief that *reason* can be used to *control* the future behaviour and success of an organization.

Planning is usually conceptualized as a 'cycle' that comprises a number of linked stages (see Dror [1973]; Leach [1982]). Each of these stages may have a separate effect on performance, or perhaps only all of them in combination allow planning to have its fullest impact:

1. Goal Clarity: Planning is premised on the belief that organizations have formal goals and that expressing these clearly is the first stage in a sequence of activities that can lead to better performance. These goals may be subject to modification as a result of subsequent stages in the cycle, but advocates of planning largely accept the management mantra that 'an organization that does not know what it is trying to achieve is unlikely to achieve anything'. Thus reducing, if not eliminating, goal ambiguity is viewed as an essential early element of a planning process.

2. Analysis of the Organization: After goals have been clarified, the next stage is to analyse the organization and its environment in order to assess the technical and political feasibility of the objectives that have been set. For example, are the required financial and human resources likely to be available, and will internal and external stakeholders support the plan? The assessment of the organization and the environment is likely to generate a lot of data that in turn will require interpretation and analysis by technical specialists and organizational strategists.

3. Performance Targets: Once goals have been refined in the light of technical and political feasibility, the next step is to set quantified targets for their achievement. This in turn requires the selection of performance indicators that accurately reflect the goals, and the identification of standards to be achieved on these indicators by a specific time (depending on the planning period—traditionally three or five years in the public sector, but more recently one year in the current era of 'government by (quick) results').

4. Formality: The extent to which objectives and strategies are expressed in a written document. This is widely viewed as an essential feature of planning. For example, in Capon et al.'s research (1987, p. 47), 'for a firm, to be classified as one that planned at all, a physical document had to be prepared'. Formality also implies that the 'procedures used are prescribed...(and) steps in the process are often scheduled and progress is controlled against the resulting timetable' (Grinyer and Norburn 1975, p. 20). Thus the existence of the formal plan is a means of guiding organizational activities and steering strategy implementation.

A comprehensive study of the effects of planning would require all four of these elements to be examined. As will be seen below, this condition is rarely met in empirical tests of the impact of planning on public service performance.

HYPOTHETICAL EFFECTS OF PLANNING ON ORGANIZATIONAL PERFORMANCE

Planning is believed to lead to positive organizational outcomes for a number of reasons (see Camillus [1975]; Capon et al. [1987]; Kay [1995]). Strategic planning forces leaders to clarify their objectives, and thereby provides a framework for allocating resources in line with the purposes of the organization. Furthermore, the objectives can be communicated to all staff who can then channel their efforts accordingly. The process of planning allows external events and internal changes to be anticipated and brought into alignment. The potential for 'panic reactions' to unforeseen circumstances is thereby reduced. It has been argued that the need for long-term planning is especially great in decisions that involve capital investment (Kukalis 1991), and when many circumstances in an organization's environment are changing rapidly (Dror 1973). By contrast, incrementalism may suffice in a simple and stable environment. Rational planning also allows decisions between alternative strategies to be taken on the basis of comprehensive information, rather than intuitively on the basis of incomplete or inaccurate data. Finally, planning contributes to the integration of the diverse activities in an organization. Separate functions can be combined and coordinated into a corporate whole, instead of working at cross-purposes.

Planning supposedly brings logic, unity, and synergy to decision-making, all of which are believed to stimulate superior performance. The critics of planning, however, dispute all of these points. The extensive critique of rational decision-making in public agencies has concentrated on three main issues. First, planning poses many technical problems: Relevant data are difficult to obtain and even more difficult to analyse. Thus planning is defeated by the intellectual limitations of the planners. This criticism reflects

Simon's argument (1961, p. xxiv) that decision-makers must 'satisfice because they have not the wits to maximize'. Secondly, planning is politically difficult: The effective development and enforcement of a plan implies a concentration of power that may be inconsistent with the realities of organizational life. As Wildavsky (1973, p. 132) argues: 'There can be no planning without the ability to cause other people to act differently than they would otherwise act. Planning assumes power. Planning is politics'. Strategic planning may require that a single view of objectives and strategies for their achievement can be embraced by the whole organization. However, most organizations resemble a set of shifting coalitions rather than a military dictatorship. Lindblom (1959) argues that the test of a good policy is, therefore, whether it commands sufficient support to be adopted, not whether it will actually achieve some grand objective. Thirdly, planning is widely considered to have a voracious appetite for financial and human resources (Bryson and Roering 1988; Mintzberg 1994). This is partly because of the time and technology required to undertake the planning cycle, each stage of which can be expensive because organizational resources are displaced towards planning rather than delivering services. Lindblom (1959, p. 80) argues that planning is absurd 'when the time and money that can be allocated to a policy problem is limited, as is always the case'. In short, the costs of planning are a burden that must be added to organizational overheads. This implies that even if planning helps to boost service outputs and outcomes, this will come at a price of lower efficiency and reduced cost-effectiveness.

Criticisms of the effects of planning systems that are actually implemented are numerous (see Camillus [1975] and Mintzberg [1994] for a summary). Two important sources will be reviewed briefly here in order to give a flavour of the arguments. In a widely cited study, Quinn (1980) argues that the strategies of successful organizations emerge from incremental rather than rational processes. Even when planning procedures are followed, they are of little relevance to the progress of the organization: 'Most important strategic decisions seem to be made outside the formal planning structure, even in organizations with well accepted planning cultures' (Quinn 1980, p. 2). Thus, planning may be decoupled from the real events of strategy formation and therefore have little impact on performance. Furthermore, in the organizations studied by Quinn, 'successful executives announced relatively few goals to their organizations. These were frequently broad and general, and only rarely were they quantitative or measurably precise' (1980, p. 66). Although these criticisms of planning are sharp, it should be noted that they are drawn from a very weak methodological base. Quinn presents no evidence on the performance of his small ($n = 9$) sample of private organizations, and does not compare the decision processes in these organizations with those in a control group. For all we know, unsuccessful organizations may formulate their strategies in exactly the same way as Quinn's supposedly successful organizations. In short, his criticisms of planning amount to little more than interesting assertions.

In a similar vein, Brunsson (1982) argues that rational analysis is an impediment to good performance. The process of planning can destabilize an organization by creating uncertainty and conflict, which in turn reduces the motivation and commitment of staff. Brunsson (1982, p. 33) concludes that 'effective decision processes break nearly all the rules for rational decision-making: few alternatives should be analysed, only positive consequences of the chosen actions should be considered, and objectives should not be formulated in advance'. However, in direct contrast to Brunsson's arguments, subsequent case studies of organizational behaviour in the private sector suggest that 'formal analysis acts as a kind of glue within the social interactive processes of generating organizational commitment and ensuring action' (Langley 1989, p. 626). The jury is still out on whether planning creates or destroys organizational commitment.

In recent years the target element of planning regimes has attracted substantial criticism, not least in the United Kingdom where central government has set thousands of quantified objectives for public services (Hood 2006). Two criticisms of targets are particularly relevant here. First, targets distort organizational behaviour and service delivery by focusing attention on what is being measured (Smith 1993). Yet this is precisely what a set of targets in a planning regime is intended to do: prioritize some elements of performance over others. Provided that targets accurately reflect the objectives of key stakeholders, then no 'distortion' occurs. This is most likely to be true if targets reflect service outcomes (e.g. better health, greater prosperity, cleaner and safer environment, more equity between social groups). By contrast, dimensions of performance such as economy or efficiency are not ends in themselves, and if used as targets may result in perverse outcomes (e.g. lower cost per unit of unwanted output). Second, targets lead to a displacement of political and managerial effort from providing services to 'playing the indicators'. Evidence of fraudulent behaviour in the pursuit of targets has been found by various bodies responsible for auditing and inspecting government agencies (Bevan and Hood 2006), and is corroborated by systematic academic studies (Bohte and Meier 2000). The scope for cheating is likely to be minimized if the extent to which targets have been achieved is visible to service users and the public at large. For example, hospital administrators are likely to fiddle the figures more easily on waiting lists than on patient mortality. Cheating is also much more difficult if performance figures are externally and independently audited.

In sum, a range of contradictory theoretical arguments on the costs and benefits of rational planning can be identified. It remains to be determined whether the results of empirical studies provide a clearer picture of the relationship between planning and performance.

Empirical evidence on planning and organizational performance

EMPIRICAL STUDIES AND THEIR CHARACTERISTICS

Empirical research on planning in the public sector is largely concerned with the obstacles to rational decision-making (Boyne et al. 2004; Downs and Larkey 1986; Rhodes 1979; Sharkansky 1970). For example, during the 1970s and early 1980s, there were many studies of a major attempt at planning in UK local government, the 'corporate revolution', but none of these analysed its impact on performance (Gray 1982). More recent studies of planning in the public sector have described the characteristics of strategic processes (Collinge and Leach 1995; Stokes-Berry and Wechsler 1995) or have prescribed particular methods of strategic planning (Bryson 1995; Caulfield and Schultz 1989; Lavery and Hume 1991). The latter studies make the implicit assumption that planning works, but offer no hard evidence either way.

Empirical evidence on the actual effect of planning on public service performance was identified through a Web of Science search process (see Chapter 1 for details). Closer inspection of the studies identified by this search revealed only eight that contain evidence on the link between planning and performance in the public sector. These studies, which are summarized in Table 4.1, are limited not only in number but also in their geographical and service coverage. First, all but one of them (Andersen 2008) has been conducted on organizations in the United Kingdom and United States, and all during the last decade when planning was promoted by proponents of NPM as a 'business practice' that would work in the public sector (Hughes 2004). Secondly, three of the studies have been conducted on the education sector, which is a context that may be favourable to planning because of objectives that are widely agreed (other things being equal, it is good for pupils to obtain qualifications) and quantifiable (e.g. percentage of pupils passing exams). Another limitation of the evidence is that measures of the impact of planning rely solely on managers' or employees' perceptions in four of the studies.

On the other hand, the set of evidence on planning has a number of strengths: It covers national and local governments, multi-purpose and single-purpose organizations, and typically is based on large samples of organizations, which enhances the external validity of the findings in the relevant national and service contexts. Also, all of the studies use different data sets, so the results are not loaded towards the relationship between planning and performance in a particular set of organizations (e.g. the three 'Cardiff studies' are on English local governments, Welsh local governments, and English local authority education departments). Finally, seven of the eight studies use formal tests of statistical significance (so the planning effects that

Table 4.1 Summary of empirical evidence

Study	Dimension of planning	Country and sector	Sample and time period	Measure of performance	Finding
Boyne and Chen (2007)	Performance targets	England, education	147 local authorities, 1998–2003	Percentage of school pupils passing exams	Performance targets associated with improvement in performance
Boyne and Gould-Williams (2003)	Targets, environmental and organizational analysis, formal plans	Wales, local government	186 service departments, 1998–2000	Managers' perceptions of service quality, efficiency, and effectiveness	Number of targets negatively related to performance; environmental and organizational analysis no effect; presence of formal plan no effect
Chun and Rainey (2005)	Goal clarity	US, federal government	49 federal agencies, 2000	Employee perceptions of productivity	Goal clarity is associated with higher performance
Hyndman and Eden (2001)	Performance targets	Northern Ireland, civil service	9 Executive Agencies, 1999	Officials perceptions of service effectiveness	Targets lead to better performance
Lan and Rainey (1992)	Goal clarity	US, federal, state, and local governments	92 agencies in Syracuse, 1990s	Managers' perceptions of organizational effectiveness	Goal clarity is associated with better performance
Walker and Boyne (2006)	Targets	England, local government	117 local authorities, 2001 and 2002	Archival; managers' perceptions	Setting targets makes little difference; target ownership by managers is associated with higher performance
Weiss and Piderit (1999)	Goal clarity	US, education	304 schools in Michigan	Exam performance of school pupils	No effect of goal clarity on performance
Andersen (2008)	Formal plans	Denmark, education	740 secondary schools, 2001–3	Exam scores, equity between socio-economic groups	Positive effect on exam scores; negative effect on equity

are uncovered by them are likely to be greater than would occur by chance alone), and use multivariate models that test the net effect of planning when some other potential influences on performance are held constant.

Evidence from the studies

Three of the studies have investigated the effects of *goal clarity* on performance. Lan and Rainey (1992) examine goal clarity in ninety-two organizations in the US city of Syracuse in New York state. The survey items for goal clarity were 'the goals of my organization are clearly defined' and 'it easy to measure the degree to which this organization achieves its goals', and that for performance was 'overall, this organization is effective in achieving its goals'. They find that goal clarity is positively related to managers' perceptions of organizational effectiveness, but the extent of this effect may be inflated by a common source bias that arises from the response to all of the survey items by the same managers.

Chun and Rainey (2005) provide evidence on the relationship between goal ambiguity (the opposite of clarity) and performance in US federal agencies. They distinguish between four dimensions of goal ambiguity: 'mission ambiguity' (how easily understandable is the organization's mission statement?), 'directive ambiguity' (the room for interpretation in translating organizational missions into concrete activities), 'evaluative ambiguity' (how precise and measurable are the organizational objectives?), and 'priority ambiguity' (the level of interpretative leeway in weighting different goals). Unlike the earlier Lan and Rainey (1992) study, these aspects of goal clarity are operationalized using archival rather than perceptual measures, and are largely derived from data and text in planning documents produced by the agencies. One measure in the study taps managers' perceptions of organizational performance: 'In the past two years the productivity of my work unit has improved'. The results show that this variable is negatively related to the first three dimensions of goal ambiguity, but is unrelated to the measure of priority ambiguity. Thus, Chun and Rainey (2005, p. 549) conclude that 'goal clarity is good' and 'high quality strategic planning provides one path towards goal clarification'.

The third goal-clarity study is by Weiss and Piderit (1999), who examine the link between the content of mission statements and pupils' exam performance in Michigan schools. Weiss and Piderit (1999, p. 195) note that proponents of mission statements argue that they 'make explicit organizational goals and priorities, leading to better communication with employees about what they should be doing', but that critics argue that they may contain confusing signals or communicate goals that employees reject, thereby generating internal conflict. One of the explanatory variables in this study is 'focus'—the number of themes (ranging from 1 to 10) in the mission statement, which can be taken as a measure of goal clarity (the weaker the focus, the greater is the goal ambiguity). Goal clarity was also measured directly by using the Gunning Fog Index to assess the readability of the organizational mission. These variables turn out to be statistically insignificant, which suggests that the focus and clarity of schools' missions neither helps nor hinders their perform-ance. Weiss and Piderit (1999, p. 220) note that an important limitation of their study is the absence of 'data about the process within each school for developing or using the mission statements'. As discussed below, this is a potentially serious flaw because theoretical arguments emphasize that staff 'buy-in' is likely to mediate the impact of mission clarity on performance.

The impact of *environmental and organizational analysis* has been exam-ined in only one study of public service performance. Boyne and Gould-Williams (2003) test the impact of this aspect of planning on the performance of local authority service departments in Wales. The measures of planning and performance are derived from managerial perceptions but from different sets of survey respondents in May and December 1999, respectively. The extent of environmental analysis is based on the extent of consultation with service users, participation in benchmarking clubs with other local author-ities, and comparisons of performance against 'market leaders'. The measure of organizational analysis comprises two elements: consultation with staff and the development of performance indicators to track progress on the depart-ment's own objectives. The seven perceptual measures of performance cover service quality, efficiency, and cost-effectiveness. Although this appears to be a comprehensive approach to the assessment of the link between planning and performance, very few significant results are produced. Thus the safest infer-ence is that, in this set of organizations, organizational and environmental analysis makes little difference to service improvement.

The most widely examined aspect of planning is *performance targets*, which has been included in four studies. Hyndman and Eden (2001) undertake a qualitative study of 'rational management' in nine executive agencies in the Northern Ireland civil service. Their data and conclusions are based on interviews with the chief executives of these agencies, and no direct measures of the use of targets or organizational performance are provided. This group of interviewees was 'chosen because of its seniority, assumed detailed know-ledge of the issues and its ability to provide an overview of the entire operations of the agency' (Hyndman and Eden 2001, p. 584). The rationale for the creation of such executive agencies was to provide a clearer framework for reporting and improving performance, partly through the use of indica-tors and targets, and for holding top managers to account. Perhaps unsur-prisingly then, 'all of the respondents perceived that focusing on mission, objectives, targets and performance measures had improved the performance of the agency for all stakeholders' (Hyndman and Eden 2001, p. 592).

Whether other stakeholders (such as middle managers, front-line staff, and service users) agreed with this statement is unknown.

Boyne and Chen (2007) provide a more comprehensive and less perceptual study of the impact of targets in 147 English local authorities between 1998 and 2003. The target regime they analyse was known as 'Local Public Service Agreements' (LPSAs). Under an LPSA, each local authority attempted to hit twelve targets negotiated with central government, in exchange for a maximum financial reward of 2.5 per cent of its revenue budget. The targets could be spread across many services or concentrated on a few services. Each authority selected from a long menu of performance indicators provided by central government, so the question 'do targets make a difference' can be answered directly by comparing the achievements of local authorities with and without an LPSA target on each indicator. Boyne and Chen (2007) assess target effects on four measures of pupils' exam performance in secondary schools, using a panel data set that covers the periods before and after the introduction of the LPSA regime. This analytical method allows a simultaneous 'before and after' and cross-sectional comparison of target effects. The results show that authorities with a target on an indicator performed better than authorities without a target, and performed better than themselves in the pre-target period. As Boyne and Chen (2007) note, this need not imply that the net effect of targets on educational performance is as positive as the results suggest, because non-targeted aspects of education provision may have been neglected during this period. Furthermore, the nature of LPSAs makes it impossible to disentangle the impact of targets *per se* from the impact of the financial rewards associated with the targets. Whether targets alone would have the same positive effect remains an open question. A further issue that is investigated in this study is the impact of the number of educational targets on exam results. Planning theory implies that a small set of precise objectives may provide a clear focus for improvement and help to mobilize effort and resources in the desired direction, whereas a large number of targets could lead to confusion and demotivation. Boyne and Chen's results suggest the opposite effect of the number of targets: More LPSA targets for education are associated with better exam results. The range of this variable is, however, quite restricted (1–6), so perhaps the impact becomes negative only at a higher number of targets.

Boyne and Gould-Williams (2003) also examine the impact of the number of targets (from 0 to 9) on the achievements of local authority service departments in Wales. They found that a higher number of targets was associated with lower managerial perceptions of performance on two measures of service quality and one measure of efficiency, but was unrelated to the other four performance measures in their data set. It would be helpful to know whether this negative relationship is linear (i.e. performance declines steadily as the number of targets grows) or whether it is at first positive but then turns downwards only after a threshold of 'too many' targets is reached (which would be consistent with the Boyne and Chen 2007 result), but this issue is not investigated in this study. Thus whether the impact of target numbers on performance is positive, negative, linear or non-linear remains unresolved by the available evidence.

Walker and Boyne (2006) examine the influence of 'target setting' and 'target ownership' on the performance of 117 upper-tier local authorities in England. The target measures were derived from a large survey of managers in 2001. The target-setting variable reflects the extent to which measurable objectives were (*a*) based on the authority's political priorities, and (*b*) were ambitious. The target ownership variable is taken from survey questions on (*a*) whether targets were agreed by those responsible for meeting them, and (*b*) whether the targets were viewed as achievable. These variables were tested against four measures of organizational success: the archival 'core service performance' element of the 2002 Comprehensive Performance Assessment (CPA), and local authority officers' perceptions of service efficiency, responsiveness, and effectiveness. The latter variables were also derived from the survey of local authorities in 2001. The statistical results show that the measure of target setting had very little impact on either the CPA score or the perceptual measures of performance. Thus linking targets to political priorities, and setting targets that are viewed locally as ambitious, appears to make no difference to service success. By contrast, the target ownership variable had a significant positive relationship with all four measures of service achievements. In other words, whether service performance is measured objectively or subjectively, a target regime is more likely to work if it is accompanied by consultation with the staff responsible for service delivery and if the targets are viewed as realistic.

Finally, the link between the presence of a *formal planning document* and performance has been investigated in only two studies. In their survey of local authority managers in May 1999, Boyne and Gould-Williams (2003) asked whether a written 'action plan' had been produced that contained a programme of activities for service improvement. A test of this variable against perceptions of performance in December of the same year yielded no significant results, but this may be too short a period for the formal plan and the associated actions to lead to any consequences for performance. An examination of the impact of formal plans over a longer time period is provided by Andersen's study (2008) of the performance of secondary schools in Denmark, as measured by the exam scores achieved by pupils and the equity of the distribution of these results by social class. The measure of planning includes 'annual steering documents', 'written goals', and 'written evaluation of student results'. Exam results are tracked over four years, with a lag between formal planning and performance of between one and three years. The results show a small but positive effect of planning on exam performance, and a more pronounced *negative* effect on equity: Students with low socio-eco¹ status perform worse at schools that have adopted formal plans. Unfortunately, Andersen (2008) offers no theoretical explanation for the adverse effect of planning on equity, but one interpretation might be that more 'business-oriented' secondary schools are more likely both to adopt formal planning and be more responsive to the demands of middle-class parents. In any event, this study poses the intriguing question of whether any average performance gains from planning are worth a redistribution of service outcomes from poor to prosperous sections of society.

In sum, the empirical studies offer some patchy support for a positive relationship between planning and public service performance. In particular, on the basis of the small body of evidence that is available, *goal clarity* and *performance targets* are associated with higher achievements by public organizations. Thus, claims that 'planning fails everywhere it has been tried' (Wildavsky 1973, p. 128) and that it 'certainly does not pay in general' (Mintzberg 1994, p. 94) should be rejected. Nevertheless, the empirical evidence is limited in a number of important ways, and a large research agenda awaits further studies of planning and performance.

UNRESOLVED RESEARCH ISSUES

Three main areas of further research on planning can be identified. These are questions about planning itself, and the internal and external contingencies that might moderate the relationship between planning and performance.

Elements of the planning process

As noted above, empirical evidence is beginning to accumulate on the impact of goal clarity and targets on public service performance. By contrast we know very little about other elements or sub-elements of the planning process. What is the impact of organizational and environmental analysis on performance? What is the relative importance of these two types of analysis, and how does this vary across organizations? For example, is environmental scanning more important for 'prospectors' that are innovative and developing new services, while internal analysis is more important for 'defenders' that are sticking with their existing services and seeking to become more efficient (Miles and Snow 1978)? Similarly, although two studies have examined the impact of formal plans on performance, their results are contradictory and their evidence does not move beyond the mere existence of the plan. Indeed, Andersen's evidence (2008) is consistent with the view that a written plan has a significant effect even if it is not implemented. It would be very helpful for both theory and practice to know a lot more about the impact of different implementation styles (e.g. the extent of flexibility in objectives, timescales, and prescribed actions) on organizational success.

Better and more comprehensive evidence on the dimensions of performance that are affected by planning is also required. The performance measures in existing studies are based too much on managers' perceptions, and the archival measures focus mostly on effectiveness. This is an important dimension of performance, but the evidence needs to be broadened to include service quality, consumer satisfaction, efficiency, and cost-effectiveness. Evidence on these last two aspects of performance would be especially helpful in resolving debates on whether planning adds financial costs that are disproportionate to service benefits. A broader array of performance measures would also allow trade-offs between them to be investigated, and reveal whether higher performance on some comes at the price of lower performance on others, as implied by Andersen's results (2008) on effectiveness and equity.

Existing studies have examined separate elements of the planning process, but not the connections between them. However, planning theory suggests that it is the adoption of the *whole cycle* that makes a difference to performance. In other words, the connections between the stages are synergistic, and the cycle is more than the sum of the parts. An assessment of this argument would require future studies to collect data on all of the stages of planning, and to examine whether they interact to produce especially positive effects on performance. This in turn, however, raises the possibility that 'too much planning' may have negative effects on performance and that rigorously completing all stages of the cycle may be a liability. At the very least, there may well be a point where further planning efforts yield smaller and smaller performance gains, or even result in 'paralysis by analysis' (Lenz and Lyles 1985).

Internal contingencies

The relationship between planning and performance may be moderated by a number of organizational characteristics. First, the quality of the planning process is likely to be influenced by the technical expertise at the corporate centre of an organization. Existing studies have examined *whether* elements of the planning cycle are undertaken, but not *how well* this is done. For example, inaccurate or incomplete scanning of the organization and its environment may lead to a poor plan that makes performance worse. Similarly, the selection of inaccurate or unreliable performance indicators is likely to lead to distorted targets that undermine organizational performance. Larger organizations are likely to have more 'corporate capacity' to devote to the technical quality of planning processes, which in turn implies that the impact of planning may vary with organizational size.

Critics of planning often argue that it flounders because of internal political opposition. Political conflict may arise from the clarification of organizational goals, the internal or external benchmarks and data that are used to assess their feasibility, the performance indicators and the targets that are set, and the actions that are prescribed for achieving them in the written plan. Thus, it can be expected that internal support will positively moderate the relationship between planning and performance. Such support in turn is likely to be greater when goals and targets are set with the involvement of those responsible for achieving them, rather than imposed from on high (Locke and Latham 2002). Some fragments of evidence from the empirical analyses of planning in public organizations are consistent with this view. The Cardiff studies in particular (Boyne and Chen 2007; Boyne and Gould-Williams 2003; Walker and Boyne 2006) provide strong hints that 'participative planning' is associated with better results. This needs to be explored more systematically in future studies by including not only measures of the elements of the planning cycle but also the support of organizational members for them. A plausible hypothesis is that planning only works if managers and staff are committed to making it work and are engaged in the planning process.

External contingencies

The generic management literature emphasizes that the impact of particular strategies is contingent on the environmental context of the organization (see Chapter 2). Relevant aspects of the task environment include *complexity* (the number of variables which influence an organization's performance), *munificence* (whether the environment is conducive to organizational growth), and *uncertainty* (the predictability of changes in complexity and munificence.). None of the existing studies of public service organizations has considered whether these variables might act as moderators of the relationship between planning and performance. Planning might be especially helpful when the environment is complex (because of the need to understand the service needs of a heterogeneous population), but less necessary when the environment is simple (e.g. only one client group with uniform needs). Planning is likely to be easier in a munificent environment because resources are abundant, but more urgent when resources are scarce and action is needed to cut costs in a sustainable way. Similarly, uncertainty both makes planning more difficult and potentially more effective as a means of developing a menu of responses to deal with the variety of circumstances that may emerge. Further studies of planning, therefore, need to include environmental contingencies in their models, and work through the theoretical logic and empirical evidence on these arguments.

Finally, studies of planning need to examine the effects of not only the task environment but also the institutional environment—in other words, the political and professional pressures that bestow legitimacy on particular managerial practices (Ashworth et al. 2009). As noted above, existing studies of planning have been conducted at a time when governments in western nations have been in the grip of the collective mania of new public management. Thus, evidence on the effects of planning during this period in Denmark, the United Kingdom, and the United States might reflect the legitimacy of clarifying goals, setting targets, and formally allocating responsibilities for their achievement. Such legitimacy, bestowed by government, its agencies, and management consultants might enhance the effects of planning in two ways. First, managers and staff within public organizations may be more willing to support planning if institutional pressures lead them to believe that it is a fashionable management practice that is likely to be effective. Secondly, external stakeholders are more likely to provide financial and political support to organizations that are viewed as legitimate, so the adoption of planning may lead the institutional environment of an organization to become more munificent, thereby in turn making it easier to perform well. Empirical investigation of these issues would require more complex study designs than have so far been attempted in research on planning. In particular it would be necessary to compare planning effects in institutional contexts of high and low legitimacy. This might be achieved by assessing the relative effects of planning in different nations, or in different historical eras in the same nation.

Conclusion

The idea that strategic planning will lead to better outcomes is seldom far from the centre of governmental thinking on public organizations. Although this idea has been widely debated, few studies have sought to examine whether it is supported empirically. In this chapter the evidence on planning and performance has been sifted and weighed, and a large research agenda of unresolved theoretical issues has been identified. The best guess on the basis of the existing evidence is that planning is likely to have a positive rather than a negative impact on public service effectiveness. This appears to be especially so for two elements of the planning process: goal clarity and performance targets. By contrast, little is known about the impact of organizational and environmental analysis or formal action plans. Furthermore, the impact of planning on other dimensions of performance, such as efficiency, consumer satisfaction, and cost-effectiveness is largely unknown.

Major opportunities exist for further research on planning and public service improvement. Prominent amongst these is the need for evidence on more nations and a wider set of services, and for studies to include measures of all stages in the planning cycle, and measures of staff involvement in (and commitment to) these stages. Beyond this baseline, more sophisticated models of the internal and external moderators of planning effects need to be theorized and tested. In particular, the task and institutional environments of organizations that attempt planning needs to be given more consideration. The current set of evidence, produced during a period when the doctrines of NPM have bestowed legitimacy on planning, is consistent with the view that it is not only planning *per se* that works, but also the adoption of practices that are endorsed by powerful public service stakeholders.

REFERENCES

Andersen, S. (2008). The impact of public management reforms on student performance in Danish schools. *Public Administration* 86, 541–58.

Ashworth, R., Boyne, G. and Delbridge, R. (2009). Escape from an iron cage? Organizational change and isomorphic pressure. In the public sector. *Journal of Public Administration Research and Theory* 19, 165–87.

Bevan, G. and Hood, C. (2006). What's measured is what matters: targets and gaming in the English national health care system. *Public Administration* 84, 517–38.

Bohte, J. and Meier, K. (2000). The motivation for organizational cheating. *Public Administration Review* 60, 173–82.

Boyne, G. and Chen, A. (2007). Performance targets and public service improvement. *Journal of Public Administration Research and Theory* 17, 455–77.

—— and Gould-Williams, J. (2003). Planning and performance in public organizations. *Public Management Review* 5, 115–32.

—— Law, J., Gould-Williams, J. and Walker, R. (2004). Problems of rational planning in public organizations: an empirical assessment of the conventional wisdom. *Administration and Society* 36, 328–50.

Brunsson, N. (1982). The irrationality of action and action rationality: decisions, ideologies and organizational actions. *Journal of Management Studies* 19, 29–44.

Bryson, J. (1995). *Strategic Planning for Public and Non-profit Organisations*. San Francisco, CA: Jossey-Bass.

—— and Roering, W. (1988). Initiation of strategic planning by governments. *Public Administration Review* 42, 995–1004.

Camillus, J. (1975). Evaluating the benefits of formal planning systems. *Long Range Planning* 8, 33–40.

Capon, N., Farley, J. and Hulbert, J. (1987). *Corporate Strategic Planning*. New York, Columbia University Press.

Caulfield, I. and Schultz, J. (1989). *Planning for Change: Strategic Planning in Local Government*. London: Longman.

Chun, Y. and Rainey, H. (2005). Goal ambiguity and organizational performance in U.S. federal agencies. *Journal of Public Administration Research and Theory* 15, 529–57.

Collinge, C. and Leach, S. (1995). Building the capacity for strategy formation in local government. *Local Government Studies* 21(3), 343–52.

Downs, G. and Larkey, P. (1986). *The Search for Government Efficiency.* New York: Temple University Press.

Dror, Y. (1973). *Public Policy Making Re-examined.* Bedfordshire: Leonard Hill.

Friedman, J. (1987). *Planning in the Public Domain.* Princeton, NJ: Princeton University Press.

Gray, C. (1982). Corporate planning and management: a survey. *Public Administration* 60, 349–55.

Grinyer, P. and Norburn, D. (1975). Planning for existing markets: perceptions of executives and financial performance. *Journal of the Royal Statistical Society* 138, 70–97.

Hood, C. (2006). Gaming in targetworld: the targets approach to managing British public services. *Public Administration Review* 64, 515–21.

Hughes, O. (2004). *Public Management and Administration.* London: Macmillan.

Hyndman, N. and Eden, R. (2001). Rational management, performance targets and executive agencies: views from agency chief executives in Northern Ireland. *Public Administration* 79, 579–98.

Kay, J. (1995). *Foundations of Corporate Success.* Oxford: Oxford University Press.

Kukalis, S. (1991). Determinants of strategic planning systems in large organisations: a contingency approach. *Journal of Management Studies* 28, 143–60.

Langley, A. (1989). In search of rationality: the purposes behind the use of formal analysis in organisations. *Administrative Science Quarterly* 34, 598–631.

Lavery, K. and Hume, C. (1991). Blending planning and pragmatism: making strategic planning effective in the 1990s. *Public Money and Management* 11(4), 35–41.

Lan, Z. and Rainey, H. (1992). Goals, rules and effectiveness in public, private, and hybrid organizations: more evidence on frequent assertions about differences. *Journal of Public Administration Research and Theory* 2, 5–28.

Leach, S. (1982). In defence of the rational model, in S. Leach and J. Stewart (eds.), *Approaches in Public Policy.* London: Allen & Unwin.

Lenz, R. and Lyles, M. (1985). Paralysis by analysis: is your planning system becoming too rational? *Long Range Planning* 18(4), 64–72.

Lindblom, C. (1959). The science of muddling through. *Public Administration Review* 19, 79–88.
—— (1979). Still muddling, not yet through. *Public Administration Review* 39, 517–26.

Locke, E. and Latham, G. (2002). Building a practically useful theory of goal setting and task motivation. *American Psychologist* 57, 705–17.

Miles, R. and Snow, C. (1978). *Organizational Strategy, Structure and Process.* New York: McGraw Hill.

Mintzberg, H. (1994). *The Rise and Fall of Strategic Planning.* London: Prentice-Hall.

Poister, T. and Streib, G. (2005). Elements of strategic planning and management in municipal government: status after two decades. *Public Administration Review* 65, 45–56.

Pollitt, C. and Bouckaert, G. (2004). *Public Management Reform: A Comparative Analysis.* Oxford: Oxford University Press.

Quinn, J. (1980). *Strategies for Change: Logical Incrementalism.* Homewood, IL: Richard D. Irwin.

Rhodes, R. (1979). Ordering urban change: corporate planning in the government of English cities, in J. Lagroye and V. Wright (eds.), *Local Government in Britain and France.* London: George Allen & Unwin.

Sharkansky, I. (1970). *Public Administration.* Chicago, IL: Markham.

Simon, H. (1961). *Administrative Behaviour.* New York: Macmillan.

Smith, P. (1993). Outcome-related performance indicators and organizational control in the public sector. *British Journal of Management* 4, 135–51.

Stokes-Berry, F. and Wechsler, B. (1995). State agencies' experience with strategic planning: findings from a national survey. *Public Administration Review* 55, 159–68.

Van Gunsteren, H. (1976). *The Quest for Control.* London: Wiley.

Verheijen, T. and Dobrolyubova, Y. (2007). Performance management in the Baltic States and Russia: Success against the odds? *International Review of Administrative Sciences* 73, 205–15.

Walker, R. and Boyne, G. (2006). Public management reform and organizational performance: an empirical assessment of the U.K. Labour government's public service improvement strategy. *Journal of Policy Analysis and Management* 25, 371–93.

Weiss, A. and Woodhouse, E. (1992). Reframing incrementalism: a constructive response to the critics. *Policy Sciences* 25, 255–75.

Weiss, J. and Piderit, S. (1999). The value of mission statements in public agencies. *Journal of Public Administration Research and Theory* 9, 193–226.

Wildavsky, A. (1973). If planning is everything, maybe it's nothing. *Policy Sciences* 4, 127–53.

5 Leadership

Nicolai Petrovsky

Introduction

Amongst all the possible levers (Wright 2003) to pull in the quest for public service improvement, leadership is one of the most discussed. There is a large literature on the topic in the private sector (for a comprehensive review, see Bass [1990*a*]). Yet without modifications, lessons from it cannot be brought into the public organizations of any advanced democracy. The reason is that there the leadership is like the tango: it takes two. Elected and appointed officials both lead in the provision of public services, each in specific ways. There is virtually no area where only politicians or only managers and bureaucrats lead. Consequently, studying leadership in the public sector is even more difficult than in the private sector. The majority opinion in the large literature on leadership in the private sector is that leadership matters for outcomes. Some systematic empirical research corroborates this assertion (for a broad review, see House and Aditya [1997]). Yet, since leadership is almost always co-produced in public organizations, whether and how it matters for public service improvement is an open question. This chapter provides a systematic review of the best available evidence to answer it.

A priori, one would expect leadership to make a difference for public services just as in the private sector because systematic and sustained improvements in public service performance are very unlikely to occur without some impulse. Those who formally hold the overall responsibility for organizational performance can indeed exert such impulses. Yet the duality of leadership in the public sector—elected and appointed officials both lead—makes the picture more complicated. To learn when and how leadership can improve public services, one needs to understand a number of things. First, how does leadership play out in the public sector? Second, how is leadership theoretically related to public service improvement? Third, do these hypothesized relationships hold up when confronted with empirical observations? And finally, what are the contingencies that make a certain type of leadership more or less effective for improving public services? The present chapter tackles these four questions in order to probe the leverage of leadership for public service improvement. The first step is to find a definition of leadership that is useful for this purpose.

Defining leadership

It is important to be clear about the definition of leadership because of the breadth of leadership studies. This entire chapter could easily be filled with different definitions of leadership, and still not all would have been covered. To allow space for the discussion of theoretical arguments on the role of leadership for public service improvement and for the review of empirical research on the topic, a very primitive, cut-and-dried definition of leadership by Stogdill (1950, p. 4; cited in Stogdill 1974, p. 10) is adopted here: 'Leadership may be considered as the process (act) of influencing the activities of an organized group in its efforts toward goal-setting and goal achievement.' The rationale for adopting Stogdill's definition is that it is particularly useful for reviewing possible effects of leadership on public service performance and improvement, as the following discussion will show.

Public service improvement is clearly an instance of goal achievement. In addition, the focus of this book is on the different levers or influences that can achieve this goal. Consequently, Stogdill's definition (1950) is very useful here. The definition also contains goal-setting. Indeed, in a few select cases, public organizations engage in goal-setting. While they often have broad strategic (and sometimes even specific operational) goals imposed upon them by legislation or orders from elected officials at higher levels of government, there may nevertheless also be some room for goal-setting. For example, District of Columbia Metropolitan Police Chief Burtell Jefferson was able to redefine the organization's unwritten goals and thus open up opportunities for African Americans (Williams and Kellough 2006). As another example, while legislation clearly defines the overall goals of the American Internal Revenue Service, Commissioner Charles Rossotti was nevertheless able to change the mission of the organization towards a greater focus on customer service (Rainey and Thompson 2006). Still, while leadership also involves setting the overarching goals for an organization, that is, its mission (Selznick 1957, p. 26), in public organizations this occurs rarely. Goal setting is clearly not a routine aspect of public leadership (Learned, Ulrich, and Booz 1951; Selznick 1957).

The major shortcoming of Stogdill's definition (1950) is that it carries the danger of concept stretching (Sartori 1970) as it also covers what are normally considered management activities, such as Planning, Organizing, and Coordinating from Luther Gullick's POSDCORB. Rost's definition (1991) of leadership is aesthetically more pleasing than that by Stogdill (1950): 'Leadership is an influence relationship among leaders and followers who intend real changes that reflect their mutual purposes' (Rost 1991, p. 102). It is a focused definition and it clearly does not overlap with management, unlike that by Stogdill (1950). Yet the problem with Rost's definition (1991) for the purposes of this chapter is that it is too precise; in other words, it is too narrow. As can be seen in the review of empirical research below, no studies testing the effect of leadership on public service improvement would satisfy this definition.

On the other hand, Stogdill's definition (1950) is usable here and now, and is very useful because all organizations charged with delivering public services, be they local governments, school districts, ambulance services, or police authorities, are undertaking efforts towards goal achievement. Amongst other things this necessarily includes the defence of their institutional integrity and ordering of internal conflict (Selznick 1957, p. 63). The latter is very important in public organizations, which have goals that are marked by 'vagueness, multiplicity, and mutual conflict' (Rainey and Steinbauer 1999, p. 20). Defining leadership in terms of the acts of influencing an organized group towards goal setting and achievement is broader than equating leadership with efforts at change, as Rost (1991) does (also see Kellerman and Webster [2001, p. 487]). Of course change is often required, and it has rightly been the focus of research on transformational leadership (Burns 1978).

Nevertheless, in this chapter it is not useful to equate leadership with efforts at change. The reason is fairly obvious: Sometimes a lot of influence is required to maintain things in a desirable state. Indeed, slowly improving services may be the current condition of an organization, and any efforts at change would halt or reverse the improvements. Yet skilled leadership might be required to maintain them on course. In addition, democratic principles sometimes require leadership for them to remain vivid and survive through adversity (Denhardt and Campbell 2006; Terry 1995). It would be strange not to consider the brave remaining democrats in late Weimar Germany leaders. In particular because it does *not* equate leadership with change, Stogdill's definition (1950) is the most useful for assessing leadership's influence on public service improvement.

In summary, the emphasis of Stogdill's definition (1950) is on the efforts of someone (the leader or leaders) in influencing the other members of the organization. This maps well onto what most consumers of public services as well as most members of public organizations have in mind when they think of leadership: The actions and efforts of the identifiable set of people formally at the top of an organization. In public services, this normally includes both elected officials and appointed top managers. Having clarified the meaning of leadership, the next section provides an outline of leadership in the public sector.

Leadership in the public sector

Leadership in public organizations is distinctive for three reasons: (*a*) its dual nature, (*b*) the multiplicity of goals it faces, and (*c*) the greater constraints it operates under. An appreciation of these three reasons helps one to understand the limits of applying insights about leadership in the private sector to the question of the role of leadership for public service improvement. The next paragraphs discuss these three reasons.

The first issue that distinguishes leadership in the public sector is its dual nature. Elected and appointed officials both lead. Only in a few areas is leadership the exclusive purview of one type of official. In a local government, an example of exclusive leadership by elected officials is a move to elections every four years as opposed to having one in three out of every four years, whereas an example of exclusive leadership by appointed officials is a shift in the focus of frontline staff, for instance where street cleaners are encouraged to not just empty bins as stated in their job description but also to ensure that the area next to the bins is clean as well. In the majority of situations, however, elected and appointed officials lead jointly. More often than not, such joint leadership is cooperative. For example, in most British local governments, the highest elected official is the leader of the majority party and the highest appointed official is the chief executive. In the majority of cases, they work in a cooperative fashion, allowing for a better anticipation and resolution of crises and better policies (Isaac-Henry 2000, p. 135). Yet the leadership exercised by elected and appointed officials may also be conflictive, as exemplified in the British television series 'Yes Minister' and 'Yes Prime Minister', where the senior civil servant Sir Humphrey often but not always outwitted the minister Jim Hacker. In any case, the interaction between elected and appointed officials is a major characteristic of leadership in public sector organizations. Managers recruited from the private sector tend to find the political interactions required by their new role to be a burden (Mellon 1993). This suggests that careful preparation is key for lateral entrants into a managerial position in the public sector.

The second issue that distinguishes leadership in the public sector is the multiplicity of goals in most public organizations, which tend to be not only vague (Chun and Rainey 2005; Rainey 1993) but also conflicting. An example is provided by the U.S. Customs and Border Protection mission statement, which includes the sentence 'We steadfastly enforce the laws of the United States while fostering our Nation's economic security through lawful international trade and travel' (Customs and Border Protection 2009). Even though improved databases allow for somewhat better screening without much additional hassle, there is still an inevitable trade-off between the degree of customs and immigration law enforcement and the extent to which the 'Nation's economic security' is fostered through lawful trade and travel, because a greater degree of enforcement inevitably entails more inconvenience even for fully compliant traders and travellers, some of whom may no longer find transactions across the US borders worthwhile. Another example is the tension in the U.S. Internal Revenue Service's (IRS) activities between a focus on enforcement and a focus on improving customer service for the taxpayer.

The relative emphasis on these two goals has been shifting back and forth over time (Dicker 2006, p. 24). Overall, while goal conflict is particularly visible in agencies that combine enforcement and service functions, such as Customs and Border Protection and the IRS, it is a phenomenon shared by many public organizations (Rainey et al. 1976, pp. 239–40), and therefore a challenge many leaders in the public sector have to contend with, often without the possibility to resolve the goal conflict.

The third and final issue that distinguishes leadership in the public sector is that leadership tends to be more constrained in public organizations because of the requirements of democratic accountability and the rule of law and due process (Denhardt 1984; Hooijberg and Choi 2001, p. 406; Savoie 2006). Whereas in 'private administration the law generally tells the administrator what he *cannot* do; in public administration the law tells him what he *can* do' (Berkley [1981, p. 10]; emphasis in the original; cited in Hooijberg and Choi [2001, p. 410]). The experience of Sir Gerry Robinson in the Rotherham District General Hospital in England is a good example. The chairman of private Granada television was recruited by the hospital to reduce waiting lists for operations. An Open University television series showed his experiences (Open University 2006). While Robinson soon became frustrated with the large number of rules and constraints in the organization, it also emerged that many of these constraints are required to ensure patient safety and comply with government policy. Overall, there tend to be greater constraints on leadership in public as opposed to private organizations, but these constraints are necessary to maintain democratic accountability and citizen trust. Lateral entrants into a managerial position in the public sector might require time to adjust to these constraints. Nevertheless many of them will also find that they still prefer to keep these constraints in place in case they find themselves at the receiving end of unchecked leadership by a public organization.

The three main features that distinguish leadership in the public sector—duality, multiplicity of goals, and greater constraints—all suggest that leadership in the public sector is an even greater challenge than in the private sector. The next section provides an overview of major theoretical arguments of when and how leadership contributes to public service performance and improvement.

Theories of the effect of leadership on public service improvement

There are three main strands of theory on the effect of leadership on public service improvement. The first is concerned with differences in the people formally at the top positions of public organizations and how these lead to differences in their influence activities. The second is concerned with a broad distinction between two types of influence activities—transactional versus transformational leadership. The third is concerned with the interactions between political and managerial leaders. While the first two strands of theory are also prominent in research on the private sector, the third is specific to public organizations and crucial because by understanding it one can gauge how much leverage leadership is likely to provide for public service improvement in a specific case.

First, the most fundamental theoretical argument about the influence of leadership on public service performance and improvement suggests that leaders differ in their capacity to bring about performance improvements and in their fit to a given organizational context. Boyne and Dahya (2002) present a theoretical framework wherein successions of chief executives, the top administrative leaders of an organization, affect its performance. More precisely, chief executives' motives, means, and opportunities affect public service performance and improvement. Motives tend to differ among three classes of chief executives: (*a*) pragmatists, (*b*) altruists, and (*c*) egotists. They also differ between those who were already working at the same organization and those who were not (Boyne and Dahya [2002]; also see Pfeffer and Salancik [1977]). Means are important because chief executives need to have resources at their disposal to influence public service performance. Boyne and Dahya (2002) point out that those chief executives will be more likely to affect public service performance if they additionally hold another post at the same time that carries a lot of formal influence (p. 188). Opportunities are crucial for chief executives; that is, they must not be completely constrained. It has been a recurrent theme in public administration that an absence of leadership change is associated with higher organizational performance, as the theoretical work by Rainey and Steinbauer (1999, p. 19) and a number of illustrative case studies (Behn 1991; DiIulio 1994; Doig and Hargrove 1987; Rainey 1990; Rainey and Rainey 1986; Riccucci 1995) suggest. Yet it remains an open question whether this holds generally. Boyne and Dahya's theoretical argument (2002) suggests that it depends, and a succession that results in a new organizational leader with more appropriate motives and means will improve public services, given there is opportunity. Also, some work on the private sector suggests that leadership change does improve organizational performance if the baseline is low or when the same leaders have been in place for too long (for instance, see Lubatkin et al. [1989]; Miller [1991]; for a systematic review of this literature see Karaevli [2007]). There is initial evidence that the former finding also carries over to initially low-performing local governments in England, where chief executive successions and increases in the rate of top management team turnover are associated with a greater rate of performance improvement than in local governments that keep their existing chief executives or do not increase their top management team turnover rate (Boyne et al. 2008*a*, 2008*b*). The debate about which characteristics of leaders help to improve organizational fit with the environment and thus improve public service performance is ongoing.

Second, a fundamental distinction exists between two types of leadership behaviour: transactional and transformational leadership (Burns 1978). Transactional leadership is marked by an exchange: Those in formal positions of leadership set out expectations of what behaviour or results are expected of the led, and devise incentives to achieve this. These incentives are both positive, in terms of compensation and rewards—hence the transactional element—and negative, in terms of discipline or dismissal. As Burns (1978) and Bass (1985) have suggested, while transactional leadership works well for maintaining given standards of performance, it does not normally allow organizations to make great performance leaps. Essentially, transactional leadership assumes the members of an organization are fixed in their prefer-ences and abilities, and it then optimizes within these constraints. Yet to take a public service beyond mediocrity—for example, consider a secondary school that does impart some skills in its pupils but leaves them ill-prepared to make the most out of themselves—tends to require more than incentives. It requires the members of the organization to grow and to change their preferences, to internalize the quest for excellence. Achieving this is the essence of transform-ational leadership, which 'occurs when leaders broaden and elevate the interests of their employees, when they generate awareness and acceptance of the purposes and mission of the group, and when they stir their employees to look beyond their own self-interest for the good of the group' (Bass 1990*b*, p. 21).

Nevertheless, for better or for worse, transactional leadership is the norm in public organizations (Maddock 2008), because—as discussed above—leader-ship in the public sector is generally marked by less discretion than in the private sector due to the requirements of democratic accountability and the focus on due process. Indeed, unchecked attempts at transformation espe-cially by managerial leaders would be a cause of great concern since there is no reason citizens would share these leaders' visions (Van Wart 2003). However, occasionally there exist opportunities for transformational change in the provision of public services. The next set of theoretical arguments helps to identify situations where this is the case—namely those where elected and appointed leaders share the same vision and have developed a good working agreement.

The final strand of theories on the effect of leadership on public service performance and improvement is concerned with the interactions between political and managerial leaders. Improvements in public service performance tend to be co-produced by both sets of leaders. For all areas of service provision, they tend to negotiate spaces that are left to one or the other as well as a space where they work jointly (Baddeley 2008). There is a *public service bargain*—an often implicit agreement between political and managerial leaders on where the responsibilities and entitlements of each lie (Hood 2002, p. 318). This agreement is not static but shifts over time (pp. 319–24). Given an uncontested agreement between both sets of leaders is in place, transformational leadership is possible in situations where political leaders have both the incentives and the support of able managerial leaders to carry out fundamental change to the way a service is provided.

The next two sections review the best available evidence to answer the question of how much leverage leadership provides for public service improvement. All studies are summarized in Table 5.1. First, the evidence is examined thematically. The subsequent section discusses the effect of contingencies.

Evidence on leadership and public service improvement

How do the theoretical arguments on the effects of leadership on public service performance and improvement fare against empirical evidence? This section provides a thematic review of existing empirical research on this topic. Ten systematic studies contain evidence where leadership is tested as a variable explaining public service performance or improvement. These studies are summarized in Table 5.1.

The studies testing a direct linkage between leadership and public service performance cover four main dimensions of the influence of leadership on public service performance and improvement: (*a*) the overall strength and visibility of leadership, (*b*) the people in formal leadership positions and the characteristics of these people, (*c*) specific aspects of leadership behaviour, and (*d*) the interaction of political and managerial leaders. All of these play a role for public service performance and improvement, yet there are many nuances.

First, there is a lot of variation between public organizations in the overall strength and visibility of leadership. Both Andrews et al. (2006) and Forsberg et al. (2004) show that it is positively related to the performance of public organizations; local governments in the former case and hospitals in the latter. While it is difficult to generalize from two very diverse studies, the presence of a positive relationship between overall strength and visibility of leadership and public service performance across countries and types of public organization suggests that it may be indicative of a general relationship.

Table 5.1 Summary of empirical evidence

Study	Aspect(s) of leadership	Country and sector	Sample and time period	Measure(s) of performance	Finding
Andrews, Boyne, and Enticott (2006)	Leadership strength	England, local government	Cross section: 120 local governments, 2002	Service performance score from the Comprehensive Performance Assessment (CPA)	Political and managerial leadership strength positively associated with service performance score
Avellaneda (2008)	Mayors' education and job-related experience	Colombia, local government	Yearly panel: 40 local governments, 2000–5	Percentage of eligible children actually attending school	Mayors' education level positively associated with percentage of eligible children attending school; on the other hand, only some types of job-related experience matter
Fernandez (2005)	Leaders' experience, delegation to subordinates, and active promotion of change	USA (Texas), school districts	Yearly panel: 400 + school districts, 1995–9	Overall pass rate on the Texas Assessment of Academic Skills (TAAS) exam	Experience positively related to performance only where task difficulty is large, otherwise no relationship; delegation positively related to performance only where task difficulty is very large and negatively only where task difficulty is very small, otherwise no relationship; active promotion of change negatively related to performance (relationship gets stronger with task difficulty)
Forsberg, Axelsson, and Arnetz (2004)	Index covering several aspects of leadership	Sweden, hospitals	Cross section: Hospitals in 11 county councils, 1998	Quality of medical care index	Leadership index and quality of care index positively associated (lacks control variables)
Gottschalk (2007)	Decision and communication leadership	Norway, police	Cross section: 101 police officers in charge of criminal investigations, year of survey not listed	Police investigation performance index	Decision leadership positively associated with police investigation performance; no relationship between communication leadership and performance

Hill (2005)	Person of the leader and their origin (from inside or outside the organization)	USA (Texas), school districts	Yearly panel: 400 + school districts, 1995–9	Year-on-year change and 5-year change in the overall pass rate on the Texas Assessment of Academic Skills (TAAS) exam	Negative relationship between externally hired leader and year-on-year change in performance; positive relationship between leadership change and five-year change in performance
Javidan and Waldman (2003)	Charismatic and transformational leadership index	Canada, whole range of government organizations	Cross section: 51 top managers assessed by 203 intermediate subordinates, data gathered 1994–6	Subordinates' work motivation and work unit performance	Charismatic leadership only modestly related to subordinates' work motivation and unrelated to work unit performance
Meier and O'Toole (2002)	Superintendent quality	USA (Texas), school districts	Yearly panel: 400 + school districts, 1995–9	11 indicators of school district performance	Superintendent quality positively associated with 10 of the 11 performance indicators; no relationship with percentage of students tested
Turner and Whiteman 2005	Interaction of ruling politicians and top managers in turning around a poorly performing local government	England, local government	Longitudinal comparative case studies of 15 local governments, 2002–4	Comprehensive Performance Assessment (CPA)	Consensus amongst political executive and top managers about a performance-oriented strategy for the poorly performing local government related to faster and more thorough performance turnaround
Vigoda 2000	Quality of leadership: professional standards and vision of ruling politicians and top managers	Israel, local government	Cross-section: 281 residents of a large city	Perceptions of local government's responsiveness	Quality of leadership positively associated with overall responsiveness and satisfaction with operations; no association between quality of leadership and satisfaction with services

Second, a number of studies test whether and how the people in formal positions of leadership and their characteristics affect public service performance and improvement. As suggested by theoretical arguments on the importance of leader characteristics, leaders who have higher levels of inherent or acquired ability or quality know more about how to influence organizations that they are elected or appointed to lead, which in turn results in a higher performance for these organizations compared to organizations led by less able people. Looking at the most basic question, whether new leaders make a difference, Hill (2005) finds that Texas school districts initially experience a decline in performance after hiring a new superintendent, yet five years after the change performance increases over and above what would be expected in the absence of a such a leadership change.

To unpack this finding, it is helpful to look at studies that examine the effects of specific characteristics of people in formal positions of leadership on public service performance and improvement. Avellaneda (2008), Meier and O'Toole (2002), and Vigoda (2000) conceptualize the quality of leaders in different ways, yet all find a positive relationship between the presence of higher-quality leaders at the helm of a public organization and the performance of the core services it provides. Avellaneda (2008) specifies leaders' quality as educational background, Meier and O'Toole (2002) specify it as the salary premium given to a top manager over and above what is to be expected given their background and the characteristics of the job, and Vigoda (2000) specifies it as the extent of professional standards and vision that leaders possess. In spite of starkly different settings—Avellaneda (2008) in Colombia, Meier and O'Toole (2002) in Texas, and Vigoda (2000) in Israel—there is a clear positive relationship between the quality of leaders and the performance of the public services they steer.

While Avellaneda (2008) finds this positive relationship for the formal education level achieved by Colombian mayors and Meier and O'Toole (2002) find it for labour market premiums paid to Texas school district superintendents, it is likely that they tap the same underlying dimension. The difference is that in Colombia there is still so much variation in the mayors' capacity to exert their leadership role that it can be measured by their formal education level, whereas US school district superintendents' capacity is not that well proxied for by their formal educational qualifications but rather shows up in salary premiums paid to high-capacity superintendents. The mechanism behind Avellaneda's finding (2008) is that mayors with higher qualifications are better able to devise ways to convince parents to keep their children in school and to tap and reallocate the resources necessary for achieving this. In Colombia, as in other developing countries, compulsory school attendance laws often do not work very well because there are many incentives for parents and children to avoid school. Mayoral leadership can reduce dropout rates by convincing parents of the greater benefits of keeping their children in school. This can sometimes include material inducements given to the parents.

Vigoda's research (2000) illuminates the linkage between the quality of people in formal positions of leadership and public service performance from a different angle—by looking at citizen perceptions of professional standards of the elected leaders and top managers of the local government of a large city. Yet even though this is potentially very different from the leader quality captured by Avellaneda's (2008) and Meier and O'Toole's measures (2002); Vigoda (2000) also finds a positive influence of leader quality. More specifically, the higher citizens perceive leaders' professional standards to be, the higher they perceive the local government's general responsiveness and the higher is their satisfaction with operations.

Overall, while these studies have yet to be replicated in other contexts, the presence of a positive relationship between the capacity of people in positions of leadership and public service performance and improvement across a number of settings and types of organizations—local governments in Avellaneda (2008) and Vigoda (2000), school districts in Meier and O'Toole (2002), and Hill (2005)—again suggest that it may be indicative of a general relationship.

Third, two studies test whether specific aspects of leadership behaviour affect public service performance and improvement. Examining Canadian governmental organizations, Javidan and Waldman (2003) test the ability of top managers to encourage initiative by employees, a crucial element of any attempt at improving public service performance. They find a willingness to engage in risk-taking to be unrelated to work unit performance. Gottschalk (2007) draws on Mintzberg's concepts (1994) of decision leadership and communication leadership. The former denotes leadership decisions on how to allocate resources. The latter denotes leaders' activities in communicating information and clarifying issues. Testing these aspects of leadership against data on the Norwegian police, Gottschalk (2007) finds decision leadership to be positively associated with police investigation performance. On the other hand, there is no relationship between communication leadership and police investigation performance.

Finally, the interaction of political and managerial leaders characterizes leadership in the public sector. Public service improvement is co-produced by both types of leader, which is visible in a number of studies. Examining change over time in fifteen local governments in England with initially failing services, Turner and Whiteman (2005) show that consensus amongst the political leaders and top managers about a performance-oriented strategy preceded a faster and more thorough turnaround in service performance than in local governments where this consensus was lacking. It remains an open question under what conditions such consensus arises. There appears to be an increasing tendency for elected leaders—at least in English local government—to search for top managers who share their vision (Leach and

Wilson 2002, p. 669). Yet it is far from clear whether the electoral process always suffices to motivate elected leaders to strive for public service improvement, in particular going beyond mediocrity. James and John (2007) found that the publication of the first wave of the Comprehensive Performance Assessment (CPA), an overall quality of service grade for each local authority in England, resulted in vote share losses for incumbent administrations of local governments graded as low performers, while there was no reward for performers at the top end. Given the apparent weakness of the ballot box for inducing high public service performance, there remains a crucial role for appointed top managers in providing leadership to strive towards public service improvement. Some corroborating evidence is provided by Andrews et al.'s finding (2006), also for local government in England, that the relationship between managerial leadership and quality of services provided is stronger than the relationship between political leadership and service quality.

Overall, there are a number of findings suggesting that leadership is a positive influence on public service improvement. However, to make these findings more relevant, it is helpful to test under what circumstances a positive association between leadership and public service performance holds, and under what circumstances it is particularly important. As this book reviews all the different levers that the overseers of public organizations might pull in an attempt to improve public service performance, it would be most helpful to know when leadership has the greatest leverage. After all, searching for new top managers, where this is possible, is a costly and disruptive activity, and it might be worth pulling another lever in circumstances where the leadership lever can be expected to achieve comparatively little.

CONTINGENCIES ENABLING OR LIMITING THE EFFECT OF LEADERSHIP ON PUBLIC SERVICE IMPROVEMENT

The same aspects of leadership may well have very different effects in different circumstances. This is very relevant for anyone interested in improving public service performance. The major factors moderating what leadership may achieve are the external circumstances and constraints an organization faces. This is commonly referred to as the organizational environment. A number of scholars are adamant that it severely constrains the efforts of the organization's leaders to achieve changes in performance, in particular to achieve improvements (Whittington 1988). Authors subscribing to the organizational population ecology point of view (Hannan and Freeman 1977; Kaufman 1991) argue that leaders' attempts to change their organization will generally worsen its performance, as their attempts tend to reduce the fit between the organization and its environment.

Even within a set of similar public organizations, variations in the organizational environment moderate any effect that leadership may have. On the basis of interviews of secondary school principals from areas that vary widely in socio-economic status, Currie, Boyett, and Suhomlinova (2005) suggest that 'any generic prescription for leadership, transformational or otherwise, is better replaced with an approach that facilitates the ability of principals to enact leadership as they perceive appropriate to school context' (p. 291). Yet what are the contingencies that one needs to know for determining how much leverage leadership can provide in improving a given service? Unfortunately this is still largely uncharted territory.

The exemplary study by Fernandez (2005) provides a blueprint for how future research into leadership can incorporate and test for contingencies, so that its applicability to particular contexts is based on a better understanding. Fernandez (2005) tests whether the characteristics of leaders—school district superintendents—and their leadership strategies are related to education service performance using data on Texas school districts. The novel contribution of Fernandez's work is the incorporation of formal tests for whether any influences of leadership on service performance are contingent on task difficulty. He finds that superintendents' experience is positively related to performance only where task difficulty is large, otherwise there is no relationship. Superintendents' willingness to delegate to subordinates is positively related to performance only where task difficulty is very large and negatively only where task difficulty is very small, otherwise there is no relationship. Finally, superintendents' active promotion of change is negatively related to performance, and the more negatively so the greater task difficulty becomes. Yet Fernandez's approach (2005) is of even greater usefulness than these findings. Other studies could benefit from explicitly testing for contingencies, both task difficulty and other factors.

There are many other potential contingencies of the effect of leadership on public service performance. Most of them concern the organizational environment (see the preceding discussions). They are likely to moderate the findings of the first three sets of studies reviewed in this chapter, namely, those covering (*a*) the overall strength and visibility of leadership, (*b*) the people in formal leadership positions and the characteristics of these people, and (*c*) specific aspects of leadership behaviour. Nevertheless, there is a trade-off between how precise one is in specifying contingencies and the usefulness of lessons from research. Too many contingencies make the findings overly specific to the particular cases studied and therefore no longer provide helpful insights. Indeed, this has led to a certain 'disillusionment with contingency theories' in research on leadership in the private sector (Bryman 1996, p. 280). Nevertheless, considering contingencies—more than the majority of public sector studies of the contribution of leadership to public service improvement currently do—is likely to make these studies more precise and consequently more helpful.

An agenda for future research

Still fairly little is reliably known about effects of leadership on public service improvement, and there is room for future researchers to make serious contributions. Before considering the most promising avenues for future work, it is helpful to briefly consider the limitations of the knowledge reviewed in this chapter. For this purpose, it is worth considering for a moment what one would need to do to confidently answer the question 'does leadership affect public service performance?' Since randomized controlled trials are infeasible, the best one can do is to systematically analyse the historical record after the fact (e.g. after leadership styles changed and indicators of public service performance were collected). Inevitably, two major problems for drawing inferences about causal effects of leadership arise. First, differences other than leadership among organizations could explain the differences in public service performance between them. This problem is sometimes called 'omitted variable' bias, a very broad issue that can include the presence of immeasurable differences between public organizations and the presence of inertia. Any omitted factor can be partly or fully responsible for an apparent effect of leadership on public service improvement. Therefore, quantitative and qualitative research is better the more it takes into account the possibility of such alternative explanations. It is fortunate that nearly all studies reviewed here attempt to address the problem of omitted variable bias by including control variables in the case of quantitative studies or by carefully considering alternative narratives in the case of qualitative research. Second, the causal arrow might go the other way. What is observed as leadership might be a result of rather than an influence on public service performance. This problem is sometimes called 'simultaneity' bias. It is extremely difficult to address outside of true experiments. Generally what is needed is some truly exogenous and unanticipated variation that affects public service performance only through leadership. Yet at a minimum, the possibility that causation goes the other way should be discussed theoretically. The idea of leadership as a by-product of performance rather than as a cause has always been lingering. For example, see Stogdill's remark (1974) that there is a folk understanding of leadership where a leader is viewed as 'a person who is kept one pace ahead of the group so that he will not be run over' (p. 8). Also, studies completely based on survey data may suffer from people's tendency to over-attribute outcomes to leadership. Meindl et al. (1985)

carefully made this point. They call this tendency 'the romance of leadership'. Amongst the studies reviewed here, Vigoda (2000) is most vulnerable to simply having captured variation in citizens' degree of romanticism.

Nevertheless, citizens interested in well-functioning public services will continue to inspire research on leadership as a means for achieving them. Two avenues for research are both particularly promising and feasible: (*a*) research on leadership successions, and (*b*) research examining the contingencies affecting how much leverage leadership can provide in a given situation. Research on leadership successions—focusing on whether new leaders with different qualities make a difference to public service performance—can be conducted across a variety of public sector organizations in different countries with different institutions. While the data collection can be burdensome, there are relatively few measurement concerns in determining whether the same person as last year leads an organization or whether there is a new leader. The special benefit of succession research is that it is an excellent way to probe the importance of agency to public service improvement. Indeed, it is essentially an 'acid test' of leadership. Succession studies will not resolve the debate over the relative importance of structure and agency, even in particular types of public organizations, but they might help to focus it and in this way shed further light on how much leverage leadership provides for improving public services. The second avenue for future research is fully compatible with succession research. In addition, research into the contingencies affecting influences of leadership on public service improvement can inform almost any aspect of leadership that is a potential contributor to public service improvement. By testing in which contexts a particular lever works well and in which contexts it does not, some costly future mistakes might be prevented. This alone would already serve as a powerful validation of research on the effect of leadership on public service improvement.

Conclusions

Overall, all ten studies reviewed here show at least one positive relationship between leadership and public service improvement. Nevertheless, each only considers some aspects of leadership, and there is wide variation in services and contexts. Selznick (1957) was spot on for both research and practice when he wrote that 'we shall not find any simple prescription for sound organizational leadership; nor will it be purchased with a bag of tricks and gadgets' (p. ix). A few lessons do emerge from the review conducted here, and they are best considered jointly since their value is enhanced or diminished by whether or not all of them are considered. First, it is worth investing serious effort into the selection of people for formal leadership posts, as all available evidence points to positive performance effects of more highly qualified leaders. Second, fostering a shared vision between political and managerial leaders is also likely to have a positive effect on public service performance. In each individual case, the possibility of a trade-off between these two lessons needs to be considered. Finally, careful considerations of local contingencies, such as the particular difficulties of the task at hand, are more likely to lead to the improvement of a particular service than the adoption of a generic strategy.

REFERENCES

Andrews, R., Boyne, G. A. and Enticott, G. (2006). Performance Failure in the Public Sector. *Public Management Review* 8(2), 273–96.

Avellaneda, C. N. (2008). Municipal Performance: Does Mayoral Quality Matter? *Journal of Public Administration Research and Theory* Advance Access published online on 19 February 2008, doi: 10.1093/jopart/mun001.

Baddeley, S. (2008). 'Political-Management Leadership', in K. Turnbull James and J. Collins (eds.), *Leadership Perspectives: Knowledge into Action*. Basingstoke: Palgrave Macmillan.

Bass, B. M. (1985). *Leadership and Performance Beyond Expectations*. New York: Free Press.

——(1990a). *Bass & Stogdill's Handbook of Leadership: Theory, Research, and Managerial Applications*. New York: Free Press.

——(1990b). From Transactional to Transformational Leadership: Learning to Share the Vision. *Organizational Dynamics* 18(3), 19–31.

Behn, R. D. (1991). *Leadership Counts: Lessons for Public Managers from the Massachusetts Welfare, Training, and Employment Program*. Cambridge, MA: Harvard University Press.

Berkley, G. E. (1981). *The Craft of Public Administration*, Third edition. Boston, MA: Allyn & Bacon.

Boyne, G. A. and Dahya, J. (2002). Executive Succession and the Performance of Public Organizations. *Public Administration* 80(1), 179–200.

——James, O., John, P. and Petrovsky, N. (2008a). 'Does Chief Executive Succession Affect Public Service Performance?' Presented at the Thirtieth Annual Association for Public Policy Analysis and Management Research Conference, Los Angeles, California.

——————(2008b). 'Should the Bureaucrats Stay or Go? The Impact of Top Management Team Turnover on Public Service Performance', Working paper, Cardiff University.

Bryman, A. (1996). 'Leadership in Organizations', in S. R. Clegg, C. Hardy, and W. R. Nord (eds.), *Handbook of Organization Studies*. London: Sage.

Burns, J. M. (1978). *Leadership*. New York: Harper & Row.

Chun, Y. H. and Rainey, H. G. (2005). Goal Ambiguity and Organizational Performance in U.S. Federal Agencies. *Journal of Public Administration Research and Theory* 15(1), 1–30.

Currie, G., Boyett, I. and Suhomlinova, O. (2005). Transformational Leadership within Secondary Schools in England: A Panacea for Organizational Ills. *Public Administration* 83(2), 265–96.

Customs and Border Protection (2009). 'CBP Mission Statement and Core Values', http://www.cbp.gov/xp/cgov/about/mission/guardians.xml (last accessed January 30, 2009).

Denhardt, J. V. and Campbell, K. B. (2006). The Role of Democratic Values in Transformational Leadership. *Administration & Society* 38(5), 556–72.

Denhardt, R. B. (1984). *Theories of Public Organization.* Pacific Grove, CA: Brooks/ Cole.

Dicker, E. J. (2006). 'Thou Shalts'. . . and Better Ways. *The Tax Executive* 58(1), 24–5.

DiIulio, J. D. (1994). Principled Agents: The Cultural Bases of Behavior in a Federal Government Bureaucracy. *Journal of Public Administration Research and Theory* 4(3), 277–318.

Doig, J. W. and Hargrove, E. C. (eds.) (1987). *Leadership and Innovation: A Biographical Perspective on Entrepreneurs in Government.* Baltimore, MD: The Johns Hopkins University Press.

Fernandez, S. (2005). Developing and Testing an Integrative Framework of Public Sector Leadership: Evidence from the Public Education Arena. *Journal of Public Administration Research and Theory* 15(2), 197–217.

Forsberg, E., Axelsson, R. and Arnetz, B. (2004). The Relative Importance of Leadership and Payment System—Effects on Quality of Care and Work Environment. *Health Policy* 69(1), 73–82.

Gottschalk, P. (2007). Predictors of Police Investigation Performance: An Empirical Study of Norwegian Police as Value Shop. *International Journal of Information Management* 27(1), 36–48.

Hannan, M. T. and Freeman, J. (1977). The Population Ecology of Organizations. *The American Journal of Sociology* 82(5), 929–64.

Hill, G. C. (2005). The Effects of Managerial Succession on Organizational Performance. *Journal of Public Administration Research and Theory* 15(4), 585–97.

Hood, C. (2002). Controls, Bargaining, and Cheating: The Politics of Public-Service Reform. *Journal of Public Administration Research and Theory* 12(3), 309–32.

Hooijberg, R. and Choi, J. (2001). The Impact of Organizational Characteristics on Leadership Effectiveness Models: An Examination of Leadership in a Private and Public Sector Organization. *Administration & Society* 33(4), 403–31.

House, R. and Aditya, R. (1997). The Social Scientific Study of Leadership: Quo Vadis. *Journal of Management* 23(3), 409–73.

Isaac-Henry, K. (2000). 'Chief Executives and Leadership in a Local Authority: A Fundamental Antithesis', in K. Theakston (ed.), *Bureaucrats and Leadership.* Basingstoke: Palgrave Macmillan.

James, O. and John, P. (2007). Public Management at the Ballot Box: Performance Information and Electoral Support for Incumbent English Local Governments. *Journal of Public Administration Research and Theory* 17(4), 567–80.

Javidan, M. and Waldman, D. A. (2003). Exploring Charismatic Leadership in the Public Sector: Measurement and Consequences. *Public Administration Review* 63(2), 229–42.

Karaevli, A. (2007). Performance Consequences of New CEO Outsiderness: Moderating Effects of Pre- and Post-Succession Contexts. *Strategic Management Journal* 28(7), 681–706.

Kaufman, H. (1991). *Time, Chance, and Organizations: Natural Selection in a Perilous Environment*, Second edition. Chatham, NJ: Chatham House Publishers.

Kellerman, B. and Webster, S. W. (2001). The Recent Literature on Public Leadership Reviewed and Considered. *The Leadership Quarterly* 12(4), 485–514.

Leach, S. and Wilson, D. (2002). Rethinking Local Political Leadership. *Public Administration* 80(4), 665–89.

Learned, E. P., Ulrich, D. N. and Booz, D. R. (1951). *Executive Action*. Boston, MA: Harvard Graduate School of Business Administration.

Lubatkin, M. H., Chung, K. H., Rogers, R. C. and Owers, J. E. (1989). Stockholder Reactions to CEO Changes in Large Organizations. *Academy of Management Journal* 32(1), 47–68.

Maddock, S. (2008). 'Public Sector Leader Change Strategies: A Focus on Technical or Collaborative Solutions', in K. Turnbull James and J. Collins (eds.), *Leadership Perspectives: Knowledge into Action*. Basingstoke: Palgrave Macmillan.

Meier, K. J. and O'Toole Jr., L. J. (2002). Public Management and Organizational Performance: The Effect of Managerial Quality. *Journal of Policy Analysis and Management* 21(4), 629–43.

Meindl, J. R., Ehrlich, S. B., and Dukerich, J. M. (1985). The Romance of Leadership. *Administrative Science Quarterly* 30(1), 78–102.

Mellon, E. (1993). Executive Agencies: Leading Change from the Outside-in. *Public Money & Management* 13(2), 25–31.

Miller, D. (1991). Stale in the Saddle: CEO Tenure and the Match Between Organization and Environment. *Management Science* 37(1), 34–52.

Mintzberg, H. (1994). Rounding out the Manager's Job. *Sloan Management Review* 36(1), 11–26.

Open University (2006). 'Can Gerry Robinson Fix the NHS?', http://www.open2.net/ nhs/index.html (last accessed 13 February 2009).

Pfeffer, J. and Salancik, G. R. (1977). Organizational Context and the Characteristics and Tenure of Hospital Administrators. *Academy of Management Journal* 20(1), 74–88.

Rainey, G. W. (1990). 'Implementation and Managerial Creativity: A Study of the Development of Client-Centered Units in Human Service Programs', in D. J. Palumbo and D. J. Calista (eds.), *Implementation and the Policy Process*. New York: Greenwood.

—— and Rainey, H. G. (1986). 'Breaching the Hierarchical Imperative: The Modularization of the Social Security Claims Process', in D. J. Calista (ed.), *Bureaucratic and Governmental Reform: JAI Research Annual in Public Policy Analysis and Management*. Greenwich, CT: JAI Press.

Rainey, H. G. (1993). 'Toward a Theory of Goal Ambiguity in Public Organizations', in J. L. Perry (ed.), *Research in Public Administration*, Volume 2. Greenwich, CT: JAI Press.

—— Backoff, R. W. and Levine, C. H. (1976). Comparing Public and Private Organizations. *Public Administration Review* 36(2), 233–44.

——and Steinbauer, P. (1999). Galloping Elephants: Developing Elements of a Theory of Effective Government Organization. *Journal of Public Administration Research and Theory* 9(1), 1–32.

——and Thompson, J. (2006). Leadership and the Transformation of a Major Institution: Charles Rossotti and the Internal Revenue Service. *Public Administration Review* 66(4), 596–604.

Riccucci, N. M. (1995). *Unsung Heroes: Federal Executives Making a Difference.* Washington, DC: Georgetown University Press.

Rost, J. C. (1991). *Leadership for the Twenty-First Century.* New York: Praeger.

Sartori, G. (1970). Concept Misformation in Comparative Politics. *American Political Science Review* 64(4), 1033–53.

Savoie, D. J. (2006). 'What Is Wrong with the New Public Management?', in E. E. Otenyo and N. S. Lind (eds.), *Comparative Public Administration: The Essential Readings.* Amsterdam: Elsevier JAI.

Selznick, P. (1957). *Leadership in Administration: A Sociological Interpretation.* Evanston, IL: Row, Peterson and Company.

Stogdill, R. M. (1950). Leadership, Membership and Organization. *Psychological Bulletin* 47(1), 1–14.

——(1974). *Handbook of Leadership: A Survey of Theory and Research.* New York: Free Press.

Terry, L. D. (1995). *Leadership of Public Bureaucracies: The Administrator as Conservator.* Thousand Oaks, CA: Sage.

Turner, D. and Whiteman, P. (2005). Learning from the Experience of Recovery: The Turnaround of Poorly Performing Local Authorities. *Local Government Studies* 31(5), 627–54.

Van Wart, M. (2003). Public-Sector Leadership Theory: An Assessment. *Public Administration Review* 63(2), 214–28.

Vigoda, E. (2000). Are You Being Served? The Responsiveness of Public Administration to Citizens' Demands: An Empirical Examination in Israel. *Public Administration* 78(1), 165–91.

Whittington, R. (1988). Environmental Structure and Theories of Strategic Choice. *Journal of Management Studies* 25(6), 521–36.

Williams, B. N. and Kellough, J. E. (2006). Leadership with an Enduring Impact: The Legacy of Chief Burtell Jefferson of the Metropolitan Police Department of Washington, D.C. *Public Administration Review* 66(6), 813–22.

Wright, T. (2003). *British Politics: A Very Short Introduction.* Oxford: Oxford University Press.

6 Organizational Culture

Rachel Ashworth

Introduction

Cultural change has been a key element of public service reform, with governments across the world viewing culture as a means to transform public service organizations (Newman 1994). It has been argued that non-profit organizations have been characterized by a public service culture, as demonstrated by numerous studies of the public service ethos and tests of specific theories of public service motivation (Wise 2000). In recent years, however, policy-makers seeking to improve the performance of public services have encouraged organizations to develop performance-oriented and consumer-based cultures, which, they argue, are more likely to deliver improvement in the quality and efficiency of services. However, the extensive literature on organizational culture suggests that government attempts to reform public organizations in this way are not guaranteed to be straightforward or successful. A review of academic work reveals a series of intense discussions and debates around whether it is possible to identify a distinct organizational culture and the extent to which organizational cultures can be identified, labelled, measured, and 'managed'. Moreover, there is considerable contention around the nature and direction of any potential relationship between organizational culture and performance.

In order to assess whether cultural change delivers improvements in public service performance, this chapter firstly defines the concept of organizational culture within a public service context, before tracing the development of the theoretical link between culture and performance. Subsequently, the chapter draws on existing research evidence on the relationship between culture and performance in the public sector. Finally, the chapter outlines implications for future research on culture and service improvement and highlights the urgent need for longitudinal, multi-methodological and institutionally sensitive studies, based upon public sector typologies of culture, which explore the extent to which cultural change is associated with public service improvement.

What is organizational culture?

Organizational culture is described by Ogbonna and Harris as ᵕ. most popular concepts in the fields of management and organizatio᠁ theory' (2000, p. 768), and also by Rainey and Steinbauer as 'probably the most overused and loosely used term in contemporary management discourse' (1999, p. 17). Culture has been interpreted, analysed, and tested extensively within the field of organization studies over the last forty years but remains a contentious and complex phenomenon (Smirchich 1983). Davies et al. (2000) have described culture as 'fraught with competing interpretations and eluding a consensual definition' (p. 3). However, many scholars seem able to cohere around the widely used explanation offered by Schein (1985), who describes organizational culture as:

A pattern of shared basic assumptions that the group learned as it solved its problems of external adaptation and internal integration, that has worked well enough to be considered valid and, therefore, to be taught to new members as the correct way to perceive, think and feel in relation to these problems. (p. 12).

It is commonly argued that culture is multi-dimensional and that consequently it is possible to identify a number of different levels, or layers, of culture. Newman (1994), writing on culture and the public sector, presents a three-layered model comprising 'symbols' which are visible signs of what is of importance and value to an organization (e.g. logos and mission statements); 'practices' which are less visible but can be observed (ways of doing things); and 'values' which are deeply held are taken for granted and have developed over considerable periods of time. Needless to say, she argues that such deep-set values are almost impossible to observe and relearn.

This multi-dimensional interpretation of organization culture has come to be widely accepted, but the way in which organizational culture has been researched and analysed has not always reflected that multi-layered approach. This has provoked some debate, particularly in relation to methodological application. For example, initial analyses of organizational culture had been qualitative in design in order to allow an in-depth understanding of unique individual organizational settings (Denison 1995). Business and management scholars have frequently studied organizational culture in quantitative terms through the application of survey-based instruments. This has provoked some criticism from those who claim that it is difficult to capture the multi-dimensional elements of culture within such quantitative measures. This has prompted many quantitative researchers to develop a keen interest in the concept of 'organizational climate'—a term which loosely corresponds to surface-level cultural attributes and perceptions (Scott et al. 2003a) and more readily lends itself to survey-based operationalization. In contrast to culture, climate is viewed as temporary, open to control and manipulation, limited to aspects of work organization easily perceived by employees, and more empirically accessible (Denison 1996; Wallace et al. 1999).

Debate on the definition, interpretation, and operationalization of the concept of organizational culture continues, but having reviewed these debates it seems appropriate that a rounded and therefore multi-dimensional interpretation of organizational culture should be adopted for this chapter, as outlined by Schein, Newman, and others. Furthermore, as both academic theory and government reform focus on culture change, the chapter concentrates on reviewing evidence on the link between organizational *culture* (rather than climate) and performance in the public sector.

The theory of improvement through cultural change

Interest in organizational culture as a concept developed largely due to the widely argued link with organizational performance. Most studies of culture and performance are private-sector based and, over time, research findings have had key implications for the theoretical link between organizational culture and performance, resulting in revised views on the nature, and direction, of the relationship between culture, performance, and other organizational variables. The extensive study of organizational culture in the 1980s by the excellence writers such as Peters and Waterman (1982) and Deal and Kennedy (1982) led to the promotion of the concept within the wider management community. These studies were vitally important in proposing an initial connection between culture and performance as they argued that organizations have unified and distinctive cultures; that there is a relationship between organizational culture and performance; and that organizational culture can be 'managed' in order to impact on performance (Scott et al. 2003*b*). However, each of these assumptions has been the subject of intense debate—especially within the public service context—and therefore we will return to them at various stages throughout the chapter.

The excellence writers claimed that it was possible to identify a 'corporate' culture which could be attributed to management—which was assumed to be the dominant group, capable of devising and imposing their culture on the organization through rites, rituals, and values (Sinclair 1991). The connection between organizational culture and performance is predicated upon the important role that culture is perceived to play in securing increased competitive advantage, and it is argued that it achieves this by making employee behaviour and responses increasingly stable and predictable, thereby facilitating and shaping individual interactions within organizations (Barney 1986; Ogbonna and Harris 2000). Scott et al. (2003*b*) elaborate on this by describing what they call 'first-order' culture change strategies, which involve sustaining competitive advantage by 'doing what you do better' and second-order strategies which necessitate a wholesale shift from one culture to another. However, the idea that culture can be developed and shaped rests upon the rather contentious assumption that culture is something an organization *has* rather than its being an integral part of what an organization *is*; that is, an attribute of organizations that can be manipulated by managers (Smirchich 1983; Davies et al. 2000).

Despite the widespread claims of a potential link between culture and performance, it seems that few studies have actually examined the existence or the nature of this relationship adequately (Lim 1995). Furthermore, whilst initially popular, by the 1990s the key assertions of the excellence writers had attracted growing criticism (see, e.g. Ogbonna [1993]; Wilmott [1993]; Alvesson [1995]). Encouraging the development of a 'strong culture' in order to deliver improved performance became increasingly viewed to be an overly simplistic strategy (Saffold 1988). Criticism of the culture–performance hypothesis gathered at pace with many drawing attention to the unsubstantiated presumed existence of a unitary culture, the apparent lack of an operational definition of cultural strength, and the weak methodologies being applied (see, e.g. Scott et al. [2003*a*]).

This mounting critique led to the development of a series of more nuanced studies—see, for example, the work of Gordon and DiTomaso (1992) who highlight the importance of external environmental conditions. Others such as Ogbonna and Harris (2002*a*; 2002*b*) sought to explore the unintended consequences of attempts to achieve cultural change. They document the appropriation of culture change processes for other purposes and argue that studies of organizational culture should look beyond the positive and encompass negative, unintended, and dysfunctional outcomes that result from efforts to bring about cultural change.

These studies form part of a significant body of work which analyses the relationship between organizational culture and the performance of private firms (see, e.g. work by authors such as Denison [1995] and Lewis [1994], and Ogbonna and Harris [2002]). Whilst this chapter focuses on public services, it is clear that work on public sector organizations has been highly influenced by the private sector literature. The private sector culture–performance link is widely cited by public management academics and policy-makers as part of their rationale for studying and implementing cultural change, and many culture typologies and measures of culture have been adopted from private studies. In the private studies, the typical approach has been to identify particular types or traits of organizational culture and analyses or tests their relationship to profitability and other measures of firm performance. Often such studies are large scale, such as the substantive analysis by Kotter and Heskett (1992) which focused on 207 firms over a five-year period. This research revealed only a small correlation between 'strong' culture and long-term performance, forcing the authors to arrive at the conclusion that culture could be a mere intermediary of the impact of effective leadership or organizational structure on performance. In contrast, Gordon and DiTomaso (1992) found evidence of a relationship between culture and short-term financial performance, giving rise to a debate over the importance of consistent versus flexible cultures. Other notable works include Denison and Mishra's multi-method analysis (1995) and the work of Harris and Ogbonna (2000) who describe cultural traits as either 'competitive', 'innovative', 'bureaucratic', or 'community'-based, concluding that internally oriented cultures are bad for competitive advantage and that performance improves if cultures are linked to the external environment. The fact that private sector evidence indicates that both consistency and adaptability cultural traits are positively related to performance led Wilderom et al. (2000) in their widely cited review of culture and performance studies, to question the evidence on the culture–performance relationship. Furthermore, they reflect on the various methodologies employed to date and conclude that the predicted effects of culture remain largely unsubstantiated.

Overall, we can identify a clear theoretical argument which indicates that changing an organizational culture should increase competitive advantage, and therefore productivity, in the private sector. It should, though, be emphasized that some underlying assumptions remain under dispute. Whilst there is some empirical evidence that supports the link, in recent years research findings have questioned the direction of the relationship between culture and performance. However, a vast array of work continues to focus on the relationship between the two in the private sector, with recent analyses extending to other dimensions of performance such as brand performance (O'Cass and Ngo 2007) and strategic supply chain management (Hult et al. 2007). Furthermore, studies continue to investigate the mediating effects of culture by analysing its role alongside other organizational characteristics such as strategy (Lee et al. 2006) and leadership (Ogbonna and Harris 2000). The mixed academic evidence on the strength of the relationship between culture and performance has not discouraged management scholars from further exploring the connection between the two. Neither has it deterred policy-makers in governments across the world from seeking to bring about cultural change in a bid to transform the way in which public sector organizations operate and thereby improving the quality of public services.

Cultural change in the public sector

Public sector organizations have traditionally been characterized by an overriding public service ethos where employees are driven by 'public service motivation' which 'pertains to the process that causes individuals to perform acts that contribute to the public good as a way of satisfying their personal needs' (Wise 2000, p. 344). It has been argued that public service motivation is underpinned by a 'public services culture', which is unique and has protected the sector against inefficiency and abuse (Theobald 1997). However, from the 1980s onwards, accusations of a dominant paternalistic 'producer-culture' within the public sector encouraged pressure for reform. Newman argues that attempts to achieve cultural change have been at the heart of the rhetoric and practice of transforming the public sector where reforms have been designed in order to 'make organizations more customer-orientated, more entrepreneurial, more innovative, more flexible, more responsive' (1994, p. 59).

In the United States, influential authors such as Osborne and Gaebler (1992) talked of an identifiable 'entrepreneurial' culture which could be adopted by public service organizations and would lead to improved public management practices. Policy-makers leapt upon these ideas as a means of reforming old-fashioned and discredited bureaucratic systems of administration: 'Our goal is to make the entire federal government both less expensive and more efficient, and to change the culture of our national bureaucracy away from complacency and entitlement toward initiative and empowerment' (Gore 1993, p. 1, cited by Brewer and Selden 2000). These 'simple prescriptions' for change depicted organizational culture as an additional lever to pull (Newman 1994) and, it is argued, reflect a recognition from government that structural change alone will not deliver improvements in the performance of public services (Scott et al. 2003*a*).

Cultural change was a key component of New Public Management, and attempts to reform organizational cultures can be evidenced across a range of public services. Driscoll and Morris describe efforts to 'imbue the civil service with private sector values.... and induce more customer-friendly attitudes' (2001, p. 807) whilst Davies et al. (2000) document repeated cultural change programmes within the NHS in the United Kingdom which range from Roy Griffiths' attempt to introduce an 'overt management culture' to the Labour government's pronouncement that they are looking at 'major cultural change for everyone' (p. 112). More contemporary cultural change programmes in health-care have been reported to involve 'shifts in basic values, beliefs, and assumptions that underpin patterns of behaviour in the delivery of care' (Hyde and Davies 2004, p. 1408) whilst McNulty and Ferlie (2002) identify successive attempts to re-orient health services towards a patient-focused model of care.

There is, though, a question as to how successful those cultural change programmes have been. In seeking to estimate the impact of attempts to modify culture within education and health, Ferlie et al. (1996) identified several cross-sectoral distinctions in terms of the rate of culture change, noting that whilst there were clear changes in the relationship between head teachers and staff and a growing managerialism in the case of education, cultures of marketization and competition were not easily embedded in the health sector in the United Kingdom. A similar analysis of cultural change in the civil service revealed that staff paid 'lip service' to change programmes with little evidence of real cultural or attitudinal change (Driscoll and Morris 2001). Studies of cultural change associated with the 'reinventing government' agenda seemed to produce similar results. For example, Nufrio (2001) analysed employee perceptions of 'reinvention' cultural traits (such as discretion, promoting a learning culture, rewarding performance, and developing a customer-based approach) only to find that these values were not evident to staff within public agencies.

Two qualitative studies of cultural change within government agencies offer similar insights. Lurie and Riccucci's analysis of cultural change within welfare offices in the United States revealed a gap between the rhetorical and espoused values of those driving reform and those of managers, supervisors, and workers (2003), whilst the ethnographic work of Brooks and Bate (1994) points to the existence of a 'cultural infrastructure' at the local level which mitigated against top-down cultural change. There is also evidence that public sector organizations continue to reflect the values of hierarchical and bureaucratic cultures long after cultural change programmes have been introduced (see, e.g. Parker and Bradley's application [2000] of the competing values of internal and external orientation and control and flexibility to public service organizations in Australia). However, more recent work on institutional isomorphism in local government based upon the perceived effects of Best Value reforms suggests that several surface-level cultural characteristics of local authorities have shifted in line with government reform and, as a result, councils have begun to look increasingly similar (Ashworth et al. 2009).

Overall, it has been argued that, too often, policy-makers engaged in driving public service reform turn to culture as a simple and straightforward way of progressing from a 'stable, bureaucratic hierarchy' to a 'fluid customer-oriented' culture (Driscoll and Morris 2001). This approach has left governments open to the charge of oversimplification, with policy-makers labouring under the perception that culture is something an organization *has* rather than being an integral part of what an organization *is* (Hawkins 1997). Consequently, these attempts at reform, it is argued, may over-emphasize the symbolic and surface levels of culture and achieve some success at that level but in doing so are likely to conflict with staff interpretations of management actions and their associated meanings (Newman 1994; Theobald 1997). However, it is important to recognize that, whilst there are considerable doubts about the extent to which organizational cultures in the public sector can be shaped and managed in line with new public management reforms, repeated government efforts to deliver cultural change have been substantial enough to warrant empirical investigation (Lurie and Riccucci 2003).

It is necessary at this stage, then, to review the academic eviden‹ culture and performance relationship within the context of pub‍ organizations.

Culture change and improvement: evidence from the public sector

In contrast to the work on private firms, there is far less work on the impact of organizational culture on performance in the public sector. A systematic literature search conducted via Web of Science, using a variety of search terms including *organizational culture, public services, effectiveness, quality, efficiency, performance,* and *improvement,* resulted in the identification of 21 empirical academic papers which shed some light on the relationship between organizational culture and service improvement in the public sector. The papers fall into two bodies of work on culture and performance: in the first group are studies of organizational performance in the public sector which have incorporated measures of cultural change, amongst many other variables within an overall analysis on determinants of performance, whilst for the second group of studies, culture is the key independent variable. Whilst these papers include control variables, their main focus is to explore the relationship between culture and performance in the public sector. The studies are summarized within Table 6.1 and are discussed in more detail below.

STUDIES OF ORGANIZATIONAL PERFORMANCE

Many studies of organizational performance have incorporated dimensions of culture within their analysis. Work operationalizing theories on the effectiveness of public organizations argues that those with strong mission-oriented cultures are likely to perform better than those that do not Moynihan and Pandey (2004). Despite their strength, these cultures are considered to be sufficiently flexible to be viewed as adaptable, externally facing, and responsive (Rainey and Steinbauer 1999). Consequently, the operationalization of culture within studies of organizational performance or effectiveness in the public sector has tended to incorporate various dimensions of culture, with most authors arguing that organizations exhibit a variety of cultures rather than falling into one category or another. For example, Brewer and Selden (2000) advocate a multi-dimensional construct which they include in their test of Rainey and Steinbauer's model of effectiveness. Their admittedly 'loose' construct of culture encompasses a combination of culture and climate

Table 6.1 Summary of empirical evidence

Author	Dimension of culture	Country and sector	Sample and time period	Measure of performance	Finding
Argote (1989)	Agreement around norms between groups and agreement within groups	US Health care	30 emergency units, 463 physicians and 278 nurses	Promptness of care Quality of nursing Quality of medical care	Positive relationship between norms and effectiveness in hospital emergency units, evidence of an association between culture and performance
Brewer and Selden (2000)	Protecting employees, teamwork, efficacy, and a concern for the public interest	US federal government	9,710 federal civilian workforce (civil servants)	Six measures derived from employee perceptions	Most influential factors all contain organizational culture variables—organizational culture is a powerful predictor of organizational performance in federal agencies
Cameron and Freeman (1991)	Clan, adhocacy, hierarchy, market	US Higher education	334 HE institutions	Management perceptions of effectiveness	Cultural type more important in accounting for effectiveness than congruence ('cultural fit') or strength
Garnett et al. (2008)	Mission-oriented and rule-oriented cultures	US, government administration	274 responses	Management perceptions of effectiveness of organization in achieving its mission	Communication mediates influence of mission-oriented cultures on performance but does not positively effect performance within rule-based cultures
Gerowitz et al. (1996)	Competing values framework	US, UK, and Canada, health care	265 hospitals—120 in the USA, 100 in the UK, and 45 in Canada	PIs: Employee loyalty and commitment. External stakeholder satisfaction, Internal consistency, Resource acquisition	Cultures of top management teams were positively and significantly related to performance for clan, rational, and developmental cultures

Gerowitz (1998)	Competing values framework	US, health care	CEO and Senior Managers in 120 hospitals	Managerial perceptions of adaptability and global performance	Culture is related to performance but that TQM interventions are not linked to culture or performance change.
Heck and Marcoulides (1996)	Structure and purpose / Values / Task climate / Individual values and beliefs	Singapore Education	156 upper and lower secondary school teachers from 26 schools	Organizational Productivity	School performance can be determined from knowledge of a school's cultural environment.
Hyde and Davies (2004)	Emergent cultures	UK, health-care	Two case studies of mental health services, 14 month period	Quality	Cultural assumptions interact with service design leading to emergent cultural artefacts that impact on organizational performance. Service users are instrumental in the emergence of organizational culture—links between service users' culture and organizational performance. Relationships are complex, contingent, and recursive.
Jackson (1997)	Person, task, power, role, ideas	UK, health-care	Case study of patients and staff of UK hospital department	Non-attenders	Role culture predominant form observed. Lack of customer culture affected DNA rates
Mannion, R. et al. 2005	Competing Values Framework:	UK, health-care	197 acute trusts (60% response rate) plus / 6 acute case studies / 6 PCT case studies	NHS * ratings / PCO indicators	Acute trusts with developmental cultures more likely to be rated highly. Trusts with hierarchical cultures were more likely to perform well on waiting times, clan cultures scored better on satisfaction.

(continued)

Table 6.1 Continued

Author	Dimension of culture	Country and sector	Sample and time period	Measure of performance	Finding
Marcoulides and Heck (1993)	Structure and purpose Values Task climate Individual values and beliefs	US Education	392 respondents	Organizational productivity	Visible aspects of culture can 'guide the direction of organizations.'
Martin et al. (2006)	Performance-oriented Culture	UK local government	Local government managers and officers, 2001–2005	Best Value Performance Indicators	Quantitative data show relationship between performance-oriented culture and PIs. Qualitative data show culture as important driver in 12/42 reviews
Moynihan and Pandey (2004)	Rational Group Developmental Hierarchical	US, government administration	National Administrative Studies survey of state government health and human services officials, 2002–3	Management perceptions of effectiveness	Evidence that culture does matter for performance. Organizations with developmental cultures (focus on organization, growth, flexibility, and resource acquisition) are likely to achieve significantly higher levels of effectiveness, according to their employees. No evidence of relationship between rational, hierarchical, and group cultures and performance.
Nufrio (2001)	Freedom to act Learning culture Recognizing performance Rewarding performance Putting customers first	US, government administration	Federal government agencies (21 depts)	Management perceptions of effectiveness	Reinvention elements not embedded within government agencies with the exception of team-working which was evident in 9/21 departments.

Nystrom (1993)	Kilmann—Saxton Culture Gap Survey	US Healthcare	Senior managers and excutive secretaries in 13 US health organizations	Management perceptions of effectiveness	Organizations with a consistent strategy possess strong cultures
Parry and Proctor-Thomson (2003)	Organizational description questionnaire	New Zealand, cross-sectoral	Survey 1 388 managers Survey 2 190 managers	Managerial perceptions of effectiveness	The public sector has less of a transformational culture but is no less effective in achieving its outcomes
Rizzo et al. (1994)	Nursing unit cultural assessment tool	US Health care	235 nursing staff	Unit skill mix, Cost measures Quality assurance PIs	Cultural patterns specific to each care unit. Nurses use this to effect change
Shortell et al. (2000)	Competing Values Framework	US, health care	3045 patients from 16 hospitals	Clinical outcomes, functional health status, Patient satisfaction, Cost measures	Variation observed but association between culture and performance not supported
Shortell et al. (2001)	Competing Values Framework	US, health care	56 medical groups, 1797 respondents	Evidence-based care measures derived from informants	No relationship between culture and evidence-based care due possibly to amorphous nature of physicians associations
Zimmerman et al.1993	Organizational characteristics measured through questionnaire	US, health care	3672 ICU admissions, 316 nurses, 202 physicians	Actual / Predicted death rate Ratio actual–predicted stay	Patient centred culture identified as a superior organizational practice.
Zimmerman et al.1994	Organizational characteristics measured through questionnaire	US, health care	888 ICU admissions, 70 nurses, 42 physicians, 2 teaching hospitals	Risk-adjusted survival, Ratio, actual / predicted stay, Resource use	Lack of distinction between high and low performing units. Both had practices to emulate and avoid

measures including whether an organization values employees' opinions, promotes a spirit of teamwork and cooperation, and fosters a concern for the public interest. In addition, they include dummy variables which capture other cultural traits, such as mission-oriented cultures. They find that the culture measures are amongst the most influential within the analysis, and conclude that 'organizational culture is a powerful predictor of organizational performance in federal agencies' (2000, p. 703). However, these findings are qualified due to a heavy reliance on employee—principally managerial—perceptions of organizational performance. Similarly, Moynihan and Pandey (2004) identify organizational culture amongst a number of organizational factors which they include within their test of the relationship between management and performance in the public sector. Their analysis of data from the National Administrative Studies survey led them to conclude that developmental cultures (which focus on the needs of the organization and its ability to change) do matter for performance.

Studies of local government performance in the United Kingdom also provide some support for the culture–performance link. Longitudinal analysis conducted in order to evaluate the long-term impact of the Best Value regime reports qualitative and quantitative evidence which suggests that culture change was a key instrument of reform (Martin et al. 2006). The research shows that employees perceive that authorities increasingly developed performance-oriented cultures between 1999 and 2004, by placing heavy emphasis on continuous improvement and providing management with incentives to achieve step changes in performance. Statistical analysis of the relationship between survey-based surface-level measures of culture and objective performance indicators revealed a positive relationship between performance-oriented cultures and good performance. Furthermore, qualitative analysis reveals that a performance-oriented culture was deemed to be a possible mechanism for improvement in 12/42 change reviews with interviewees highlighting supportive cultures, although the authors also cite evidence of 'obstructive cultures', resistant to reform. Overall, it seems studies seeking to identify the determinants of organizational effectiveness in the public sector provide some empirical support for the relationship between culture and performance amongst other variables, although it should be noted that these analyses often incorporate symbolic or surface-level measures of culture.

STUDIES OF CULTURE AND IMPROVEMENT IN THE PUBLIC SECTOR

The nature of the relationship between culture and performance has probably been best investigated within the health-care field. Scott et al. (2003*a*) conducted a comprehensive review of studies on culture and performance, which resulted in the in-depth analysis of ten pieces which met their inclusion criteria. These include work by authors such as Argote (1989), Gerowitz ᴄ (1996), and Zimmerman et al. (1993, 1994). They found a huge amount of variation across the ten studies in terms of methodology, performance measures, and assessment of culture. However, they found that six of the ten were based in the United States, and whilst most studies addressed culture in terms of behaviour, artefacts, and values, they did not address the underlying assumptions.

Of all the papers reviewed, Scott et al. (2003a) found Gerowitz et al.'s application (1996) of the 'competing values framework' to top management culture in 265 hospitals the most convincing. The authors attempted to measure 'clan', 'open', 'hierarchical', and 'rational' cultures against five different performance variables. They found that management cultures varied across different health-care organizations, and whilst certain cultures impacted on performance this was only when particular elements of performance aligned with cultural values and beliefs.

At the end of their review, Scott et al. (ibid) conclude that the 'strong culture leads to good performance' link is not substantiated by the research on health care, as just four of the studies claim support for the culture and performance hypothesis. In seeking to explain this overall finding, they contended that performance is as slippery a concept as culture and raised concerns about the distinction between independent and dependent variables in some of the studies they reviewed:

It is problematic to assess the effect of espoused values on employee loyalty and commitment when such measures of performance are indeed values in themselves. Likewise, can subjective judgements of managers on their own organization's performance be viewed as external to that organization's culture? (2003a, p. 115)

There have been few in-depth qualitative studies of the impact of culture on performance in the public sector. Hyde and Davies (2004) provide a rare exception as they investigate the government's aim to shift the basic values and beliefs and assumptions that underpin patterns of behaviour in the delivery of care through a comparative case study analysis within the mental health sector. Overall, they conclude that 'cultural assumptions and deeper processes interact with service design, leading to emergent cultural artefacts that impact on organizational performance' (p. 1424). A particularly comprehensive study conducted recently within the health sector provides some more evidence of a connection between culture and service improvement. Mannion et al. (2005) analysed both quantitative and qualitative data on English NHS trusts, and conclude that different types of cultural type impact on different types of improvement. For example, trusts with hierarchical cultures were more likely to deliver shorter waiting times but poor star ratings, clan cultures scored better on measures of staff satisfaction but were also less likely to achieve a high star rating, whilst developmental cultures were much more likely to achieve a high star status.

Studies conducted on other parts of the public sector yield similar results. For example, Cameron and Freeman's analysis (1991) of higher education institutions in the United States revealed the dominance of a 'clan-based' congruent (Wilkins and Ouchi 1983) and concluded that cultural type, rather than congruence or strength, is most important in explaining organizational effectiveness, as perceived by managers. More recent studies have focused on the role of variables which mediate the culture–performance link and have produced some interesting findings. For example, Garnett et al. (2008) examined whether communication moderates or mediates the impact of culture on performance in public service organizations. Arguing that culture has been shown to be 'profoundly shaped by communication' they identify characteristics of *'role-oriented'* (formalization, structures, bureaucracy, rules, and policies) and *'mission-oriented'* (dynamic, entrepreneurial, innovation, task, and goal accomplishment) cultures. Statistical analysis of 274 survey responses derived from the National Administrative Studies Project tested for mediation and moderation effects of the two cultures. In terms of mediation, the authors conclude that mission-based cultures result in better performance because employees exhibit better-quality communication with superiors about tasks and performance. In terms of moderation, again the findings are positive in relation to mission-based cultures as 'excellent communication increases the likelihood of excellent performance'. However, in contrast, in rule-based cultures 'excellent communication increases the likelihood of average performance and decreases the likelihood of excellent performance'. The authors advocate a more thorough examination of all these variables and their impacts. A rare comparative study of leadership, culture, and performance in the private and public sectors in New Zealand (Parry and Proctor Thomson 2003) found less evidence of transformational organizational change within public sector organizations, with most characterized by transactional organizational culture, but that this did not seem to make them any less effective. They also note that organizational culture is important in 'liberating or suppressing the display of leadership' (p. 393).

To summarize, in comparison with the private sector, it seems that there has been a limited amount of work to date on culture and organizational effectiveness, performance, and improvement within a public service context. This is somewhat surprising given the attention that governments worldwide have devoted to cultural change in the public sector. The work that has been conducted falls into two groups. The first group of studies seek to explain organizational effectiveness and public service performance, and include organizational culture as one of many organizational factors under analysis. These studies tend to conclude that 'culture matters' and is a strong predictor of performance, but also concede that it is possible that high-performing organizations might develop strong or 'performance-oriented' cult, than the other way around. The second group of studies ten specifically on the culture–performance link in the public sector (altho mainly in health-care). As culture is the main focus of the analysis, in general, greater care is taken in the interpretation, construction, and measurement of culture within these studies (Scott et al. 2003a). However, some of these studies do not provide clear evidence to suggest there is a causal link between organizational culture and performance. They do, though, highlight the importance of mediating factors such as leadership and communication. Taken together and in light of the evidence on private firms, these mixed research findings have implications for the relationship between culture and performance and for future research in this area.

Culture and the improvement of public services

This review shows that evidence on the impact of culture on organizational performance is mixed with work on both public and private sectors littered with caveats and qualification. Mostly these concern the conceptualization, and subsequent operationalization, of organizational culture, and therefore raise a number of methodological questions and implications.

There are persistent claims that quantitative approaches to analysing culture have been unable to go beyond surface-level aspects, such as symbols and behaviours and are, more accurately, measures of organizational climate rather than culture (see, e.g. Brewer and Selden's admission [2000] that they treat culture and climate as one and the same). Schein (1996) has argued that scholars have failed to capture the multi-dimensional nature of culture, whilst others suggest that the widespread use of questionnaires leads to a danger of imposing one's own cultural perspective on the organization rather than uncovering its actual nature (Lim 1995). Equally, there have been relatively few examples of in-depth qualitatively based analysis of cultural change and its impact on organizations. It has been argued that many qualitative pieces tend to focus on 'best practice' examples and therefore do not make a substantial contribution to theory development (Khademian 2000). Furthermore, there are very few longitudinal studies, with many presenting a 'snapshot' analysis of culture in an organisation at a particular point in time. Further concerns have been raised about the lack of objective and independent performance measures utilized to date, with many of the studies included in this review relying on managerial evaluations of performance.

Finally, research findings continue to cast doubt over direction of causal relationship—does 'strong' culture improve performance or does improved performance lead to the development of a 'strong' culture? Hargreaves (1995) argues that school culture 'may be a cause, an object or an effect of school improvement' (p. 41), whilst Scott et al. (2003a) argue that those studying culture and performance in health care are in serious danger of confusing cause and effect and clouding any possible link. Citing the urgent need to tackle these methodological obstacles in order to allow for more work 'unpacking' the culture–performance relationship, their final conclusion is that it is more likely that culture and performance are mutually created in a reciprocal manner which is dependent upon context and other influences.

The transportation of the culture–performance link from the private sector to public services has also been criticized by public management scholars on a broader basis. Some argue that work on culture in the public sector lacks substance. For example, Khademian (2000) warns that, so far, research agendas have been driven by the needs of practitioners, and suggests that if we assume that 'every dimension of an organization is manageable in the hands of a "successful" manager, we forgo an opportunity to better understand the complexities of public management in rich institutional and organizational settings' (2000, p. 48). Newman (1994) finds a number of underlying culture–performance assumptions problematic when applied to public services. She argues against the assumption that cultures are closed societies, highlighting the fact that public sector organizations are not sealed from their environment. She also refutes the assumption that cultures are integrated wholes, highlighting professional, departmental, and functional divisions in both public and private organizations. The assumption that cultures are consensual and based upon 'shared values' is also rejected on the grounds that cultural change marks a key source of conflict and division, whilst the claim that cultures are leader-generated is also countered, as this approach pays little attention to power within organizations and the dynamics of organizational change. Finally, Newman disputes the argument that culture is a separate domain, a specific lever to pull—isolated from strategy and other aspects of change management.

Sinclair (1991) has also questioned the application of the excellence school's 'cultural control model' and other private sector-based typologies (e.g. measures of 'mission-oriented' cultures) to public services. In contrast, she has argued in favour of alternative models of culture which are better suited to the public sector context, outlining a 'sub-cultural model' (where unified cultures can impede effectiveness), a 'professional-managerial model' (which assumes cultural diversity leads to synergy and innovation), and a 'public interest/service model' (which advocates bottom-up distinctive and cohesive organizational culture). Each of these, she argues, offers an understanding of culture which is more appropriate to public service organizations which are not 'devoid of sub-cultural conflict' (1991, p. 321). This view is supported by Brooks and MacDonald (2000), who highlight the complicating nature of sub-cultural power within the health-care sector.

Conclusions

A number of conclusions can be drawn on the basis of this review of evidence on the relationship between organizational culture and improvement in the public sector. Firstly, it is clear that any study of culture should adopt a multi-dimensional and rounded interpretation of the concept or, alternatively, focus on 'organizational climate' if conceptualizations and measures more closely correspond to surface-level cultural features. Secondly, there is an evident theoretical rationale for linking types of organizational culture and levels of performance, and this chapter has demonstrated the ways in which policy-makers have seized upon cultural change as a mechanism to improve the delivery of public services with varying effects.

Thirdly, evidence to date offers some support for the culture–performance link, but doubts remain in terms of the nature and direction of the relation-ship. Much of the work on culture and improvement has been based upon private firms and that conducted on public services is uneven in its coverage. For example, whilst there is a growing body of work in health care and US agencies which attempts to establish the impact of culture on organizational effectiveness and quality of service, there has been little detailed examination of culture and improvement in key local government services like education and social care.

Overall this chapter concludes that there is an urgent need for an in-depth, longitudinal, multi-methodological, and comparative analysis of the relation-ship between organizational culture and public service improvement, such as that conducted by Mannion et al. (2005) in relation to the UK health service. Such a study should apply public service-specific typologies of organizational culture (such as those outlined by Sinclair), be mindful of the institutional context of public service organizations (Khademian 2000), and adopt a rounded interpretation of organizational culture. This kind of research is vital in assisting both academic and policy-maker understandings of the relationship between organizational culture and public service performance.

REFERENCES

Alvesson, M. (1995). *Cultural Perspectives on Organisations.* Cambridge: Cambridge University Press.

Argote, L. (1989). Agreements about Norms and Work-Unit Effectiveness: Evidence from the Field. *Basic and Applied Social Pyschology* 10, 131–40.

Ashworth, R. E., Boyne, G. A. and Delbridge, R. (2009). Escape from the Iron Cage? Organizational Change and Isomorphic Pressures in the Public Sector. *Journal of Public Administration, Research and Theory* 19(1), 165–87.

Barney, J. B. (1986). Organizational Culture: Can it be a Source of Sustained Competitive Advantage? *Academy of Management Review* 11(3), 656–65.

Brewer, G. and Selden, C. (2000). Why Elephants Gallop: Assessing and Predicting Organizational Performance in Federal Agencies. *Journal of Public Administration Research and Theory* 10(4), 685–711.

Brooks, I. and Bate, P. (1994). The Problems of Effecting Change within the British Civil Service: A Cultural Perspective. *British Journal of Management* 5, 177–90.

—— and MacDonald, S. (2000). 'Doing Life' Gender Relations in a Night Nursing Sub-Culture. *Gender Work and Organizations* 7, 4, 221–229.

Cameron, K. and Freeman, S. J. (1991). Cultural Congruence, Strength and Type: Relationships to Effectiveness. *Research in Organizational Change and Development* 5, 23–59.

Driscoll, A. and Morris, J. (2001). Stepping Out: Rhetorical Devices and Culture Change Management in the UK Civil Service. *Public Administration* 79(4), 803–24.

Davies, H. T. O., Nutley, S. and Mannion, R. (2000). Organizational Culture and the Quality of Health Care. *Quality in Health Care* 9, 111–19.

Deal, T. E. and Kennedy, A. A. (1982). *Corporate Cultures: The Rites and Rituals of Corporate Life.* Reading, Mass: Addison-Wesley.

Denison, D. R. and Mishra, A. K. (1995). Toward a Theory of Organizational Culture and Effectiveness. *Organization Science* 6(2), 204–23.

—— (1996). What is the Difference between Organizational Culture and Organizational Climate? A Native's Point of View on a Decade of Paradigm Wars. *Academy of Management Review* 21(3), 819–54.

Doig, A. and Hargrove, E. (1987) (eds.). *Leadership and Innovation: A Biographical Perspective on Entrepreneurs in Government.* Baltimore: Johns Hopkins University Press.

Ferlie, E., Ashburner, F., Fitzgerald, L. and Pettigrew, A. (1996). *The New Public Management in Action.* Oxford: Oxford University Press.

Garnett, J. L., Marlowe, J. and Pandey, S. K. (2008). Penetrating the Performance Predicament: Communication as a Mediator or Moderator of Organizational Culture's Impact on Public Organizational Performance. *Public Administration Review* 68(2), 266–81.

Gerowitz, M. B., Lemieux-Charles, L., Heginbotham, C. and Johnson B. (1996). Top Management Culture and Performance in Canadian, UK and US Hospitals. *Health Services Management Research* 9, 69–78.

—— (1998). Do TQM Interventions Change Management Culture? Findings and Implications. *Quality Management in Healthcare* 6, 1–11.

Gordon, G. and DiTomaso, N. (1992). Predicting Corporate Performance from Organizational Culture. *Journal of Management Studies* 29(6), 783–798.

Hargreaves, D. (1995). School Culture, School Effectiveness and School Improvement. *School Effectiveness and School Improvement* 6(1), 23–46.

Harris, L. C. and Ogbonna, E. (2002). The Unintended Consequences of Culture Interventions: A Study of Unexpected Outcomes. *British Journal of Management* 13, 31–49.

Hawkins, P. (1997). Organizational Culture: Sailing between Evangelism and Complexity. *Human Relations* 50(4), 417–41.

Heck, R. H. and Marcoulides, G. A. (1996). School Culture and Performance: Testing the Invariance of an Organizational Model. *School Effectiveness and Improvement* 76–95.

Hyde, P. and Huw T. O. Davies. (2004). Service Design, Culture and Performance: Collusion and Co-production in Health Care. *Human Relations* 57(11), 1407–26.

Hult, G., Tomas, M., Ketchen, D. J. and Arnfelt, M. (2007). Strategic Supply Chain Management: Improving Performance through a Culture of Competitiveness and Knowledge Development. *Strategic Management Journal* 28(10), 1035–52.

Jackson, S. (1997). Does Organizational Culture Affect Out-patient Rates? *Health Manpower Management* 23, 233–6.

Khademian, A. M. (2000). 'Is Silly Putty Manageable? Looking for the Links between Culture, Management and Context', in Brudney, et al. *Advancing Public Management: New Developments in Theory, Methods and Practice*, Washington DC: Georgetown U.P.

Kotter, J. P. and Heskett, J. L. (1992). *Corporate Culture and Performance*. New York, NY: Macmillan.

Lee, S., Yoon, S. J., Sanguk, K. and Kang, J. W. (2006). The Integrated Effects of Market-Oriented Culture and Marketing Strategy on Firm Performance. *Journal of Strategic Marketing* 14(3), 245–61.

Lewis, D. S. (1994). Organizational Change: Relationship between reactions, behaviour and organizational performance. *Journal of Organizational Change and Management* 7(5), 41–55.

Lim, B. (1995). Examining the Organizational Culture and Organizational Performance Link. *Leadership and Organizational Development Journal* 16(5), 16–21.

Lurie, I. and Riccucci, N. (2003). Changing the Culture of Welfare Offices: From Vision to the Front Lines. *Administration and Society* 34(6), 653–77.

Mannion, R., Davies, H. T. O. and Marshall, M. (2005). *Cultures for Performance in Health Care*. Maidenhead: Open University Press.

Marcoulides, G. A. and Heck, R. H. (1993). Organizational Culture and Performance: Proposing and Testing a Model. *Organization Science* 4(2), 209–25.

Martin, S. et al. (2006). *Long-term Evaluation of Best Value: Final Report*. ODPM: London.

McNulty, T. and Ferlie, E. (2002). *Reengineering Health Care*. Oxford: Oxford University Press.

Moynihan, D. and Pandey, S. J. (2004). Testing how Management Matters in an Era of Government by Performance Management. *Journal of Public Administration Research and Theory* 15, 241–439.

Newman, J. (1994). Beyond the Vision: Cultural Change in the Public Sector. *Public Money and Management* April-June, 59–64.

Nufrio, P. M. (2001). *Changing Organizational Culture: A Study of the National Government*. University Press of America.

Nystrom, P. C. (1993). Organizational Cultures, Strategies, and Commitments in Health Care Organizations. *Health Care Management Review* 18, 43–9.

O'Cass, A. and Ngo, L. V. (2007). Market Orientation versus Innovative Culture: Two Routes to Superior Brand Performance. *European Journal of Marketing* 41(7), 868–87.

Ogbonna, E. (1993). Managing Organizational Culture: Fantasy or Reality? *Human Resource Management Journal* 3(2), 42–54.

—— and Harris, L. C. (2000). Leadership Style, Organizational Culture and Performance: Empirical Evidence from UK Companies. *International Journal of Human Resource Management* 11(4), 766–88.

—— —— (2002*a*). The Performance Implications of Management Fads and Fashions: An Empirical Study. *Journal of Strategic Marketing* 10(1), 47–68.

—— —— (2002*b*). Organizational Culture: A Ten Year, Two-Phase Study of Change in the UK Retailing Sector. *Journal of Management Studies* 39(5), 673–706.

Osborne, D. and Gaebler, T. (1992). *Reinventing Government.* Reading, MA: Addison-Wesley.

Parker, R. and Bradley, L. (2000). Organizational Culture in the Public Sector: Evidence from Six Organizations. *International Journal of Public Sector Management* 13(2), 125–41.

Parry, K. W. and Proctor-Thomson, S. B. (2003). Leadership, Culture and Performance: The Case of the New Zealand Public Sector. *Journal of Change Management* 3(4), 376–99.

Peters, T. and Waterman, R. (1982). *In Search of Excellence.* New York: Random House.

Rainey, H. and Steinbauer, P. (1999). Galloping Elephants: Developing Elements of a Theory of Effective Government Organizations. *Journal of Public Administration Research and Theory* 9(1), 1–32.

Rizzo, J. A., Gilman, M. P. and Mersmann, C. A. (1994). Facilitating Care Delivery: Redesign using Measures of Unit Culture and Work Characteristics. *Journal of Nursing Administration* 24, 32–37.

Saffold, G. (1988). Culture Traits, Strength and Organizational Performance: Moving Beyond Strong Culture. *Academy of Management Review* 13(4), 546–5.

Schein, E. (1985). *Organizational Culture and Leadership.* San Francisco, CA: Jossey Bass.

Schein, E. H. (1996). Culture: The Missing Concept in Organizational Studies. *Administrative Science Quarterly* 41, 229–40.

Scott, T., Mannion, R., Marshall, M. and Davies, H. (2003*a*). Does Organisational Culture Influence Health Care Performance? A Review of the Evidence. *Journal of Health Services Research Policy* 8(2), 105–17.

—— —— Davies, H. W. T. O. and Marshall, M. (2003*b*). Implementing Culture Change in Health Care: Theory and Practice. *International Journal for Quality in Health Care* 15(2), 111–18.

Shortell, S., Jones, R., Rademaker, A., Gillies, R., Dranove, D. and Hughes, E. (2000). Assessing the Impact of Total Quality Management and Organizational Culture on Multiple Outcomes of Care for Coronary Artery Bypass Graft Surgery Patients. *Medical Care* 38, 201–17.

—— Lazzali, J., Burns, L., Alexander, J., Gillies, R. and Budetti, P. (2001). Implementing Evidence-Based Medicine. The Role of Market Pressures, Compensation Incentives, and Culture in Physician Organizations. *Medical Care* 39, 62–78.

Sinclair, A. (1991). After Excellence: Models of Organizational Culture for the Public Sector. *Australian Journal of Public Administration* 50(3), 321–32.

Smirchich, L. (1983). Concepts of Culture and Organizational Analysis. *Administrative Science Quarterly* 28, 339–58.

Theobald, R. (1997). Enhancing Public Service Ethics: More Culture, Less Bureaucracy. *Administration and Society* 29(4), 490–504.

Wallace, J., Hunt, J. and Richards, C. (1999). The Relationship between Organizational Culture, Organizational Climate and Managerial Values. *International Journal of Public Sector Management* 12(7), 548–64.

Wilderom, C., Glunk, U. and Maslowski, R. (2000). Organizational Culture as a Predictor of Organizational Performance, in Ashkanasy, N., Wilderom, C. and Peterson, M. (eds). *Handbook of Organizational Culture and Climate*. Thousand Oaks: Sage.

Wilkins, A. L. and Ouchi, W. G. (1983). Efficient Cultures: Exploring the Relationship between Culture and Performance. *Administrative Science Quarterly* 28(3), 468–81.

Wilmott, H. (1993). Strength is Ignorance: Slavery is Freedom: Managing Culture in Modern Organizations. *Journal of Management Studies* 30(4), 515–551.

Wise, L. E. (2000). 'The Public Service Culture', in R. Stillman (ed.), *Public Administration: Concepts and Cases*, New York: Houghton Mifflin.

Zimmerman, J., Shortell, S. M., Rousseau, D., Duffy, J., Gillies, R. and Knaus, W. (1993). Improving Intensive Care: Observations based on Organizational Case Studies in Nine Intensive Care Units: A Prospective, Multi-Centre Study, American Journal of Critical Care. *Critical Care Medicine* 21, 1443–51.

——————————and Wagner, D. (1994). Improving Intensive Care at Two Teaching Hospitals: An Organizational Case Study. *American Journal of Critical Care* 3, 129–38.

7 Human Resource Management

Julian Gould-Williams

Introduction

During the last two decades there has been a surge of interest in evaluating the link between human resource management (HRM) and organizational performance, to the extent that the search for 'positive' evidence between the two is now considered the subject's 'Holy Grail' (Boselie et al. 2005). Despite a call for 'a theory about HRM, a theory about performance and a theory about how they are linked' (Guest 1997, p. 263), there remains limited theoretical development in this area (Fleetwood and Hesketh 2006). In fact, Purcell and Kinnie (2007, p. 533) note that 'numerous review papers ... have found this field of research often wanting in terms of method, theory and the specification of HR practices to be used when establishing a relationship with performance outcomes'. Further, the majority of empirical evidence is based on private sector experience, with just a limited number of studies considering public sector organizations.

Given the heightened awareness of the need to engage public sector workers in securing higher standards of service, the lack of a firm empirical base on which to inform the development of theory and management practice in the public sector needs to be addressed. The context in which public sector workers now operate is becoming increasingly similar to that experienced by private sector workers who face ongoing pressure to increase sales or provide superior customer service in an attempt to boost profits. This shift in context has been attributed to the introduction of New Public Management (NPM), whereby the public sector was encouraged to move from a rule-bound culture to a performance-based culture which, according to Brown (2008), opened the way for public managers to adopt 'sophisticated HRM techniques' (p. 3).

The opening section of this chapter will outline the various approaches taken by those defining HRM. A description of the theoretical foundations between HRM and performance will then be considered, and thereafter the empirical evidence will be examined in an attempt to determine whether HRM has a positive effect on public service performance.

What is HRM?

There continues to be a lack of consensus of the definition of HRI
several decades of study in the field. HRM can be viewed broadl
people management activities in which:

HRM includes anything and everything associated with the management of employment relationships in the firm. We do not associate HRM solely with a high-
commitment model of labour management or with any particular ideology or style
of management (Boxall and Purcell 2000, p. 184).

In contrast, others consider it to be a 'philosophical' approach to managing
employees based on 'soft' or developmental HR practices (Legge 2005). For
instance, Storey associates HRM with a particular style of 'high-commitment'
management (1995, p. 5).

This view is consistent with the public sector's image of being a 'model'
employer. In fact, Brown (2008, p. 3) states: 'The notion of the model
employer encapsulated the principles of best practice, and was argued to set
an example to the private sector'. As such, this chapter will consider HRM as a
distinctive, high-commitment approach to employment management.

Combinations of HR practices have been labelled in various ways such as
High Commitment Management (Guest 1997; Walton 1985), High Performance Work Systems (Appelbaum et al. 2000; Huselid 1995), and High Involvement Practices (Lawler 1992). Of course, these labels should be viewed as
loosely describing the practices' aims or intended outcomes. However, the
question of which HR practices should be included in any specific bundle
remains unanswered (Delery 1998), with Boselie et al. (2005, p. 73) pointing
out that there is 'no accepted theory...that might classify different practices
into 'obligatory' and 'optional', 'hygiene', and 'motivators'. This, they argue,
has resulted in 'HRM...consist[ing] of whatever researchers wish or, perhaps, what their samples and data sets dictate' (Boselie et al. 2005, p. 74). In
the main, this area of research can be divided into two groups: First, the 'best
practice' perspective in which it is proposed that a prescribed set of HR
practices can be applied in the workplace regardless of national or sectoral
contexts. The alternative, 'best fit' view advocates that HR practices should
'fit' with the organization's external and internal contexts. Both these
perspectives will now be developed in turn.

THE BEST PRACTICE PERSPECTIVE

The best practice perspective advocates that a distinctive set of HR practices
should be adopted by all types of organization regardless of context, and these
will always lead to enhanced performance. Pfeffer (1994) is one of the

foremost advocates of this approach in which he initially prescribed 16 HR practices which, in his view, captured 'best practice' in this area. Later Pfeffer (1998) reduced the 16 core best practices to just seven. These are employment security, selective hiring, teamworking, high compensation contingent on performance, extensive training, reduced status differentials between management and staff, and information sharing. Pfeffer's list of best-practice HRM is by no means definitive; other commentators provide alternatives and somewhat eclectic lists of HR practices. A review of 104 articles published in refereed journals between 1994 and 2003 reported that a total of twenty-six different HR practices were used in individual studies (Boselie et al. 2005) (see Table 7.1). As such, Boxall and Purcell (2003, p. 62) state: 'It is difficult to see the underpinning logic in such a long list of practices'. It is possible, however, to identify common practices across studies. For instance, a recent review reported that the four most commonly cited HR practices were (*a*) training and development, (*b*) reward management schemes, (*c*) performance management (including appraisals), and (*d*) careful recruitment and selection (Boselie et al. 2005). On this basis it could be argued that the main purpose of HRM is to recruit and select strong performers, provide them with the skills needed to perform, and reward them on the basis of their performance.

Table 7.1 List of HR practices based on review of 104 studies

1	Training and development
2	Contingent pay and rewards
3	Performance management (including appraisals)
4	Recruitment and selection
5	Teamworking
6	Direct participation
7	'Good' wages
8	Communication and information sharing
9	Internal promotion opportunities
10	Job design (job rotation, job enrichment)
11	Autonomy and decentralized decision-making
12	Employment security
13	Benefits packages
14	Formal grievance procedures
15	HR planning
16	Financial participation (e.g. employee stocks and shares)
17	Symbolic egalitarianism
18	Attitude surveys
19	Indirect participation (consultation via unions)
20	Diversity and equal opportunities
21	Job analysis
22	Socialization, induction, social activities
23	Family-friendly policies and work–life balance
24	Employee exit management
25	Professionalization and effectiveness of HR function.
26	Social responsibility practices

Source: Boselie et al. (2005, p. 94)

In contrast to this approach, there are now emerging arguments in which it is proposed that attempts to isolate specific sets of relevant HR practices are meaningless (Purcell et al. 2009). According to this view, it is not the selection or identification of specific types of HR practices that is important, as it is possible for a range of different HR practices to be equally effective in improving performance outcomes, depending on sector and employee group (Datta et al. 2005). Thus different HR practices will have similar effects on performance outcomes depending on where they are applied and the employee group experiencing them. This view could be particularly relevant in public sector organizations with frontline workers consisting of both highly skilled and less skilled workers (contrast, e.g., refuse collectors and grounds maintenance staff with doctors, teachers, and social workers).

THE 'BEST FIT' APPROACH

The 'best fit' approach is based on the view that the effectiveness of HR practices will be contingent on how closely the practices fit the external and internal environments of the organization (Wood 1999). Commentators adopt different views relating to what particular context(s) HR practices should fit. Some stress the outer context or competitive strategy, and others emphasize the 'inner context' of existing structures and strategy, whereas still others place emphasis on the particular stage of maturity an organization has reached in its life-cycle (Hendry 1995; Purcell et al. 2009). As such, HR practices can be regarded as being most effective when they meet or fit an organization's competitive strategy (Porter 1980). Jackson and Schuler (1995) identify a range of competitive strategies and prescribe the appropriate role behaviours needed to fit each strategy. For example, a strategy based on cost leadership would require a minimal investment in the work-force, low stand-ards for recruitment and selection, relatively low levels of pay, and minimal training provision. Brown (2008, p. 5) acknowledges that the 'new models of HRM in the public sector introduced the notion of human resources having the capacity to achieve performance outcomes in line with the strategic direction of the public sector organisation ... emphasis [was placed] on securing and retaining staff who could achieve desired outcomes'. If this is so, then the relevant HR practices need to be identified and thereafter implemented by line managers before the contribution of HRM will be realized in public organizations.

It should be noted, however that the best fit perspective makes several fundamental assumptions. First, that organizations will always have a competitive strategy and that the chosen strategy is the best one for business success. Second, the best fit perspective takes no account of the possibility that organizations may adopt a mix of competitive strategies. If this is so then identifying relevant HR practices to 'fit' such a mix of strategies would be problematic. Further exacerbating these issues is the need for organizations to have a degree of flexibility in their choice of strategy in order to respond to turbulent and unpredictable business environments (Purcell et al. 2009).

It is possible, however for both the 'best practice' and 'best fit' approaches to hold some utility, in that Boxall and Purcell (2003, p. 68) suggest they are simply 'two sides of the same coin'. For instance, they propose that a core group of HR practices, such as employee development, employee involvement, and high rewards, could be broadly viewed as best practice in a particular sector, but the more detailed design of each of these practices should then be dependent on organizational context. This is consistent with Guest et al. (2004) who suggest that the implementation of HRM should be considered in terms of 'practice' and 'technique'. For instance, an organization can adopt a similar rationale towards selecting new recruits (a HR practice), but adopt a very different approach in doing so, depending on the skills and qualifications needed for the job (e.g. psychometric testing, interviews, assessment centres—HR techniques). Thus, from this perspective both the broadly prescribed universal best practice view and the more specifically designed best fit approach can be considered as relevant.

Theories of HRM and performance

There is limited higher-level theory linking HRM with performance, as much of the early research in this area was concerned with evaluating associations rather than causal connections between HRM and performance outcomes (Arthur 1994; Delaney and Huselid 1996; Huselid 1995). To date, three theoretical perspectives can be identified in the literature: (*a*) the contingent, (*b*) the value-added, and (*c*) the motivational. The first perspective argues that the adoption of HRM should take place in response to the organization's environment and should complement the organization's internal systems (contingency theory). The second perspective views HRM as adding value through the strategic development of an organization's staff, providing the organization with rare, inimitable, and non-substitutable resources (the resource-based view). The third, motivational perspective—also referred to as AMO theory (**A**bility, **M**otivation, and **O**pportunity)—proposes that a HR system should be designed to meet employees' needs for skills and motivation, and thereafter provide them with opportunities to use their abilities in various job roles. The model assumes that employees will want to achieve high standards of work and will be willing to engage in involvement schemes using their skills to contribute towards organizational performance (Purcell et al. 2003). In providing direction for future research, Boselie et al. (2005) argue that the above three theoretical frameworks provide only part of the answer to Guest's call (1997) for more theoretical development in the field of HRM. They suggest that more emphasis should be given to 'micro'-theories (these include Expectancy theory and Goal-setting theories) to understand employees' experiences of HR practice, and the subsequent impact on organizational performance.

So far the link between HRM and performance has been described as a simple, unidirectional relationship between input (HR practices) and output (performance). However, there are now several 'micro' level HRM-Performance models which isolate potential mediating variables linking HRM with organizational performance in an attempt to identify why or in what way HRM affects performance. These models point out that it is possible for the direction of causality to shift from input → output, to output → input (reverse causality) (Schneider et al. 2003). For instance, it has been observed that organizational 'success' can lead to increased employee satisfaction as most people enjoy being part of a 'winning team'. Schneider et al. (2003) tested for reverse causality and reported that it is more likely that profitability impacts job satisfaction than job satisfaction impacts profitability

Testing these models requires data at the individual, employee level as it is employees and their attitudes that need to be assessed. Also, Wright and Boswell (2002) argue that researchers should differentiate between HR *practice* and HR *policy,* in that the former refers to the actual *observable* activities as experienced by the employee, whereas the latter refers to the organization's stated *intentions.* On this basis, where commentators are interested in the effects of HR practice on worker outcomes, it would again be more appropriate to use employees' perceptions of HR practice. And yet only 11 of the 104 articles reviewed by Boselie et al. (2005) considered employees' perspectives. Due to the limited empirical evidence that has so far considered the possible links between HR practices and organizational performance, this area of research has become known as the 'HR black box' in that its contents remain uncertain (Wright et al. 2003).

As was noted above, Boselie et al. (2005) recommends that more consideration should be given to the contribution of behavioural theories to gain a better understanding of the contents of the 'black box'. This is consistent with Guest's earlier recommendation (1997) that behavioural models should be used to link employee perceptions to behavioural outcomes, which in turn should be linked to group-level performance outcomes, and thereafter to organizational performance (see also Martin-Alcazar et al. [2008]). In so doing, it becomes apparent that a range of individual and organizational performance measures should be considered. However, the recommended numbers and types of mediating links between HRM and performance differ considerably from one commentator to another. For instance, some argue that the starting point in assessing the relationship between HRM and performance should be the organization's business strategy, with the design of the HR system emerging from this strategy (Becker et al. 1997, see Figure 7.1). Guest (1997) makes a similar argument and uses Porter's strategic choice typology which distinguishes between differentiation and innovation, focus and quality, and cost reduction type strategies (see Figure 7.2). These views are consistent with the 'best fit' hypothesis. However, so far there appears to be no convincing empirical evidence that HRM should be linked with an organization's strategy (Boxall and Purcell 2003; Huselid 1995).

As illustrated in Figures 7.1 and 7.2, the different types of performance outcomes should be considered at different levels. For instance, to test Guest's behavioural model (1997) (Figure 7.2) one would need performance measures at the individual level (e.g. commitment, effort, organizational citizenship) and the unit or company level (e.g. absence rates, labour turnover, customer complaints, profit; see also the approach taken by Wright et al. [2005]). In addition, the assumption that the 'high-commitment' approach to management always lead to favourable worker experiences has been challenged by several commentators (Green 2004; Marchington and Grugulis 2000). Therefore, more recently behavioural models have included 'negative' work-related experiences along with 'positive' experiences (Godard 2001). Further, according to Guest's model, it will be necessary to collect data on a firm's strategy, but whether this should be intended or enacted strategy is not indicated. It is likely that such data will be provided by senior managers who will present either the work unit's or company's view on strategy. In the public sector this would involve identifying an organization's service priorities. Empirically testing behavioural models will present public sector researchers with several methodological challenges. We return to discuss these in the concluding section of this chapter.

Regardless of the proposed number of links between HRM and Performance, it is probable that the impact of HRM will become weaker as factors other than HRM intervene. In other words, the impact of HRM will become progressively less the further along the causal chain the performance outcome is situated. For example, we would expect HRM to have a greater impact on employee attitude (such as job satisfaction and commitment) and a much weaker effect on organizational profits. This issue has been termed the problem of 'causal distance' in that extraneous factors from both within and outside the organization can affect profits and performance. Such extraneous factors may include the introduction of new technology, marketing campaigns, mergers and acquisitions, public relations catastrophes, oil prices, global political conflict, and terrorism (Boselie et al. 2005). In public sector organizations, extraneous factors could also include a change in resource allocation, political priorities, and leadership.

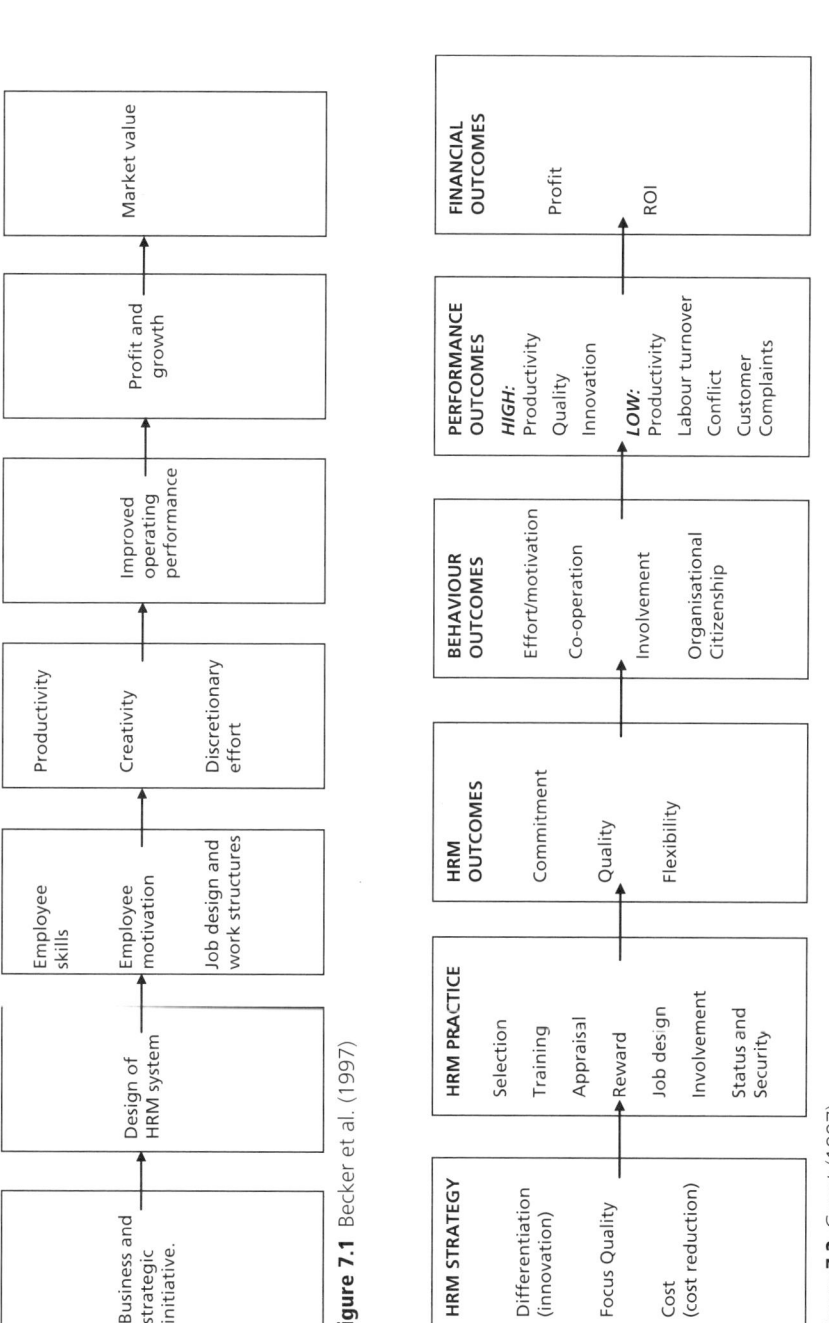

Figure 7.1 Becker et al. (1997)

Figure 7.2 Guest (1997)

Evidence on HRM and performance

CHARACTERISTICS OF THE STUDIES

There is an interesting array of empirical studies that have been conducted in public sector organizations which have assisted our understanding of the nature of HR practice and, more generally, worker environment. For instance, Procter and Currie (2004) considered the interdependency of work groups and target-based team working in the UK civil service; Currie and Procter (2003) describe the interaction between HR policies and practices and the implementation of team working in the UK Inland Revenue; Eaton (2000) provides a useful description of contrasting approaches to managing nurse aides in nursing homes in two US states: California and Pennsylvania; and Harris (2001) considered the effects of line managers' values on successfully implementing performance-related pay schemes in a mixed UK sector (which included the Health Service and Civil Service). However, as these studies did not include performance outcome measures, they have not been included in this review of the effects of HR practice on service performance.

A systematic review of the HRM literature was conducted in order to identify those public sector studies that have empirically tested the relationship between HRM and performance. The review produced a total of seventy-three articles relating to HRM and performance, but on closer examination twenty-three papers were literature reviews or prescriptions of best practice, thirty-six considered a single HR practice[1] or did not include measures of performance, and three highlighted the role of the HR department. This resulted in eleven papers being considered for this review (see Table 7.2 for a summary of the studies). The articles were published between 1999 and 2008, with three studies conducted in England, a further three in the Netherlands, with the remaining studies using samples from Australia, Canada, Israel, New Zealand, and Wales. The studies cover a relatively narrow range of public sector organizations: six studies used mixed settings, namely, either private and public sectors or multiple public sector organizations; three studies were conducted in local government service departments; two studies were conducted in nursing homes, with the remaining study conducted in UK NHS hospitals. All the studies used a questionnaire survey to collect empirical data, either by means of postal, telephone, or face-to-face interviews.

---

[1] Several articles referred to HR-related issues, such as competency frameworks, downsizing, diversity management, career planning, appraisals, using HR-software programmes, HRD, absence management, undertaking HR audits, and training expenditure. Even though these individual aspects of HR practice are important, these studies were excluded from the review as they would provide over-estimations of the effects of each of the individual HR practices on performance outcomes as noted earlier in this chapter (Lepak et al. 2006).

In considering the effects of HR practice on performance outcomes, the studies will be summarized on the basis of whether their main focus was on micro-outcomes (at the employee level) or macro-outcomes (at the organizational level). Four of the eleven studies assessed the relationship between HR practices and employee-related outcomes (Baptiste 2008; Edgar and Geare 2005; Gould-Williams 2007; Steijn and Leisink 2006); a further four considered performance at the organizational level (Boselie et al. 2003; Harel and Tzafrir 1999; Ott and van Dijk 2005; West et al. 2002); and the remaining three studies considered both employee and organizational outcomes (Gould-Williams 2003; Orlitzky and Frenkel 2005; Rondeau and Wagar 2001).

INDIVIDUAL EMPLOYEE PERFORMANCE OUTCOMES

As noted earlier, studies evaluating the effects of HR practice on employee outcomes contribute to gaining insight into 'black box' issues. The HR practices selected in these studies are generally compatible with 'high-commitment' bundles, so we would predict that the studies will report statistically significant findings between HR practices and desirable employee outcomes, such as commitment, job satisfaction, and worker effort. Of the seven studies that included individual performance measures, the most common variables considered were organizational commitment and job satisfaction (four of the five studies included both these measures); three studies included a measure of employee effort, with quit intentions, employee well-being, and work-related stress incorporated in two of the five studies. The public sector research has also captured potential negative outcomes of HR practice such as measures of work-related stress. Here, consistent with the 'high-commitment' thesis, we would anticipate HR practices to have a neutral or negative effect on work-related stress.

The studies' results do not provide convincing evidence of the 'positive' effects of HR practices on employee outcomes. For instance, just two studies reported statistically significant associations[2] between HR practices and organizational commitment and worker effort, with one study reporting statistically significant links between HR practices, job satisfaction, quit intentions, morale, and absenteeism. Given that all the studies in this review relied on respondents' views of both HR practices and performance outputs, it is likely that the relationships reported here are over-estimations due to common source bias. Nonetheless, we can infer that in some but by no means all instances, HR practices do indeed positively affect employees' experience at work.

---

[2] Given the small sample size reported by Baptiste (2008) where an *n* of 51 was achieved, it may not be surprising to note that none of the relationships between HR practices and employee outcomes were statistically significant at conventional levels.

Table 7.2 Summary of empirical evidence

	Study	HR practice(s)	Country and sector	Sample and time period	Measure of performance	Findings
1	Baptiste (2008)	Selection and internal recruitment	England, local government service department	Mixed: Senior managers, professional workers, and clerical staff ($n = 51$), cross-sectional	Employee commitment Job satisfaction	No significant associations
		Employee voice Employee involvement and information sharing High compensation contingent on performance Extensive training, learning, and development Involvement in decision-making and work teams			Employee well-being at work	
2	Boselie, Paauwe, and Richardson (2003)	Employee influence	The Netherlands; Mixed (local government, hospitals, and hotels).	HR managers focusing on application to frontline workers ($n = 132$), cross-sectional	Absence due to illness	No significant associations
		Training and skill development Participation in seminars Employee participation Teamworking rewards			Average duration of absence due to illness Employee turnover rates	
3	Edgar and Geare (2005)	Good and safe working conditions	New Zealand, Public and Private.	Multiple: Employer and employees ($n = 609$), cross-sectional	Organizational commitment Job satisfaction Organizational fairness.	Positive and significant associations between variables with the exception of EEO and satisfaction
		Training and development Equal employment opportunities (EEO) Recruitment and selection				

	Study	Context	HR practices	Sample/Design	Outcomes	Findings
4	Gould-Williams (2003)	Wales, local government	HR index Training and development Communication Status differential Teamworking Rigorous selection process Job security PRP Employee involvement	Frontline workers, supervisors, and managers ($n = 191$), cross-sectional	Job satisfaction Organizational commitment Worker effort Intention to remain Subjective organizational performance.	HR index associated with job satisfaction, commitment, workers effort, and organizational performance.
5	Gould-Williams (2007)	England, local government service departments.	Rewards Training and development Employee involvement Teamworking	Front-line workers, supervisors, and managers ($n = 3,165$), cross-sectional	Discretionary effort Motivation Intention to quit Quality of life Stress	Involvement and teamworking associated with discretionary effort and motivation; training and development associated with quit intentions (−)
6	Harel and Tzafrir (1999)	Israel, Public and Private	Recruitment Selection Internal labour market HR decisions Participation Compensation Training	Single: HR directors (or equivalent) ($n = 76$), post-predictive.	Perceived organizational performance over the past year in comparison with similar organizations.	Training associated with performance measure.

(continued)

Table 7.2 Continued

Study	HR practice(s)	Country and sector	Sample and time period	Measure of performance	Findings
7 Marlies and Han van Dijk (2005)	Personal development plan	The Netherlands, care for the elderly.	Employee survey (n = 12,193) in 2002.	(i) Behaviour of care providers;	Job-related training, performance review, predictable work schedules (-), and supportive leadership style were associated with quality of care provided
	Job-related training		Residents survey (n = 3,542).	(ii) The expertise of care providers;	
	Performance review			(iii) The promptness of care providers.	
	Departmental meetings				
	Protocol to deal with labour-shortage				
	Predictable work schedules				
	Supportive and transparent leadership style.				
8 Orlitzky and Frenkel (2005)	Communication	Australia, Public and Private	Multiple: Managers and employees, cross-sectional	Job satisfaction	HPWP and communication associated with labour productivity
	Decentralized management			Job strain	
				Labour productivity	
	Employee participation			Management competence	
				Motivation and effort	
	Fair pay			Work intensity	
	Good benefits				
	Index of HPWP*: Rigorous selection			Trust?	
	Formal training and development				
	Equal employment opportunity				
	Job discretion				
	Job insecurity				

9	Rondeau and Wagar (2001)	Communication programmes, team-based programmes, work scheduling; incentive compensation; employee counselling; employee recognition; grievance resolution; employment: selection tests; internal promotion policy; formal performance appraisal; minority recruitment.	Canada, Nursing homes. Profit and Non-profit organizations included.	Chief executive officers ($n = 283$).	(i) Employee outcomes: Employee morale, Employee absenteeism, Organizational conflict. (ii) Customer and client outcomes: Resident satisfaction, Resident food quality, Resident loyalty, Community support, Organizational reputation. (iii) Performance outcomes: Operating efficiency, Operating expenses, Use of information systems, New programmes and services, Revenue per employee	HR index associated with ALL performance outcomes with the EXCEPTION of organizational conflict and operating expenses
10	Steijn and Leisink (2006)	Appraisal interviews	The Netherlands, Public administration,	Single: Employees ($n = 21{,}791$), cross sectional	Three component employee commitment:	No significant associations for HR index; significant associations reported between satisfaction with HR policy and affective, normative, and continuance commitment

(continued)

Table 7.2 Continued

Study	HR practice(s)	Country and sector	Sample and time period	Measure of performance	Findings
	Personal development plans	Public security, Non-profit sector		Affective, normative, and continuance	
	Training plans				
	Career planning				
	Job and task rotation				
	Individual coaching				
	Competence management				
	Age-related personnel policies				
	Mobility polices (index used)				
	Single item measure of satisfaction with HR policy				
11 West, Borrill, Sawson, Scully, Carter, Anelay, Patterson, and Waring (2002)	HRM Index:	England, NHS hospital	Single: HR directors ($n = 61$), post-predictive.	Deaths following emergency surgery	HR index negatively associated with patient mortality
	Training			Deaths following non-emergency surgery	
	Teamworking			Deaths following admission for hip fractures	
	Appraisal				
	Decentralized decision-making			Deaths following admission for heart attacks	
				Readmission rates	
				Mortality index	

Organizational performance outcomes

Earlier in the chapter the issue of causal distance was raised, in which it was highlighted that the effects of HR practice on performance outcomes will become progressively weaker when assessed at the unit or organizational level. As HR practices in the public sector appear to have had a small effect on employee-level outcomes, it is anticipated that their effects on organizational performance outcomes will be even weaker.

Again, as for individual performance outcomes, the seven studies that assessed the impact of HR practice on organizational performance outcomes used a range of both subjective and objective measures of performance. Two studies used respondents' perceptions of organizational performance (Gould-Williams 2003; Harel and Tzafrir 1999), with the remaining studies incorporating objective measures based on worker productivity (Orlitzky and Frenkel 2005; Rondeau and Wagar 2001), turnover rates (Boselie et al. 2003), absence rates (Boselie et al. 2003; Rondeau and Wagar 2001), mortality rates following surgery (West et al. 2002), and client satisfaction (Ott and van Dkjk 2005; Rondeau and Wagar 2001).

The public sector studies reported statistically significant associations between HR practices and perceptions of organizational performance (Gould-Williams 2003; Harel and Tzafrir 1999), labour productivity (Orlitzky and Frenkey 2005; Rondeau and Wagar 2001), client satisfaction (Ott and van Dijk 2005), and objective measures of performance (Rondeau and Wagar 2001; West et al. 2002). From a 'high-performance' perspective, these findings are encouraging in that they provide support for the thesis that HR practices do lead to enhanced performance outcomes at the organizational level of analysis. When considering these findings in conjunction with the individual level outcomes, they provide some but not convincing evidence of mutuality. None of the studies suggest that HR practices lead to increased work-related pressure or stress, nor do they provide evidence that HR practices reduce desirable work-related attitudes, such as organizational commitment, job satisfaction, and motivation. Instead, three of the seven studies included in the review reported positive associations between HR practices and worker experiences. So on this basis it could be argued that HR practices hold potential to enhance employees' work-related experiences as well as positively effect some aspects of organizational performance. To provide more convincing evidence of the effects of HR practice on performance outcomes, future research in public sector organizations should consider the issues highlighted in the final section of this chapter.

Directions for further research

In order to advance our understanding of the impact of HRM on public service performance, a behavioural model has been developed (see Figure 7.3). This model has endeavoured to incorporate the theoretical issues identified in the review and place them in a public sector context. The model is described in this way. First, consistent with the 'best fit' perspective, public organizations need to identify their specific service priorities (Hendry 1995; Wood 1999). Depending on the nature and types of services provided, the priorities may range from reducing the numbers of homeless families living in temporary accommodation (housing management services) to providing a rapid response to emergency calls (fire and rescue service).

Second, the organizational context and climate in which HR practices are to be introduced need to be understood as, according to Datta et al. (2005), HR practices should be designed to 'fit' specific sectors and employee groups. On this basis, the model accommodates differences between sectors and work groupings, along with leadership and industrial relations climates. For instance, it is likely to be especially challenging to introduce a 'high-commitment' approach in an adversarial environment—one in which unions' propensity is to undermine management decisions. It is also possible for line managers to resist senior management's directives and challenge proposals to engage workers in decision-making processes. Further, the extent to which HR is introduced in organizations and work units is also likely to depend on the role and influence of political leaders and elected members. As with the potential for union resistance, political influence or lack of influence may impact HR policy and managers' capacity to effectively implement HRM.

Rather than making any attempt to prescribe HR practices, the model refers to 'bundles' of practices which should be selected on the basis of public service priorities, context, and work-group characteristics. The extensive list of HR practices identified in Boselie et al.'s review (2005) (see Table 7.1) could be used as a means to select and bundle together relevant core practices. It should be noted, however, that the list of HR practices lacks detailed specification of each practice, and thus runs the risk of being too vague for any practical usage unless researchers address this issue by including relevant details.

The Public Service HR Model may also consider *both* managerial and employee perspectives of HR practice (Wright and Boswell 2002). For instance, line managers should provide information on policy directives, whereas employees should provide their personal experiences of HR practice within their work unit. Such information would not only provide insight into the extent to which managers have successfully implemented policy, but any gaps identified between policy and practice can be explored. Also, the diffusion of HR practice amongst workers can be monitored to assess whether any

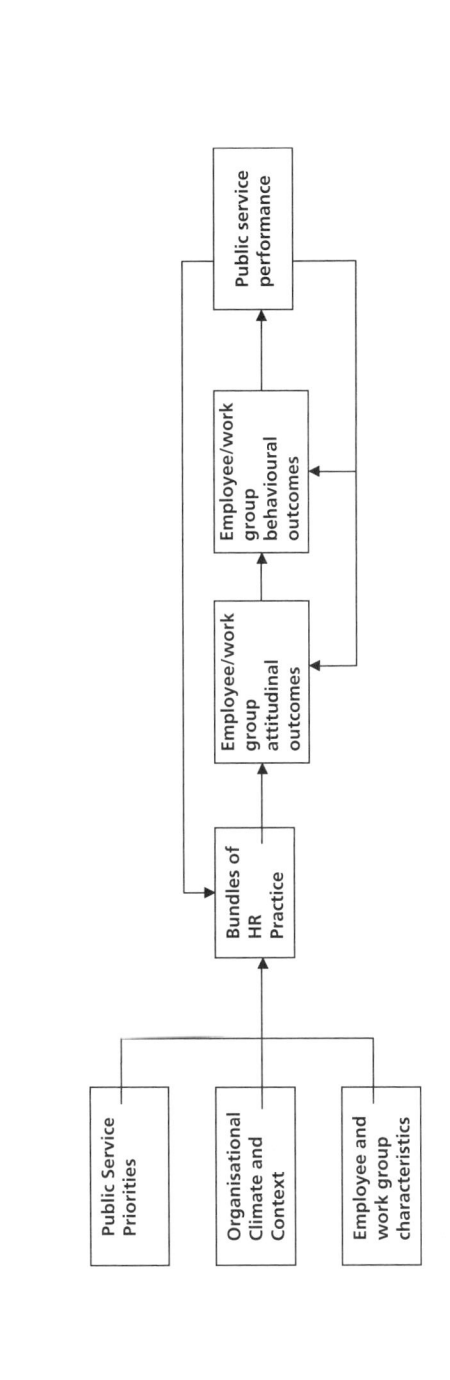

Figure 7.3 The public service HR model

The boxes in the figure read:

- Public Service Priorities
- Organisational Climate and Context
- Employee and work group characteristics
- Bundles of HR Practice
- Employee/work group attitudinal outcomes
- Employee/work group behavioural outcomes
- Public service performance

particular group is being discriminated against on the basis of, *inter alia* job type, gender, social class, race, and sexual orientation.

As outlined in the model, bundles of HR practices should affect employee or work group attitudinal and behavioural outcomes, such as employee satisfaction, motivation, commitment, trust, and organizational citizenship behaviours. These outcomes are consistent with the 'high-commitment' thesis. However, it would also be important to monitor the effects of HR practices on absenteeism rates, work-related pressure or stress, and labour turnover (Godard 2001; Green 2004; Marchington and Grugulis 2000). It is anticipated that employee or work-group outcomes will in turn affect public service performance.

As was noted in our review, it is also possible for service performance to affect the types of HR practices used by public organizations along with employee or work-group outcomes (Schneider et al. 2003). For instance, the achievement of high public service performance may lead to managers having greater discretion over budgets, which in turn may enable them to adopt more costly HR practices (e.g. provide more extensive training and use sophisticated selection procedures, such as psychometric testing and assessment centres). Employees could also feel more motivated and experience greater job satisfaction due to the achievement of higher public service performance (Schneider et al. 2003).

Compared to the amount of research undertaken in private sector organizations, the research evidence emerging from the public sector is narrow and limited. For instance, much of the early research undertaken in the private sector focused on the links between HRM and firm performance, albeit financial performance measures were used in the majority of instances. As this body of research emerged from the United States, the studies achieved respectable sample sizes at the organizational level. In contrast, the public sector research has five studies where objective measures of organizational performance were used, and in these instances the sample size was either extremely low ($n = 21$) or based on mixed, public and private responses (Boselie et al. 2003). Clearly, it will be useful for future research in the public sector to incorporate organization-level performance data to supplement the individual outcome measures. Of course, this is not to say that public sector research should focus exclusively on organizational measures of performance. This would be contrary to recent theoretical developments in the area, in which researchers are endeavouring to understand the links between HRM and performance. In fact, data are needed at the individual, unit, and organizational levels[3] in order to undertake multi-level analysis as outlined in the Public Service HR Model.

---

[3] Examples include: (*a*) *SECTOR: Local Government*: (i) *individual level* = front-line worker (refuse collector, receptionist); (ii) *unit level* = service department; and (iii) *organizational level* = authority. (*b*) *SECTOR: Hospitals*: (i) *individual level* = frontline worker (nurse, catering staff); (ii) *unit level* = ward; and (iii) *organizational level* = hospital.

Without exception, all the public sector evidence is based on cross-sectional data analysis. Where measures of organizational performance are used, these were either collected at the same time as assessments of HR practice (Boselie et al. 2003; Gould-Williams 2003), or preceded the HR measures (Harel and Tzafrir 1999; West et al. 2002). If the relationship between HRM and performance is to be evaluated, the logical temporal progression should be from HR practice to individual outcomes and then organizational performance. Such causal orderings are likely to present researchers with significant methodological challenges, especially as getting longitudinal data is problematic, either due to resource constraints or access to data sources. The following simplified approach to data collection is recommended: the first stage should incorporate measures of public service priorities, and organizational climate, context, employee, and work-group characteristics should be noted; at the second stage, measures of HR policy and practice (as perceived by managers and employees) should be noted. Individual performance measures should then be collected at the third stage, with organizational performance outcomes recorded at the final stage.

The literature review highlighted the lack of sufficient theory in determining or selecting appropriate HR practices to form HR bundles. Boselie et al. (2005) in particular suggested that it would be useful to have practices identified as 'optional', 'hygiene', and 'motivators'. Here again public sector research could make a contribution. It is possible for empirical investigation to inform the selection of these types of practices (Guest 1997). For instance, qualitative data could first be collected via case study research, where attempts are made to categorize HR practices as optional, hygiene, and motivators. Thereafter, a large-scale study could be undertaken to statistically test for such bundles (through, for example, factor analysis), and evaluate the effects of these bundles on various individual outcomes in an attempt to determine the motivators and obligatory practices.

Application of the Public Service HR model should provide useful insights into employees' working environment and reveal organizational or unit inhibitors and facilitators of improved performance. Also, although the importance of differentiating between policy and practice was highlighted, in public sector organizations the role of the locally elected council member may also need to be taken into account, as in some units their influence on service priorities and staff may be significant.

A final consideration that needs to be borne in mind when undertaking future research in the public sector is the adoption of more sophisticated data analysis techniques. Researchers have in the main progressed from simple correlation matrixes in evaluating statistical associations between variables, to multiple regression analyses. If public sector research is to make a serious contribution to HRM theory, then it is important for the sophistication of data analysis to progress further. There is now a growing call for multi-level data analysis amongst private sector researchers, and a similar call would be timely for public sector researchers too.

In conclusion, it is encouraging to see evidence of the HRM–Performance relationship beginning to emerge from across the world in the public sector. Here, the public sector research agenda is, relatively speaking, advancing at a greater pace in comparison with the private sector evidence which is predominantly of Anglo-Saxon origin. It will be welcome, too, if the research base could now incorporate a greater range of public sector organizations and multiple actors in their analysis of data.

REFERENCES

Appelbaum, E., Bailey, T., Berg, P. and Kalleberg, A. (2000). *Manufacturing Advantage: Why High-Performance Systems Pay Off.* NY: ILR Press: Ithaca.

Arthur, J. B. (1994). Effects of Human Resource Systems on manufaturing preformance and turnover. *Academy of Management Journal* 37(3), 670–687.

Baptiste, N. R. (2008). Tightening the Link Between Employee Well-being at Work and Performance. *Management Decision* 46(2), 284–309.

Becker, B. E., Huselid, M. A., Pickus, P. S. and Spratt, M. F. (1997). HR as a Source of Shareholder Value: Research and Recommendations. *Human Resource Management* 36, 39–47.

Boselie, P., Paauwe, J. and Richardson, R. (2003). Human Resource Management, Institutionalization and Organizational Performance: A Comparison of Hospitals, Hotels and Local Government. *International Journal of Human Resource Management* 14(8), 1407–29.

——Dietz, G. and Boon, C. (2005). Commonalities and Contradictions in HRM and Performance Research. *International Journal of Human Resource Management* 15(3), 67–94.

Boxall, P. and Purcell, J. (2000). Strategic Human Resource Management: Where Have We Come from and Where Should We Be Going? *International Journal of Management Reviews* 2(2), 183–203.

—— —— (2003). *Strategy and Human Resource Management.* New York: Palgrave Macmillan.

Brown, K. (2008). 'Human Resource Management in the Public Sector', in R. S. Beattie and S. P. Osborne (eds.), *Human Resource Management in the Public Sector,* London: Routledge.

Currie, G. and Procter, S. (2003). The Interaction of Human Resource Policies and Practices with the Implementation of Teamworking: Evidence from The UK Public Sector. *International Journal of Human Resource Management* 14(4), 581–99.

Datta, D. K., Guthrie, J. P. and Wright, P. M. (2005). Human Resource Management and Labor Productivity: Does Industry Matter? *Academy Of Management Journal* 48, 135–45.

Delaney, J. T. and Huselid, M. A. (1996). The impact of human resource management practices on perceptions of organisational performance. *Academy of Management Journal* 39(4), 949–969.

Delery, J. (1998). Issues of Fit in Strategic Human Resource Management: Implications for Research. *Human Resource Management Review* 8(3), 289–309.

Eaton, S. C. (2000). Beyond 'Unloving Care': Linking Human Resource Management and Patient Care Quality in Nursing Homes. *International Journal of Human Resource Management* 11(3), 591–616.

Edgar, F. and Geare, A. (2005). HRM Practice and Employee Attitudes: Different Measures—Different Results. *Personnel Review* 34(5), 534–49.

Fleetwood, S. and Hesketh, A. (2006). HRM-Performance Research: Under-Theorized and Lacking Explanatory Power. *International Journal of Human Resource Management* 17(12), 1877–1993.

Godard, J. (2001). High Performance and the Transformation of Work? The Implications of Alternative Work Practices for the Experience and Outcomes of Work. *Industrial and Labor Relations Review* 54(4), 776–805.

Gould-Williams, J. S. (2003). The Importance of HR Practices and Workplace Trust in Achieving Superior Performance: A Study Of Public-Sector Organizations. *International Journal of Human Resource Management* 14(2), 1–27.

—— (2007). HR Practices, Organizational Climate and Employee Outcomes: Evaluating Social Exchange Relationships in Local Government. *International Journal of Human Resource Management* 18(9), 1627–1647.

Green, F. (2004). Why Has Work Effort Become More Intense? *Industrial Relations* 43(4), 709–41.

Guest, D. (1997). Human Resource Management and Performance: A Review and Research Agenda. *International Journal of Human Resource Management* 8(3), 263–76.

—— Conway, N. and Dewe, P. (2004). Using Sequential Tree Analysis to Search for 'Bundles' of HR Practices. *Human Resource Management Journal* 14(1), 79–96.

Harel, G. H. and Tzafrir, S. S. (1999). The Effect of Human Resource Management Practices on the Perceptions of Organizational and Market Performance of the Firm. *Human Resource Management* 38, 185–200.

Harris, L. (2001). Rewarding Employee Performance: Line Managers' Values, Beliefs and Perspectives. *International Journal of Human Resource Management* 12(7), 1182–92.

Hendry, C. (1995). *Human Resource Management: A Strategic Approach to Employment.* Oxford: Butterworth-Heinemann.

Huselid, M. A. (1995). The Impact of Human Resource Management Practices on Turnover, Productivity and Corporate Financial Performance. *Academy of Management Journal* 38(3), 635–72.

Jackson, S. and Schuler, R. (1995). Understanding Human Resource Management in the Context of Organisations and Their Environments. *Annual Review of Psychology* 46, 237–64.

Lawler, E. E. (1992). *The Ultimate Advantage: Creating the High-Involvement Organisation.* San Francisco, CA: Jossey-Bass.

Legge, K. (2005). *Human Resource Management Rhetorics and Realities.* London: Palgrave.

Lepak, D., Liao, H., Chung, Y. and Harden, E. E. (2006). A Conceptual Review of Human Resource Management Systems in Strategic Human Resource Management Research. *Personnel and Human Resource Management* 25, 217–71.

Marchington, M. and Grugulis, I. (2000). 'Best Practice' Human Resource Management: Perfect Opportunity or Dangerous Illusion? *International Journal of Human Resource Management* 11(6), 1104–24.

Martin-Alcazar, F., Romero-Fernandez, P. M. and Sanchez-Gardey, G. (2008). Human Resource Management as a Field of Research. *British Journal of Management* 19, 103–19.

Orlitzky, M. and Frenkel, J. (2005). Alternative Pathways to High-Performance Workplaces. *International Journal of Human Resource Management* 16(8), 1325–48.

Ott, M. and Van Dijk, H. (2005). Effects of HRM on Client Satisfaction in Nursing and Care for the Elderly. *Employee Relations* 27(4), 413–24.

Pfeffer, J. (1994). *Competitive Advantage Through People. Unleashing the Power of the Work Force.* Boston: Harvard Business School Press.

—— (1998). *The Human Equation: Building Profits by Putting People First.* Boston, MA: Harvard Business School Press.

Porter, M. (1980). *Competitive Strategy Techniques for Analysing Industries and Competitors.* New York: Free Press.

Procter, S. and Currie, G. (2004). Target-Based Teamworking: Groups, Work and Interdependence in the UK Civil Service. *Human Relations* 57(12), 1547–72.

Purcell, J. and Kinnie, N. (2007). 'Human Resource Management and Business Performance', in P. Boxall J. Purcell and P. Wright (eds.), *The Oxford Handbook of Human Resource Management*, Oxford: Oxford University Press.

—— —— Hutchinson, S., Rayton, B., and Swart, J. (2003). *Understanding the People and Performance Link: Unlocking the Black Box.* London: Chartered Institute of Personnel and Development.

—— —— Swart, J., Rayton, B. and Hutchinson, S. (2009). *People Management and Performance.* London: Routledge.

Rondeau, K. V. and Wagar, T. H. (2009). Impact of human resource management practices on nursing home performance. *Health Services Management Research* 14, 192–202.

Schneider, B., Hanges, P., Smith, B. and Salvaggio, A. (2003). Which Comes First: Employee Attitudes or Organizational Financial and Market Performance? *Journal of Applied Psychology* 88, 836–51.

Steijn, B. and Leisink, P. (2006). Organizational Commitment among Dutch Public Sector Employees. *International Review of Administrative Sciences* 72(2), 187–201.

Storey, J. (1995). *Human Resource Management: A Critical Text.* London: Routledge.

Walton, R. E. (1985). From Control to Commitment in the Workplace. *Harvard Business Review* 63(2), 76–84.

West, M. A., Borill, C., Dawson, J., Scully, J., Carter, M., Snelay, S., Patterson, M. and Waring, J. (2002). The Link Between the Management of Employees and Patient Mortality in Acute Hospitals. *International Journal of Human Resource Management* 13(8), 1299–1310.

Wood, S. (1999). Human Resource Management and Performance. *International Journal of Management Reviews* 1(4), 367–413.

Wright, P. M. and Boswell, W. R. (2002). Desegregating HRM: A Review and Synthesis of Micro and Macro Human Resource Management Research. *Journal of Management* 28(3), 247–76.

—— Gardner, T. M. and Moynihan, L. M. (2003). The Impact of HR Practices on the Performance of Business Units. *Human Resource Management Journal* 13(3), 21–36.

—— —— —— and Allen, M. R. (2005). The Relationship Between HR Practices and Firm Performance: Examining Causal Order. *Personnel Psychology* 58, 409–46.

8 Innovation

Richard Walker

Introduction

The primary purpose of innovation in public service organizations has been to improve public services—to meet needs and enhance organizational performance. Organizations innovate—that is, implement new processes within the organization or deliver new services to users—because of pressure from the external environment (influenced by factors such as competition, deregulation, resource scarcity, and customer demands) or because of internal organizational choices (including gaining distinctive competencies, reaching a higher level of aspiration, and increasing the extent and quality of services). Pressures from the external environment have grown—populations are aging, gaps between the rich and poor are increasing—and organizational choices become more important to ensure that growing needs can be fulfilled. In meeting needs, improvements are made as performance gaps are isolated and filled as organizations change and adapt their behaviour to maintain or improve performance. Isomorphic pressures may also be experienced from the external environment and innovation has been adopted for other purposes, which include boosting legitimacy. However, in this latter case innovations may be adopted and not fully implemented.

Governments around the world have promoted innovation as a means to achieve higher performance targets and have put in place agencies to assist in this end. For example, the Performance and Innovation Unit was established in the early years of the Blair's Prime Ministership in the United Kingdom, while the United States had the National Institute for Government Innovation. Much is done to disseminate the lessons of innovation. To this end the English central government has established the Beacon Council Scheme for local governments; in the United States, Harvard University is the depositary of the Government Innovation Network. One may argue that innovation knows no boundaries—in China the Local Government Innovation Awards are used to promote new ways of working, as does the Foundation for Local Government Innovation in Indonesia, and the National Awards for Innovation in Local Government in Australia.

Empirical evidence clearly demonstrates that innovation is within the grasp of managers in public organizations (Borins 1998; Light 1998; Moore 1995;

Osborne 1998; Walker, Jeanes, and Rowlands 2001). Some of this innovative activity is led by central governments and mandated. For example, the Local Government Modernization Agenda in England and Wales required local authorities to implement a range of new management approaches. While some authorities had experience of aspects of the overall framework, to the majority the combination of these activities was clearly new and constituted what Boyne et al. (2005, p. 419) refer to as 'an innovative programme of management reform'. Evidently not all innovation in public organizations is top-down, and Berry and Berry (2007) have argued that this type of innovation is perhaps of least interest. Evidence collated elsewhere visibly charts the role of politicians and public servants in developing innovations. Borins' analysis (1998) of the Ford–KSG innovation awards programme in the United States shows that just under a fifth of innovations could be attributed to politicians, a further fifth to agency leaders, four-tenths to other public servants (middle managers and front-line staff), and the remainder to partner agencies such as non-profit organizations and service users and citizens. What is of interest here is the relatively large proportion of innovations attributable to the lower echelons of the organization or to external parties, indicating the wide vista of sources for innovation in public organizations.

The literature on innovation in public organizations is now large, reflecting the practices of service delivery agencies and the aspirations of higher levels of government. A number of strands of work have sought to interpret and understand innovation. Some work has asked why innovations are adopted (Berry 1994; Borins 1998; Boyne et al. 2005; Light 1998; Walker 2006); this research has examined competitive pressures from other public agencies and other service providers, demands from users and citizens and learning and networking (see Berry and Berry [2007]), and the characteristics of innovations such as the compatibility, relative advantage, complexity, and trailability (Rogers 1995). The stream of research on innovativeness, or what types of organizations are innovative, examines the characteristics associated with these organizations, and include slack, specialization, external communication, integration, size, and centralization (Borins 1998; Burns and Stalker 1961; Damanpour 1991; Light 1998; Tidd 2001). Process research explores how innovations are implemented in organizations (Golden 1990; Walker 2003). Early work examined this as a linear process (Zaltman et al. 1973) and more recently progressed to view it as a complex and iterative process (Van de Ven et al. 1999). This has examined the complex interplays between leadership, innovation champions, pilots, innovation teams, inter-organizational relationships, and implementing new ways of behaving. These approaches take innovation as the dependent variable, and typically the rate of adoption of innovations. Consequently, much of this work has not addressed the central question of this book: Does innovation result in public service improvement? This is somewhat surprising given the presumption that innovation leads to improvements in organizational processes and outcomes, but it is perhaps the strong 'pro-innovation bias' in the literature which has resulted in the accumulation of relatively limited knowledge of the consequences of innovation. At the heart of the pro-innovation bias is the notion that innovation is a beneficial process that results in improvements (Rogers 1995).

This chapter firstly defines innovation and delves into its types, as different types of innovations are assumed to have different consequences. The innovation–performance hypothesis is then explored prior to reviewing the empirical evidence. In conclusion, a research agenda is outlined that seeks to deliver more systematic evidence on the innovation–performance hypothesis.

Theories of innovation

DEFINING INNOVATION

Innovation is a process through which new ideas, objects, and practices are created, developed, or reinvented, and which are new for the unit of adoption (Aiken and Hage 1971; Kimberly and Evanisko 1981; O'Toole 1997; Rogers 1995). Because public organizations may innovate in search of legitimacy and not fully adopt an innovation it has to be more than just an idea, and implementation has to occur (Boyne et al. 2005; Damanpour and Evan 1984). Prior studies have sought to address the problem of inconsistent results by distinguishing between types of innovation, such as product and process innovations (Damanpour and Gopalakrishnan 2001; Tornatzky and Fleischer 1990), technical and administrative innovations (Damanpour and Evan 1984; Kimberly and Evanisko 1981), and radical and incremental innovations (Ettlie, Bridges, and O'Keefe 1984; Germain 1996). Product or services can be understood as *what* (e.g. what is produced, what service is delivered) and processes as *how* innovations (e.g. how a service is rendered). Within each of these types there are subtypes (see the following paragraphs). It is also possible to distinguish ancillary innovations, or innovations that are developed in partnership with other organizations.

Distinguishing between innovation types is essential to understand the adoption of innovation and its performance consequences, more so in public than private organizations. It is helpful to differentiate between innovation in public and private organizations to illustrate this point. Private organizations typically focus upon the development of one-off product innovations (and to a lesser extent process innovations) and technological change. Research and practice assumes that product innovations are radical and stand-alone, and that firms mainly organize their innovation efforts through R&D activities, hence R&D activities are often the object of much research. Further, the emphasis is upon the manufacturing sector, with little attention given to the service sector. This narrow focus has also, in turn, led to an interest in the process that led to the innovation, rather than to the impact an innovation has on firm performance.

In public organizations, one-off or stand-alone innovations are not the norm. Innovation is evolutionary rather than radical—innovations originate in the external environment and imitation is encouraged to disseminate new ideas, practices, and behaviours across public sector organizations. Evolutionary models contend that innovation will arise from the cumulative effect of a series of incremental changes (Aldrich and Ruet 2006) drawing from existing activity: an organization's 'system of strategic attributes *evolves over time* as it continually incorporates new strategic assets and new products' (Roberts and Amit 2003, p. 108). If innovation is based on continuous incremental activity, then it is necessary to consider the complementary relationships between different types of innovation. By understanding innovation in public organizations as a dynamic process it is argued that a more comprehensive account of adoption, organizational innovativeness, and performance consequences can be obtained.

TYPES OF INNOVATION

Service innovations are defined as new services offered by public organizations to meet an external user or market need: they are concerned with *what* is produced. Service innovations occur in the operating component and affect the technical system of an organization, and include the adoption of goods (which are material) and intangible services, which are often consumed at the point of production (Damanpour and Evan 1984; Kimberly and Evanisko 1981; Normann 1991). Given the focus on meeting needs in the public sector, the nature of service innovation is best understood through the relationship with users. Three types of service innovation have been identified and tested (Osborne 1998; Walker et al. 2002). 'Total' innovations involve providing new services to new users, or what Borins (1998) has referred to as 'holistic innovations'. Existing services provided to a new user group are 'expansionary' innovations. The third type is 'evolutionary' innovations, which involve delivering a new service to existing users. Osborne (1998) highlights a range of new services provided by voluntary organizations that include emergency accommodation for adolescents and sex therapy services. Of the service developments researched by Osborne, just over 70% could be classified as innovative, and the balance was towards evolutionary (47.6%), followed by total (14.8%), then expansionary (10.9%). Similar proportions of innovation were identified in Walker et al.'s study (2001) of English housing associations.

Organizational process innovations affect management and organization. They change relationships amongst organizational members, and affect rules, roles, procedures and structures, and communication and exchange among organizational members and between the environment and organizational members: They are concerned with *how* services are rendered (Abernathy and Utterback 1978; Damanpour et al. 1989; Damanpour and Gopalakrishnan 2001; Edquist et al. 2001). Process innovation made up over a half of Borins' study (1998) of innovation in US public service organizations. Research has focused on a number of types of organizational process innovation (Edquist et al. 2001) that include administrative, marketization, organization, and technological.

Marketization innovations involve modifying the organization's operating processes and systems to increase the efficiency or effectiveness of producing and delivering its services to users (Schilling 2005). The drivers of marketization innovations are primarily reduction in delivery lead-time, increases in flexibility, and lowering of operational costs (Boer and During 2001). Marketization innovations are concerned with methods to purchase and deliver services and revenue generation, and reflect the core New Public Management themes of contracting, externalization, and market pricing of public services.

Organization innovations concern structure, strategy, and administrative processes (Damanpour 1987). They include improvements in an organization's practices and the introduction of new organizational structures (Borins 1998; Light 1998; Walker et al. 2002). Organization innovations are thus concerned with primary work activity and changes in the social system.

Administrative process innovations are new approaches to motivate and reward organizational members, devise strategy and structure of tasks and units, and modify the organization's management processes (Daft 1978; Hamel 2006; Hipp et al. 2000; Kimberly and Evanisko 1981; Light 1998). Whereas technological innovations are directly related to the primary work activity of the organization and mainly produce changes in its operating systems, administrative innovations are indirectly related to the organization's basic work activity and mainly affect in its management systems (Damanpour and Evan 1984). Administrative process innovations pertain to changes in systems, knowledge used in performing the work of management, and managerial skills that enable an organization to function and succeed by using its resources effectively.

Technological innovations are new elements introduced into an organization's production system or service operation for producing its products or rendering its services to the customers and clients (Abernathy and Utterback 1978; Damanpour and Gopalakrishnan 2001; Knight 1967). The drivers of these innovations are primarily reduction in delivery time, increase in operational flexibility, and lowering of production costs (Boer and During 2001). Technological process innovations, therefore, modify the organization's operating processes and systems (Schilling 2005). In service organizations, these are primarily innovations associated with information technology (Barras 1990; Miles 2001).

Ancillary innovations are identified by Damanpour (1987) and are differentiated from other innovations because they are concerned with working across boundaries with other service providers, users, or other public agencies. Thus, their successful implementation is reliant upon others. Ancillary innovations are 'organization-environment boundary innovations' (Damanpour 1987, p. 678). In Damanpour's study of libraries these included community service programmes and after-school supplementary education programmes. What distinguishes an ancillary innovation from service and organizational process innovations is that successful adoption is dependent on factors outside an organization's control. Ancillary innovations made up 39 per cent of the Ford–KSG innovation award winners examined by Borins (1998) and included programmes that housed people with AIDS in certified private homes with public funding.

Some innovation scholars contend that innovation types are artificial distinctions and that they are conceptually and operationally alike (Archibugi et al. 1994; Edquist et al. 2001). This is clearly so for some innovations; for example, the development of new pedagogy for special needs children. Processes are developed in teaching that may result in new services to children. Separate types of service and organizational process innovations can, nonetheless, be identified. For example, a quality assurance system will put in place a range of new management practices but does not necessarily result in new services. Ancillary innovations are, however, linked to other innovation types. For example, a new service could be developed in partnership with other actors, which involves partner or user agencies undertaking joint decision-making. Alternatively, it is feasible that a number of agencies could work in conjunction and geographically decentralize services to a common 'one-stop shop'. Ancillary innovations are then a separate type, but may in practice overlap with other innovation types. It is, however, less likely that market-ization innovations will be developed in partnership with others. The distinction between innovation types is therefore useful.

Hypotheses on the innovation–performance relationship

Four sets of arguments have been made about the relationships between innovation and performance. These focus on organizational characteristics, performance gaps, innovation types, and the diffusion of innovation. Each is reviewed in turn.

The first argument focuses upon the management and organizational characteristics and capacities that public agencies develop and retain that stimulate innovation and higher levels of performance. The characteristics and capacities cited reflect those found in prior reviews of the determinants of organizational innovativeness, and include structure, specialization, professionalism, size, slack, functional differentiation, managerial tenure, and managerial attitudes towards change (see, e.g., Damanpour [1987, 1991]; Kimberly and Evanisko [1981]).

Rainey and Ryu's review (2004, p. 33) draws attention to six organizational and management characteristics that link high performance and innovation. Effective leadership is the first, and includes interactions with stakeholders and the role of innovation champions providing energy and initiative. Second, effective task design is highlighted and importance is attached to redesigning and clarifying work tasks, organizational structures, and work production processes, including the use of performance management regimes. External relationships with stakeholders are the third characteristic, and include steering the organization through the external environment to ensure ongoing support and performance enhancement. Mission valence is isolated as the fourth characteristic, which includes the importance of clear goals, shared values, and ethical standards in relation to customer orientation. The fifth set of practices associated with innovation and high performance are human resource systems that incentivize staff and offer training, development, and learning and provide empowerment, autonomy, and flexibility, and value employees. Finally, 'strong, effective organizational cultures' (Rainey and Ryu 2004, p. 33) are highlighted. Rainey and Ryu (2004, p. 35) conclude that management plays an important role: 'The results suggest that the skills, abilities, practices, and motivation of leaders and the members of the organization can overcome environmental constraints to achieve high performance.'

The organizational effectiveness framework outlined by Rainey and Ryu has strong connections to the management literature on resource dependency, the resource-based view (RBV) of the organization and dynamic capabilities. (See Bryson et al. [2007] for a review of the application of these frameworks to public organizations.) The important addition in this literature, over that presented by Rainey and Ryu, is that innovation in organizations is not just a function of internal capabilities but is also a response to environmental demands. Resource dependency theory posits that environmental constraints, such as scarcity of resources or client demands, are responded to with service and process innovations by managers who make choices over their course of action to gain organizational resources (Pfeffer 1993). The RBV of the organization hypothesizes that rare, valuable, non-substitutable, and inimitable organizational resources available across an organization are used to create distinctive competencies (Barney 1991; Bryson et al. 2007). Complementary resources and capabilities are argued to ensure organizations can innovate, which increases the positive influence of innovation on organizational performance. These theories raise the importance of internal organizational capacities and the ability of an organization to respond to external environmental stimuli that will help them to perform well.

Second, innovations may be implemented by public organizations in response to 'felt needs' (Rainey and Ryu 2004). In the management literature, this notion is conceptualized as the performance gap; that is, the difference between what an organization is actually accomplishing and what it can potentially accomplish. This approach is applicable to public organizations because motivation to change or adopt an innovation arises to reduce a perceived gap (Zaltman et al. 1973). The idea of a performance gap is also applicable to a variety of performance circumstances. Low performers may be seeking a performance boost, and high-performance organizations may have identified upcoming change in the environment for which a response is required.

The third set of arguments explores the effect of different types of innovation on organizational performance, and builds upon the RBV of the organization outlined above. Prior evidence would hold that organizations should focus their innovation efforts on one type of innovation, and build knowledge, skills, and capacities on a single innovation type in depth. Focusing on one innovation type ensures that knowledge is retained in the organization and not widely available for imitation by other organizations, and creates opportunities to enhance performance. This theory is derived from evolutionary models of radical innovations and technological change in industry, and thus the production of goods. Such a model has weakness when applied to public service organizations. Most notable is the way in which many services are consumed at their point of production; this makes radical innovation less likely (as assumed in evolutionary models), suggesting models of incremental innovation. Within public organizations the evidence base for arguments about types of innovations is limited, but suggests that product and process innovation, or 'what' and 'how' innovations (Light 1998), are important for organizational performance, and that the highest returns to organizations are for the complementary implementation of types of innovation (Borins 1998; Damanpour and Evan 1984; Damanpour et al. 1989). Light argues (1998, p. 155): '(a) [T]he organization starts with a *what* innovation of some kind, which (b) forces it to consider a *how* innovation to keep the *what* innovation alive, which (c) creates even more opportunity for *what* innovation.' While evidence is not fully developed or consistent on these relationships (see, e.g., Walker, 2008), it suggests that an even keel is more likely to have a positive effect on performance than a focus on one particular innovation type.

Argument has been presented that service and process innovations affect one another and need to be implemented in conjunction. Walker's review (2004) of the innovation–performance hypothesis supported this assumption, indicating that organizations that implement process and product innovations are the most likely to achieve higher levels of organizational performance. Lastly, different types of innovation are projected to have different performance impacts. Process innovations are suggested to have the greatest impact on efficiency and services on effectiveness. Given the typical requirement in a public service organization is to meet multiple performance goals, a consistent focus on one type of innovation is more likely to be harmful for performance.

The fourth area of literature draws upon the longstanding body of knowledge on the diffusion of innovations amongst public organizations. Evidence is presented that indicates that contextual, organizational, and individual variables offer explanation (Berry 1994; Boyne et al. 2005; Rogers 1995; Walker 2008). Much of this literature presumes that innovation results in higher levels of performance (Rainey and Ryu 2004), following the pro-innovation bias. This view is reflected in public policies. For example, the Beacon Council scheme, which seeks to diffuse innovations through approaches that borrow from inter-organizational learning, offers 'reward for higher performing councils' (Rashman and Hartley 2002, p. 523). Research studies that take innovation diffusion as their conceptual framework therefore seek to isolate organizations at the forefront of new developments—what the private sector literature would refer to as 'first movers'. While studies that focus on learning offer one mechanism to share the benefits of an innovation, the studies examined by Rainey and Ryu (2004, p. 35) were unable to identify where benefits accrue, beyond noting that they may be in contexts with favourable environments. The impacts of the alternative diffusion mechanisms of competition and public pressure have not been explored in a performance context (Walker 2008). The extent to which the performance gains achieved by early adopters are available to other organizations again remains an empirical question.

Alongside these arguments innovations may be adopted through coercive programmes of innovative management reform (Boyne et al. 2005) or to attain organizational legitimacy (Feller 1981). It is likely that such approaches will not have a clear or positive relationship with organizational performance, though this should not be fully discounted and is similarly an unresolved empirical question. The empirical evidence that examines the extent to which 'innovation equals high performance' is now examined.

Evaluating the innovation–performance hypothesis

EMPIRICAL STUDIES AND THEIR CHARACTERISTICS

The number of studies that examine the innovation–performance hypothesis is limited to around thirty in total across the public and private sectors

(Walker 2004). In the management literature, many studies do not take an organizational measure—the dependent variable focuses on the performance of the new product. When we turn to the public sector, authors have been plentiful in classifying innovation (Moore and Hartley 2008; Walker et al. 2002), discussing factors leading to its adoption, and the characteristics of innovators (Berry 1994; Borins 1998; Golden 1990). However, they have been less likely to examine the performance consequences at the level of the organization. Rainey and Ryu's review (2004) of high performance and innovativeness notes that the measurements of innovation and performance are not always crisp: for example, high performance is taken as read because organizations are stated to be high performers, or it is equated with organizational processes rather than outputs or outcomes. The consequence of this is that there are only four published studies that systematically examine innovation and performance in public organizations, and these derive from only two data sets.[1] The key characteristics of these studies and their findings are laid out in Table 8.1.

Table 8.1 Summary of empirical evidence

Study	Dimension of innovation	Country and sector	Sample and time period	Measure of performance	Finding
Damanpour and Evan (1984)	Technical and process innovation	US, public libraries	99 public libraries, 1982	Library PIs and subjective assessments	More innovation is found in high-performing organizations
Damanpour (1990)	Technological, administrative, ancillary	US, public libraries	99 public libraries, 1982	Library PIs and subjective assessments	The adoption of innovation is positively related to performance
Walker and Damanpour (2008)	Process and service innovations	England, local government	94 local authorities, 2001–4	Comprehensive Performance Assessment and subjective measures	Innovation has a positive, though weak and somewhat uncertain, relationship with performance
Damanpour, Walker, and Avellaneda (2009)	Service, administrative, and technological innovation	England, local government	412 local authorities, 2001–5	Comprehensive Performance Assessment	Innovation has a positive relationship with performance, focusing on one type of innovation harms performance, and divergence from the norm is beneficial

[1] A further study based upon Damanpour's public library dataset includes theory and evidence on the relationship between organizational size, innovation, and performance (Damanpour et al. 1989). Data are displayed as ranks within a contingency table, and the results are ambiguous and not discussed in this chapter.

Such a limited evidence base raises clear external validity concerns—knowledge is derived from public libraries in six north-eastern states in the United States (with populations over 50,000) and upper-tier English local governments. Further, the library study was undertaken in the early 1980s and the English local government studies at the beginning of the twenty-first century. Second, innovation and performance are operationalized in quite different ways in each study. Damanpour and Evans (1984) derived a list of current innovations in libraries and asked respondents to indicate if they had implemented any of these over the period 1970–82. The approach resulted in the identification of sixty-seven innovations. The English local government studies rely upon respondent's perceptions of the extent to which they implement different types of innovation (Damanpour et al. 2009; Walker and Damanpour 2008). Both studies draw upon respondents' assessments of the performance of their organization and objective measures. External stakeholder measures include the Comprehensive Performance Assessment and performance indicators collected by Damanpour, some of which measured inputs, and two of which were single-item measures. Having noted these limitations, the chapter now moves on to examine the empirical evidence.

EVIDENCE FROM THE STUDIES

Damanpour and Evan (1984) use an organizational lag model to test the relationship between the rate of adoption of different types of innovation and performance. Innovations are defined as administrative (occurring in the social system of an organization—rules, roles, procedures, structures, communication, etc.) and technical (new products or services in an organization's production process or service operation). Organizational lags are concerned with the differential rate of adoption of different types of innovation, and presume a higher rate of adoption of technical innovations, though administrative innovations are hypothesized to result in the adoption of technical innovations. Higher levels of innovation adoption are anticipated in high-performing organizations. Damanpour and Evan (1984) find that high-performing organizations do indeed adopt more innovations than low-performing ones, and that this relationship is stronger when efficiency (an objective measure) is used as the dependent variable. Administrative innovations are shown to trigger the adoption of technical innovations over time; however, the consequences of this relationship are not tested on performance. It is important to note that the data structure used by Damanpour and Evan predicts a performance–innovation relationship rather than an innovation–performance one, and thereby indicates that high-performing organizations are more likely to adopt innovations than are low performers.

Damanpour (1990) extends the above analysis to include managers' rating of the effectiveness of innovation types as a moderator of the innovation-type–performance hypothesis in the same data set. The analysis also includes ancillary innovations alongside administrative and technological. The results show a lagged effect of the impact of an index of all innovation types on indexes of subjective and objective measures performance. When individual innovation types are considered, technological innovation has an association with subjective performance within the same time period, whereas administrative and ancillary have lagged relationships. However, the associations are weak, and the highest recorded correlations are low (below $r = 0.3$). Innovations assessed as highly effective are shown to moderate the innovation–performance relationship, but in unanticipated ways. A positive moderation effect occurs for technological innovations and the total index of innovation for subjective performance, but a negative correlation coefficient is found for administrative and ancillary innovations with the objective measure of performance. The conclusions point towards weak and uncertain relationships between innovation and organizational performance, and raise questions about the contingent nature of these relationships.

Walker and Damanpour (2008) examine the effects of service and process innovation (including measures of administrative and technological innovation) on subjective and objective measures of organizational performance, and include lags of one, two, and three years. The results generally supported the notion that innovation has a positive effect on organizational performance but did not find consistent support across types of innovation or measures of performance. For example, a three-year lag was noted for service and process performance when innovation was regressed against the internal measure of performance, The evidence for the external, or objective measure of performance showed a one-year lag, and then only for service innovations. These results cast some doubt on arguments about the importance of adopting across a number of types of innovation, or at least raise questions about the relative importance of service and process innovations, the length of time lag for innovation type, and the role of internal and external measures of performance. The findings recorded in this study display some similarities with the Damanpour (1990) article: that of uncertain relationships between innovation and performance. One of the main developments between the earlier and subsequent studies is the inclusion of control variables that take into account the organizational environment. All studies, however, including that reported below, do not control for other internal organizational characteristics, or other management strategies which might mediate the innovation–performance relationship.

Damanpour, Walker, and Avellaneda (2009) examined the combined effects of innovation types on organizational performance in a panel of 428 English local authorities for the period 2001–5. Innovation types include service, administrative, and technological, and performance is measured using the Audit Commission's Core Service Performance variable. Because the majority of knowledge on innovation is derived from private sector studies, prior research has presumed that innovation follows a technological trajectory. This trajectory assumes that organizations invest knowledge in one type of innovation and use this to build organizational capacity and in turn higher levels of performance. Damanpour et al. (2007) postulate that the performance goal can be accomplished by offering new and improved services to existing or new users (service innovation) as well as introducing process innovations in the internal systems of the organization (technological and administrative innovations). Results show that innovation, as measured through an index of all types, does matter for performance. They also indicate that if public service organizations focus on one type of innovation, rather than keeping an even keel across a number of types of innovation, it will harm performance. Organizations do not need to maintain consistent balance in their innovation focus over time, but the findings point towards the value of diverging from the sector norm as a means to achieve higher levels of performance. This research provides the most systematic empirical evidence to support the notion that innovation unfolds in different ways across public organizations and that innovation does indeed matter for performance.

UNRESOLVED RESEARCH ISSUES

The piecemeal way in which innovation research has developed means that there are typically no comprehensive theories on the innovation–performance hypothesis and clearly no empirical tests of such theories. Figure 8.1 presents initial thoughts on this process. Diffusion variables and internal and external organizational determinants are related to innovation characteristics, and this

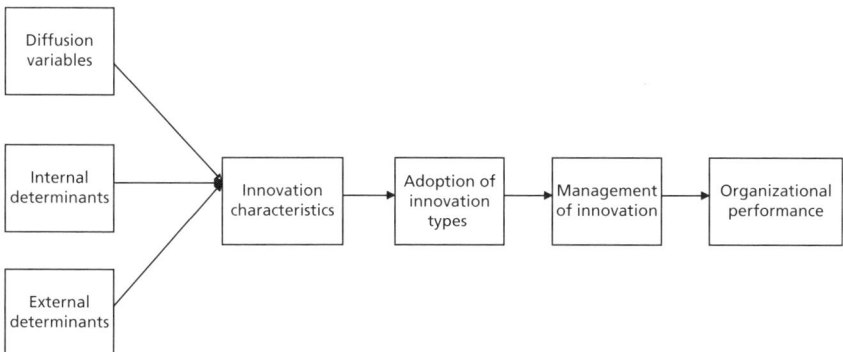

Figure 8.1 Combined influences on the diffusion of innovation

influences the adoption of different types of innovation. Adopted innovations have to be managed, and it is through the successful management and implementation of innovation that performance consequences are recorded by an organization. It is likely that this process is not linear, that there are feedback loops, and that some relationships may be moderated and mediated.

In public management it is rare that entire theories are tested; rather, an *ad hoc* approach is seen where testable and manageable components are explored to build up a picture of the overall model. Research to date does not come near the whole framework as proposed, or parts of it. The four studies discussed above examine the relationship between the adoption of innovation and organizational performance. As noted earlier in this chapter, theory abounds on the potential relationships between different types of innovation and performance. In public service organizations this needs to be traced back to the multiple and sometimes conflicting goals of public agencies and the incremental ways in which innovation occurs in this sector. An extensive variety of innovation types was outlined earlier in this chapter, and these need to be explored in greater detail to ensure that research findings are generalizable. Furthermore, a variety of timescales require examination. While we may find relationships between the combinative adoption of in-novation and performance (Damanpour et al. 2009) studies to date do not confirm the presumption (best articulated by Light [1998]) that *what* innovations result in *how* innovations which then produce additional *what* innovations. The evidence indicates that there are lagged relationships between the adoption of innovation and performance, but no conclusive evidence has been presented. Damanpour (1990) suggests that it could be up to seven years, while Walker and Damanpour (2008) speculate on one to three years. To date, time spans have been practically constrained by the available data—which is clearly problematic.

The presumption of this chapter has been that innovation influences performance. Damanpour and Evan (1984) tested the reverse of this relation-ship. The question of whether innovation influences performance or per-formance influences innovation is a critical one (not mapped in Figure 8.1). Many of these limitations have occurred because most of the studies are cross-sectional or have relied upon testing the consequences of a single innovation type. Implicit in the literature is a virtuous relationship between innovation and performance; until we know which drives which, and whether the relationship is sustainable over the long term, we will be unable to build better theory or offer insightful comments to the policy community.

A multitude of studies have examined the factors influencing the adoption of innovations. These have come from the diffusion traditions (see Berry and Berry [2007] for a review of studies examining their diffusion model and Rogers [1995] for a more general overview). Others have explored organiza-tional and environmental characteristics (see Damanpour [1991] for a review of antecedents in the management literature). This literature is edging towards an understanding of some of the influences on the adoption of different types of organization. Most recently, Walker (2008) has suggested that these are likely to be configurations of internal and external characteristics, but this has not been subjected to a test on service performance.

Implementation and performance is a rarely explored topic amongst public management scholars. Literature abounds on factors that influence the successful implementation of policies, but as Andrews et al. (2006) note, the implementation of management strategies is unlikely to receive attention. The same is so for studies of innovation in public services. Golden (1990) and Walker et al. (2001) offer case-study material on the management of innovation and suggest that it is a complex and iterative process. Walker (2003) builds on the Van de Ven et al. (1999) model of innovation management to show that the path from the decision to adopt to final implementation is often multifaceted—suggesting that this is more complex than the linear or rational implementation frameworks first suggested by Zaltman et al. (1973). This work again signals the importance of lagged relationships between innovation and performance because the adoption of innovation can be uncertain. The level of uncertainly is very likely correlated to the magnitude of the innovation—a classification of innovation noted above. While the adoption of innovations in public service organizations is likely to be incremental, such innovations can, nonetheless, be highly disruptive. The evidence base can again be bolstered by future studies that include variables that measure the way in which innovation is managed, and include these in multivariate models of the innovation–performance hypothesis.

Considering innovation as a complex process returns to one of the theories discussed earlier. Innovation in organizations does not happen in isolation; rather it is a response by organizational managers and others to external signals in the environment and the capacities of an organization to adopt those innovations. This would suggest that the most fruitful line of enquiry for the ideas outlined here would be to take the RBV of the organization and the notion of dynamic capacities as the underlying framework to build future studies. Such an approach may also be able to place parameters around the extent of innovation in public organizations. It is clear that an organization cannot innovate *ad infinitum*, and that too much innovation will be bad for an organization and likely result in reductions in performance as new activities are traded off with service provision. While no research has explicitly addressed this issue in public agencies, an approach based around resources and dynamic capacities might permit some understanding of organizational innovation. Similarly, research based upon this perspective might also be able to examine instances of failures to innovate. While failure is typically off the public management radar (for exceptions see the recent interest in disaster management), the pro-innovation bias in the literature means that little is written about when things go wrong, or when innovations are aborted and the consequences of this. Finally, the data requirements of what is outlined here are onerous and will take many years for scholars to build. They include measures of all the variables outlined in Figure 8.1, and should be tested across different types of organizations, in different contexts, and through time.

Conclusions

Innovation is a central public service improvement strategy adopted by governments around the world. It is clearly in the grasp of public organizations, and a growing amount of literature attests to agencies developing new procedures and a wide range of new services. These are in response to changing external environments (see Chapter 10) and the activities of managers and leaders in organizations. Theory—the more robust of which is from the management literature—is developing to explain and help research, policy, and practice. What is somewhat surprising is the lack of research on the service improvement implications of a strategy of innovation. This is a remarkable comment to make after several decades of government exhortations for public service innovation. In conclusion it is, therefore, suggested that innovation is omnipresent, yet the extent to which, and the way, it impacts on performance remain opaque. Energy needs to be directed towards filling this glaring gap in our knowledge on public service improvement over the coming years.

REFERENCES

Abernathy, W.J. and Utterback, J. (1978). Patterns of industrial innovation. *Technology Review*, 80(June–July), 40–7.
Aiken, M. and Hage, J. (1971). The organic organization and innovation. *Sociology* 5, 63–82.
Aldrich, H. and Ruet, M. (2006). *Organizations Evolving*. Thousand Oaks, CA: Sage.
Andrews, R., Boyne, G.A. and Walker, R.M. (2006). Strategy content and organizational performance: An empirical analysis. *Public Administration Review* 66, 52–63.
Archibugi, D., Evangelista, R. and Simonetti, R. (1994). 'On the definition and measurement of product and process innovations', in Y. Shionoya and M. Perlman (eds.), *Innovation in Technology, Industries and Institutions: Studies in Schumpeterian Perspectives*. Ann Arbor, MI: The University of Michigan Press, pp. 7–24.
Barney, J.B. (1991). Firm resources and sustained competitive advantage. *Journal of Management* 17, 99–120.
Barras, R. (1990). Interactive innovation in financial and business services: The vanguard of the service revolution. *Research Policy* 19, 215–37.

Berry, F.S. (1994). Innovation in public management: The adoption of strategic planning. *Public Administration Review* 54, 322–30.

——Berry, W.D. (2007). 'Innovation and diffusion models in policy research', in P. Sabatier (ed.), *Theories of the Policy Process*, Second edition. Boulder, CO: Westview Press, pp. 169–200.

Boer, H. and During, W.E. (2001). Innovation, what innovation? A comparison between product, process, and organizational innovation. *International Journal of Technology Management* 22, 83–107.

Borins, S. (1998). *Innovating with Integrity: How Local Heroes are Transforming American Government.* Washington, DC: Georgetown University Press.

Boyne, G.A., Gould-Williams, J.S., Law, J. and Walker, R. M. (2005). Explaining the adoption of innovation: An empirical analysis of public management reform. *Environment and Planning C: Government and Policy* 23, 419–35.

Bryson, J.M., Ackermann, F. and Eden, C. (2007). Putting the resource-based view of strategy and distinctive competencies to work in public organizations. *Public Administration Review* 67, 702–17.

Burns, T. and Stalker, G.M. (1961). *The Management of Innovation.* London: Tavistock Publications.

Daft, R.L. (1978). A dual-core model of organizational innovation. *Academy of Management Journal* 21, 193–210.

Damanpour, F. (1987). The adoption of technological, administrative, and ancillary innovations: Impact of organizational factors. *Journal of Management* 13, 675–88.

——(1990). 'Innovation effectiveness, adoption and organizational performance', in M.A. West and J.L. Farr (eds.), *Innovation and Creativity at Work. Psychological and Organizational Strategies,* Chichester: John Wiley & Sons.

——(1991). Organizational innovation: A meta-analysis of effects of determinants and moderators. *Academy of Management Journal* 34, 555–90.

——Evan, W.M. (1984). Organizational innovation and performance: The problem of 'organizational lag'. *Administrative Science Quarterly* 29, 392–409.

——Gopalakrishnan, S. (2001). The dynamics of the adoption of product and process innovations in organizations. *Journal of Management Studies* 38, 45–65.

——Szabat, K.A. and Evan, W.M. (1989). The relationship between types of innovation and organizational performance. *Journal of Management Studies* 26, 587–601.

——Walker, R.M. and Avallenda, C. (2009). Combinative effects of innovation types on organizational performance: a longitudinal study of public services. *Journal of Management Studies* 46, 4, 650–675.

Edquist, C., Hommen, L. and McKelvey, M. (2001). *Innovation and Employment: Process Versus Product Innovation.* Cheltenham: Edward Elgar.

Ettlie, J.E., Bridges, W.P. and O'Keefe, R.D. (1984). Organization strategy and structural differences for radical versus incremental innovation. *Management Science* 30, 682–95.

Feller, I. (1981). Public-sector innovation as 'conspicuous consumption'. *Policy Analysis* 7(1), 1–20.

Germain, R. (1996). The role of context and structure in radical and incremental logistics innovation adoption. *Journal of Business Research* 35, 117–27.

Golden, O. (1990). Innovation in public sector human service programs the implications of innovation by 'groping along'. *Journal of Policy Analysis and Management* 9, 219–48.

Hamel, G. (2006). The why, what and how of management innovation. *Harvard Business Review* 84(2), 72–84.

Hipp, C., Tether, B.S. and Miles, I. (2000). The incidence and effects of innovation in services: Evidence from Germany. *International Journal of Innovation Management* 4, 417–53.

Kimberly, J.R. and Evanisko, M.J. (1981). Organizational innovation: The influence of individual, organizational, and contextual factors on hospital adoption of technological and administrative innovation. *Academy of Management Journal* 24, 689–713.

Knight, K.E. (1967). A descriptive model of the intra-firm innovation process. *Journal of Business* 40, 478–96.

Light, P.C. (1998). *Sustaining Innovation. Creating Nonprofit and Government Organizations That Innovate Naturally.* San Francisco, CA: Jossey-Bass.

Miles, I. (2001). *Services Innovation: A Reconfiguration of Innovation Studies.* Manchester: PREST, University of Manchester.

Moore, M. (1995). *Creating Public Value: Strategic Management in Government.* Cambridge MA: Harvard University Press.

—— Hartley, J. (2008). Innovations in governance. *Public Management Review* 10, 3–20.

Normann, R. (1991). *Service Management.* Chichester: Wiley.

O'Toole, L.J. Jr. (1997). Implementing public innovations in network settings. *Administration and Society* 29, 115–38.

Osborne, S. (1998). *Voluntary Organizations and Innovation in Public Services.* London: Routledge.

Pfeffer, J. (1993). Barriers to the advance of organizational science: Paradigm development as a dependent variable. *Academy of Management Review* 18, 599–620.

Rainey, H.G. and Ryu, J.E. (2004). 'Framing high performance and innovativeness in government', in P.W. Ingraham and L.E. Lynn (eds.), *The Art of Governance: Analyzing Management and Administration.* Washington, DC: Georgetown University Press.

Rashman, L. and Hartley, J. (2002). Leading and learning? Knowledge transfer in the Beacon Council Scheme. *Public Administration* 80(3), 523–42.

Roberts, P.W. and Amit, R. (2003). The dynamics of innovative activity and competitive advantage: The case of Australian retail banking, 1981 to 1995. *Organization Science* 14, 107–22.

Rogers, E. (1995). *Diffusion of Innovation.* New York: The Free Press.

Schilling, M.A. (2005). *Strategic Management of Technological Innovation.* New York: McGraw Hill.

Tidd, J. (2001). Innovation management in context: Environment, organization and performance. *International Journal of Management Reviews* 3, 169–83.

Tornatzky, L.G. and Fleischer, M. (1990). *The Process of Technological Innovation.* Lexington, MA: Lexington Books.

Uchupalanan, K. (2000). Competition and IT-based innovation in banking services. *International Journal of Innovation Management* 4, 455–89.

Van de Ven, A., Polley, D.E., Garud, R. and Venkataraman, S. (1999). *The Innovation Journey.* New York: Oxford University Press.

Walker, R.M. (2003). Evidence on the management of public services innovation. *Public Money and Management* 23, 93–102.

—— (2004). 'Innovation and organizational performance: Evidence and a research agenda'. Advanced Institute for Management Research Working Paper Number 2, London, AIM Research, www.aimresearch.org

—— (2006). Innovation type and diffusion. An empirical analysis of local government. *Public Administration* 84, 311–36.

—— (2008). An empirical evaluation of innovation type and organizational and environmental characteristics: Towards a configuration framework. *Journal of Public Administration Research and Theory* 18(4), 591–615.

—— Damanpour, F. (2008). 'Innovation type and organizational performance: An empirical exploration', in C. Donaldson, J. Hartley, C. Skelcher, and M. Wallace (eds.), *Managing Improvement in Public Service Delivery: Progress and Prospects.* Cambridge: Cambridge University Press.

—— Jeanes, E. and Rowlands, R.O. (2001). *Managing Public Services Innovation: The Experience of English Housing Associations.* Bristol: Bristol University, The Policy Press.

—— —— —— (2002). Measuring innovation: Applying the literature-based innovation output indicator to public services. *Public Administration* 80, 201–14.

Zaltman, G., Duncan, R. and Holbek, J. (1973). *Innovations and Organizations.* New York: Wiley.

9 Collaboration

Tom Entwistle

Introduction

The public services, like their private counterparts, are increasingly charac-terized by hybrid forms of organization variously described as partnerships, collaborations, networks, or alliances. Inter-organizational collaboration has indeed assumed a central place in the international tool-kit of public manage-ment reform. With the promise of realizing goals beyond the scale or scope of the 'lonely organisation' (Hjern and Porter 1981, p. 212), inter-organizational partnerships—variously embracing the public, private and voluntary sector—are now used to design and deliver public services from small-town refuse collection to national-scale infrastructure projects.

Resistant to snappy definition, the new partnerships fall into the organiza-tional middle ground between hierarchies and markets. They rely, as Ronald Dore (1983) puts it, on a 'spirit of goodwill' in which organizations collab-orate on the basis of equality, trust, and agreed goals. Neither highly formal-ized bureaucratic structures nor fleeting contractual relationships between purchasers and providers, partnerships are treated here as a relatively endur-ing and at least reasonably formalized network arrangement. Reflecting their hybrid status, the partnership literature can be found under headings as diverse as collaboration, networks, partnerships, alliances, co-production, joining up, and so on. While that diversity provides a wealth of different perspectives, it can easily take us a little too far away from our core business. Boundaries need to be drawn.

The first of two boundaries drawn in this chapter serves to exclude the networking activity of individuals. Of course, all inter-organizational rela-tionships rely on interpersonal contacts of one form or another. Similarly, much empirical research relies at some point on individual-level data in the form of interview transcripts or survey responses. On the basis of extensive analysis of networking behaviour in Texas schools, O'Toole and Meier conclude, however, that 'the networking behaviour of managers (and others) is not the same thing as the structural interdependence that often binds elements of networks together' (O'Toole and Meier 2004, p. 491; Keast et al. 2004, p. 364).

The second boundary—focused on the distinction between public and private services—is a little fuzzier. Huge literatures consider the effectiveness of alliances, networks, and joint ventures in private management. Parts of that theory read across the sectoral divide very well (Isett and Provan 2005). Much of the work on the micro-contingencies of partnership behaviour, for example, seems equally applicable to public and private management. Similarly some of the points about structure—life-cycles and the scale of collaboration—seem likely to be applicable to public services and therefore deserving of inclusion. There are, however, important differences between the sectors which justify a distinctively public service take on the collaboration agenda. Probably the most important of these differences is focused on the purposes and outcomes of collaboration. Whereas private organizations collaborate to advance their own organizational interests, public (and to some extent voluntary or third-sector organizations) collaborate to advance public or community goals. Typically those evaluating private collaborations use the yardsticks of organizational performance and ask whether an alliance has increased sales or profitability. While improved organizational performance at this level can be translated into improved public services, public management researchers are more likely to ask whether partnerships have ameliorated problems felt at the community or society level (Provan and Milward 2001).

Within these boundaries, this chapter considers whether public service partnerships deliver the outcomes they promise. The answer in a nutshell is that it all depends. It depends, according to the literature, on a series of specific contingencies ranging from the socio-economic context to the individual behaviour of the partners sitting around the table. Commentators have focused on three sets of contingencies in their efforts to explain the successes and failures of collaborative forms of government.

At the micro-level, a number of studies have pointed to a series of behaviours associated with successful collaboration. We are told that commitment, coordination, communication, trust, and joint problem-solving are the key ingredients (Huxham 1993; Huxham and Vangen 1996; Mohr and Spekman 1994; Shortell et al. 2002). At the strategic level, commentators have considered some of the structural qualities of networks, like the size of collaborations, sector of partners, formalization, density, and integration. Finally at the environmental level, commentators have looked at a series of considerations beyond the grasp of partners like the policy context, resource munificence, stability, and the life-cycle of collaborative endeavours.

Before considering these issues in greater depth, this chapter will examine the prospectus for partnership as developed by its advocates. Why should working in partnership lead to public service improvement? Following a detailed examination of the specific contingencies of public service partnership at the behavioural, structural, and environmental levels, the chapter will conclude with a discussion of the prospects for partnering before suggesting some new avenues of inquiry.

The theory of improvement through partnership

Agranoff and McGuire (2003) define collaborative public management as 'the process of facilitating and operating in multi-organizational arrangements to solve problems that cannot be solved, or solved easily by single organizations' (p. 4). The huge interdisciplinary scope of the partnership and network literature gives an indication of the range of the very demanding challenges put at the door of the new collaborative agenda. From integrating the delivery of health and human services to the provision of large-scale transport infra-structure, governments turn to partnership in the hope of solving a bewilder-ing variety of challenging problems. This complicated picture can however be distilled down to four main rationales or anticipated outcomes of partner-ship: advantages of scale, scope, supervision, and learning.

The scale rationale suggests that partnerships allow public services, like their private counterparts, to maximize the return from scarce resources (Hennart 1988; Prager 1994). Lowndes and Skelcher suggest that partnership allows public managers to 'increase resource efficiency', 'reduce duplication', 'share overheads', and 'add value by bringing together complementary ser-vices' (1998, p. 315). Hardy et al. talk about 'building organizational capaci-ties through the transfer or pooling of resources' (2003, p. 324). The scale rationale is particularly relevant to partnerships between agencies tradition-ally divided by geographical boundaries (Warner 2006); it focuses attention on the size of collaborations, the resources they unlock, and the efficiency dimension of performance.

The management literature describes economies of scope as the result of bringing together different product lines. In place of economies and products, public management talks about improvement through the joining-up of policies and programmes. As Ling explains, a perception grew in the 1990s 'that important goals of public policy cannot be delivered through the separate activities of existing organizations but neither could they be delivered by creating a new "super agency"' (2002, p. 616). He describes 'the emergence of a class of problems whose causes are so complex, and whose solutions are so multi-factorial, that they require a multi-agency response' (Ling 2002, p. 622). Likewise, Keast et al. highlight the recent growth of issues which 'defy precise definition, cut across policy and service areas and resist solutions offered by a single agency or silo approach' (2004, p. 363). Although not the only way of joining-up (6 Perry 2004), collaboration at the sharp end of service delivery offers a relatively new way of plugging holes in statutory mandates and ameliorating the unintended consequences or 'negative externalities' of policies delivered through narrowly defined departments or programmes (6 Perry 2004, p. 107; Lowndes and Skelcher 1998). The scope rationale underlines the importance of the organizational membership of a partnership and the capacity to develop 'consistency between the organizational arrangements of programs, policies or agencies, which may enable them to collaborate' (6 Perry 2004, 106). The scope rationale is particularly associated with improvements in the effectiveness and equity of service delivery and progress on the wicked issues that cut across public sector jurisdictions.

Although widely cited in the literature as a goal of collaboration, in truth the benefits of increased scale and scope could be delivered by other forms of inter-organizational working. It is quite easy to conceive of increasing the scale or scope of service delivery through organizational mergers or contracting arrangements. Unfortunately very few studies have sought to compare the relative performance of partnership against merger or contracting-type approaches (although see Bazzoli et al. [2000]).

Surprisingly, perhaps, commentators have said rather less about two other rationales which genuinely seem more distinctive to partnership forms of coordination. The supervision rationale engages with the principal–agent problems associated with hierarchies and markets. Hierarchies build complex processes of control and accountability to ensure that subordinates do what they are supposed to do. Markets rely on contracts to enforce the obligations of buyers and sellers. Either way, principal–agent problems impose significant transaction costs on coordination through hierarchies and markets. At least in theory, trusting forms of coordination solve this problem by abolishing the distinction between principals and agents, uniting the intentions of partners in common goals. Partnerships promise lower transaction costs, because partners do not, at least in theory, need to be supervised; they can be trusted to do the right thing because everyone is working towards the same goals (Podolny and Page 1998, p. 65). The supervision rationale draws attention to the importance of a series of behavioural characteristics like agreed goals, trust, and communication (Edelenbos and Klijn 2007). These in turn should generate reduced transaction costs which could be used to improve any dimension of performance.

Finally, the learning rationale posits that by engaging different groups and sectors in enduring and relatively equal consultative arrangements it is possible to make better strategic decisions about service delivery. In this way the new partnerships promise deeper and broader participation than can be realized through the traditional institutions of representative democracy (Klijn and Skelcher 2007; Leach et al. 2002). According to Fung (2006, p. 67): 'The principal reason for enhancing citizen participation in any area of contemporary governance is that the authorized set of decision-makers—typically elected representatives or administrative officials—is somehow deficient.' Whereas hierarchies and markets assume away the challenges of marshalling complicated information with notions of rational choice and perfect knowledge, network forms of organization offers a methodology for 'the creation and circulation of knowledges' (Thompson 2003, p. 119). As Podolny and Page put it: 'Network forms of organization foster learning because they preserve greater diversity of search routines than hierarchies and they convey richer, more complex information than the market' (1998, p. 62). The learning rationale emphasizes the number of collaborative ties and diversity of partners (Hardy et al. 2003, p. 326). Suggesting that participation can be evaluated as an end in itself, Mathur and Skelcher point to a number of different ways of assessing both the hardware and software of these initiatives (2007). Others argue, however, that the benefits of broader participation should be apparent in improved public services; improvements likely to be most discernible to those excluded by the traditional institutions of representative democracy (Andrews and Entwistle (forthcoming)). The learning rationale may then be particularly associated with equity dimensions of performance.

Evidence of improvement

Having clarified why public agencies choose to collaborate, the rest of this chapter considers the evidence of its effectiveness (Table 9.1). As suggested in the preceding paragraphs, hardly any studies have sought to evaluate the relative efficiency or effectiveness of collaboration against other forms of organization. We just do not know whether working in partnership is better than working alone. In place of this question researchers have sought to understand the contingencies which affect partnership working. Most studies consider, for example, whether certain forms of behaviour, types of structure, or organizational environment are more conducive to collaboration than others.

The measurement of improvement is also problematic. While some studies use relatively uncontroversial outcome measures—like client perceptions, or independently audited performance indicators—time-lags and the changing goals of partnership sometimes make the use of these inappropriate (Agranoff 2008). Accordingly, other studies use intermediate measures of performance such as shared resources, accessed knowledge, or expanded trust. Agranoff, for example, measures performance through 'the perceptions of participants regarding how professional and organizational value is added by the network'

Table 9.1. Summary of evidence

Study	Dimension of partnership	Country and sector	Time period and sample	Measure of performance	Finding
Agranoff (2008)	Behaviour	US, various	Date not specified, 14 networks	Partner perceptions of 'personal', 'agency', 'network', and 'tangible' outcomes	'The importance of management in the traditional supervisory sense has decreased. Today's managers must place as much emphasis on organizing communities and building knowledge-friendly cultures' (p. 345).
Andrews and Entwistle (forthcoming)	Structure	UK, local government	2002, 46 service departments	Government performance indicators of efficiency, effectiveness, and equity	'Public–public partnership is positively associated with effectiveness, efficiency and equity, but public–private partnership is negatively associated with effectiveness and equity. Public-non-profit partnership is unrelated to performance' (forthcoming).
Bazzoli et al. (2000)	Structure and environment	US, health	1995, 2,159 hospitals	Financial performance indicators	'Unified hospital ownership has financial advantages over interfirm health networks' (p. 247) but there were diminishing returns to 'centralization for system-affiliated hospitals' (p. 248).
Chan et al. (1999)	Structure and environment	US, health	1992, 335 rural hospitals	Financial performance indicators	'All dependent variables have a curvilinear association with group size. The optimum group size is somewhere in the neighborhood of 45. This reveals the benefits of collective action (i.e. scale economies and/or synergy effects) and the issue of complexity as group size increases' (p. 9).
Eden and Huxham (2001)	Behaviour	UK, children	Date not specified, 1 partnership	Stakeholder and researcher perceptions of partnership health	'There are at least some characteristic episodes that recur' during the discussion of purpose or goals. Interventions based on the recognition of those episodes will 'increase the probability of success' (p. 387).
Entwistle et al. (2007)	Environment	UK, various	Date not specified, 10 partnerships	Partner perceptions of various outputs	'The majority of our partnerships complained predominantly of a mix of hierarchical and market dysfunctions' (p. 76).
Grimshaw et al. (2002)	Behaviour and structure	UK, public–private	Date not specified, 2 partnerships	Partner perceptions of costs and innovation	'The public sector partner tended to underestimate the time and resources needed to negotiate ad manage the terms and conditions of the partnership contract. This put the private sector in the driving seat' (p. 499).
Hardy et al. (2003)	Scale and learning	Palestine, children	Date not specified, 8 partnerships	Acquisition of distinctive resources; creation of knowledge; and inter-organizational influence.	'Collaborations that have high levels of involvement will be positively associated with the acquisition of distinctive resources' (p. 339). 'Collaborations with high levels of involvement and high levels of embeddedness will be positively associated with the creation of knowledge' (p. 340).

(continued)

Table 9.1. Continued

Study	Dimension of partnership	Country and sector	Time period and sample	Measure of performance	Finding
Hicks et al. (2008)	Behaviour	US, mothers/children	1999–2003, 16 partnerships	Withdrawal rates from the programme	'There is a clear and identifiable relationship between the quality of the collaborative process and community health program success' (p. 474).
Johnston and Romzek (2008)	Environment, stability	US, social welfare	1996–2005, 2 networks	Client perceptions of quality and turnover of case managers	'The effects of instability in the Kansas child welfare system are observable and pervasive, and they impose high organizational costs on the contracting agencies' (p.139).
Klijn and Teisman (2003)	Behaviour and structure	Netherlands, PPP	Date not specified, 3 partnerships	Success at realizing various partnership goals	PPPs are doomed by fundamental differences in the strategies and values between the sectors.
Leach et al. (2002)	Behaviour and environment	US, water management	1999–2000, 44 partnerships	Six measures of performance: effect on the watershed; human and social capital; restoration; education; monitoring and levels of agreement	A mixed picture of the ability of watershed partnerships to achieve their stated goals and objectives. . . One of the clearest findings is the positive relationship between each of the evaluation criteria and the age of the partnership' (p. 665)
Lemieux-Charles, et al. (2005)	Structure	US, health	1999–2002, 4 networks	Partner perceptions of service delivery and administrative effectiveness	'The most effective network shared information broadly, was highly formalized and with a broad scope of activities' (pp. 462–3).
Nylen (2007)	Structure	Sweden, health	3 years, not specified 7 networks	Various measures of service quality	'Effectiveness depends upon degree of formalization and intensity of collaborative activity.'
Perrons and Skyers (2003)	Environment	UK, regeneration	Date not specified, 1 partnership	Stakeholder involvement	'In the absence of transformative redistribution—formal mechanisms for inclusion—'can do little to redress the processes leading to social disadvantage' (p. 282)
Provan and Milward (1995)	Structure and environment	US, health	1991–2, 4 networks	Client and manager perceptions of service outcomes	'Differences in network effectiveness could be explained by aspects of network structure and context namely centralized integration, external control, stability and resource munificence' (p. 27).
Provan and Sebastian (1998)	Structure	US, health	1991–2, 3 networks	Client perceptions of service outcomes	'To be most effective, clique integration must be intensive, involving multiple and overlapping links both within and across the organizations that compose the core of the network' (p. 460).

Source	Focus	Context	Data	Measure	Findings
Selden et al. (2006)	Structure and environment	US, children	Date not specified, 20 collaborations	Client and stakeholder perceptions of service outcomes	Teachers more satisfied, wider range of services and greater child readiness for school. 'interagency collaboration in early education and care can be a positive organizational tool for improving the ability of providers to achieve these outcomes' (p. 421).
Shortell et al. (2002)	Behaviour	US, health	1995–2000, 25 partnerships	Stakeholder perceptions across four dimensions of performance (pp. 60–2)	The authors identify 'six characteristics that distinguished the top performing sites from the bottom five performing sites': ability to manage size and diversity; multiple components of leadership; maintain focus; manage conflict; ability to hand off the baton and patch' (p. 64).
Vangen and Huxham (2003a)	Behaviour	UK, various	Various	Stakeholder and researcher perceptions of partnership health	'Trust management requires the assessment of each collaborative situation . . . and whether trust can be built incrementally through a small wins approach or whether a more rapid and comprehensive approach to trust development is required' (p. 27).
Vangen and Huxham (2003b)	Behaviour	UK, various	13 partnerships	Stakeholder and researcher perceptions of partnership health	The leadership of collaborations needs to be both facilitative and directive.
Warner (2006)	Comparison of cooperation to contracting	US, local government	1992–2002, 1,031 local governments	ICMA survey and local government expenditure per person	'Inter-municipal cooperation presents a means to reach economies of scale in public service delivery at the municipal level 'although without monitoring, efficiency seems to decline over time (p. 234).

(2008, p. 327). Some of these intermediate measures of improvement can, however, lead to quite circular analysis. Trust, for example, is sometimes treated as both an ingredient and an intermediate outcome of collaboration. They further presume causal connections—that high-trust partnerships are more efficacious than low-trust ones, for example—which have not been demonstrated.

The next three sections consider the evidence provided by these studies under three headings suggested by their predominant focus.

BEHAVIOUR

One of the most important lines of analysis within the partnership and network literature focuses on behaviour within the partnership. Commentators have identified a series of ingredients associated with the effective management of partnerships or networks. Typically, the ingredients of good partnership practice include: agreeing to common goals or aims, dispersed forms of leadership, trust, communication, and conflict resolution (Huxham and Vangen 1996, 2004; Lasker et al. 2001; Shortell et al. 2002). Although some commentators use a different vocabulary—Weiner and Alexander, for example, focus on turf and territoriality, community, accountability, and growth and development (1998); Agranoff and McGuire talk of activation, framing, mobilizing, and synthesizing (2001)—the same core set of ingredients or behaviours are discernible.

Although a great deal could be said about each of these, only three of the most cited ingredients will be considered here. Top of that list is the repeated assertion that successful collaboration presumes 'an explicit vision of what is to be accomplished' (Shortell et al. 2002, p. 83). As Eden and Huxham put it: 'Most of the collaborations that appear successful have small numbers of member organizations, a well defined goal and high level of resource' (2001, p. 385). They go on to explain, however, that most collaborations do not enjoy these benefits, indeed they characterize the archetypal partnership as having 'multiple stakeholders', a focus on 'complex social issues', and 'many areas of tension' (2001, p. 385). Pointing to the inevitable conflicts between the goals of the individual people, the organizations they represent, and the emergent ambitions of the collaboration itself, Eden and Huxham argue that the key ingredient of success is not so much a single goal, as 'the group members' capacity to manage the tensions' (2001 p. 385). Reporting similar findings, Shortell et al. describe their more successful partnership as 'anticipating problems and likely trouble spots', working 'to create interdependencies', 'continually maintaining a high degree of trust', and creating 'a process of decision making that was perceived to be fair and open to all' (2002, p. 75).

Under closer scrutiny the advocates of common purpose propose a second-best solution of conflict resolution.

Second on the list of ingredients is trust. Trust is important, according to Vangen and Huxham, because with at least 'the ability to predict others' behaviour' (2003*a*, p. 26) 'more ambitious ventures can be undertaken as trusting attitudes develop' (2003*a*, p. 12). Vangen and Huxham are clear, however, that trust has to be built in a cyclical fashion and that this 'probably means aiming for modest but achievable outcomes, in the first instance, becoming more ambitious only as success breeds a greater level of trust' (2003*a*, p. 15). Shortell et al. talk about 'the need to first accomplish some doable projects to gain legitimacy with the community and to gain momentum to take on larger tasks' (2002, pp. 77–8). Lack of trust, Vangen and Huxham conclude, does not inevitably lead to failure (2003*a*); it just implies the need for relatively modest objectives.

While arguing that common goals and trust are good for collaboration, Huxham, Shortell, and their associates make the point that very few real world partnerships exhibit these qualities. Indeed, the key challenge for partners, as they frame it, turns on the ability to negotiate progress when goals are confused or conflicting and inter-organizational trust is low. Leadership is key to collaborating in these sub-prime conditions.

Although again commentators have used different vocabularies, there is an emerging consensus around the key elements of collaborative leadership. McGuire describes four activities—activation, framing, mobilizing, and synthesizing (2002, pp. 602–3); Vangen and Huxham (2003*b*) talk about embracing, empowering, and mobilizing members of the partnership. Embracing means facilitating the 'active involvement of those who are critical to ensuring a partnership's aims' (Huxham and Vangen 2000*a*, p. 1170). Empowering means 'creating an infrastructure in which people and organizations can be enabled to participate' (Vangen and Huxham 2003*b*, p. S67). Mobilizing involves ensuring that 'member organizations benefit from their involvement' (p. S68) and that 'representatives are acting as conduits to the resources of their organization' (Huxham and Vangen 2000*a*, p. 1170). Shortell et al. refer to three component leadership which included 'a dedicated executive director who enjoyed the respect of the whole group', an external sponsoring organization 'that provided important stability and legitimacy' and finally subsidiary leadership, the practice—as Shortell et al. describe it—of 'delegating to people and groups closest to a given problem the authority and resources to deal with the problem' (2002, p. 69).

Collaborative leadership is not, however, all about 'relational skills such as patience, empathy and deference' (Vangen and Huxham 2003*b*, p. S70). Working with members 'who are not on board', are 'ill informed', or 'cannot mutually communicate' (Vangen and Huxham 2003*b*, p. S70) sometimes calls for 'collaborative thuggery' (Vangen and Huxham 2003*b*, p. S69) to move the collaboration in an 'appropriate direction' (Huxham and Vangen 2000*a*, p. 1169). Huxham and Vangen describe a need for leaders to manipulate the collaborative agenda by using 'the power of their position, tools or skills to influence the activities of a collaboration' (2000*a*, p. 1169). Sometimes this means manipulating discussions, other times it calls for empowering certain groups or 'shifting deeply held mind sets', (Huxham and Vangen 2000*a*, p. 1169) and 'political manoeuvring' involving 'sorting out those who are and are not worth the bother' (Vangen and Huxham 2003*b*, p. S72). Huxham and Vangen conclude that 'it is paradoxical that the single-mindedness of leaders appears to be central to collaborative success' (2000*a*, p. 1171).

Although the behavioural aspects of partnership have received a lot of attention in the public management literature, much of the work has been formative rather than summative in character. The assessment of partnership has been made on the basis of partners' reported experience of trying to collaborate rather than on the final outcomes of their endeavours. Reviewing this type of evidence many commentators think they have seen enough to conclude that the prospects of collaboration are not that good. Huxham and Vangen warn: 'Don't do it unless you have to... Unless the potential for real collaborative advantage is clear, it is generally best if there is a choice, to avoid collaboration' (Huxham and Vangen 2004, p. 200).

While Huxham and Vangen's caution is an important corrective to the excessive enthusiasm voiced by some government agencies, there are reasons to think that this is an unnecessarily bleak prescription. While summative evaluations—designed to assess the overall effectiveness of different ap-proaches to partnership management—are much thinner on the ground, Hicks et al.'s study of the nurse–family partnership in Colorado found that 'the quality of the process of building community collaboration' accounted for a significant proportion of the variation in the performance of the partnerships they studied (2008, p. 469). Their measure of process quality gauged, amongst other things

whether stakeholders perceive the process as free from undue influence from special interests outside the process, whether the process itself can generate binding decisions rather than simply confirming decisions already made, and whether the stakeholders perceive that they have equal standing (Hicks et al. 2008, p. 464).

Similarly, Agranoff reports a number of benefits emerging from networks characterized by 'investment, exploration, discussion, testing, compromise, and all the other elements of co-practice' (2008, p. 344). Work of this type is consistent with a much larger literature in private management, which sug-gests a positive association between the ingredients of what is taken to be good partnership practice and performance (Mohr and Spekman 1994).

STRUCTURE

The second line of inquiry pursued by theorists of partnership is focused on the structures of partnership activity. Whereas behavioural approaches to partnership emphasize the agency of the individuals or organizations which make up a network, the structural perspective focuses on the institutional rules or 'social infrastructure', as Klijn describes it (2001, p. 158), which guides behaviour. The distinction between behaviour and rules—like that of agency and structure (Giddens 1986)—is contingent. Klijn explains: 'Through their sustained interactions actors create network structures: rules and resources that (will) have a structuring effect on future interactions in the network' (2001, p. 135). Network structures are then both constructed by, and constructive of, the behaviour of agents who make up a network. The rules described by Klijn, amongst other things, define the focus of collaborative activity, furnish actors 'with a sort of policy paradigm' (2001, p. 139), specify the position or status of actors in the network, and 'regulate the mode of interaction between actors' (2001, p. 140). By structuring the behaviour of agents, network rules influence the outcomes of collaborative activity.

Not all of the rules are constructed wittingly or unwittingly by actors in the network. Analysts have focused also on the rule-making activities of higher levels of government which sometimes direct the activities of existing networks or else require their creation in the first place. In a study of the Dutch fishery network, van Buuren and Klijn describe the EU's attempts to impose quotas, professionalize, liberalize, and raise environmental awareness. They conclude that the network was 'restructured' in an 'important way' by EU interventions (van Buuren and Klijn 2006, p. 411). The structuring activities of higher levels of government are, however, considered in the next section.

Perhaps the most important structural quality of a collaboration is its size. Larger collaborations should be able to call on a wider range of resources and in due course benefit from economies which result from a greater scale of production. Shortell et al. argue that the partnerships they studied needed to 'achieve sufficient size and heterogeneity to be seen as relevant and credible in their local communities' (2002, p. 65). They warn, however, that size brings with it 'significant management and policy implementation challenges involving coordination, communication, conflict management, priority setting, and monitoring activities' (2002, p. 65). Although stretching the definition of public service, Chan et al.'s analysis of the performance of eighty-five consortia of rural hospitals in the United States found a curvilinear-shaped relationship between the size of the consortia and the individual operating profits of the hospitals. They estimate that profits are maximized at a consortium size of forty-three; after this point they suggest that the complexity of coordinating a larger consortium results in increased costs from diseconomies of scale (Chan et al. 1999).

In a number of articles published over the last decade or so, Provan and Milward, and a number of other researchers, have investigated the performance effects of network integration. 'Integration', 'interconnectedness', or 'density' (Provan and Milward 1995, p. 10) can be measured 'through the commitment of network members to one another as reflected in their engagement in multiples types of links and exchanges' (Lemieux-Charles et al. 2005, p. 459).

In their path-breaking paper of 1995, Provan and Milward found that 'networks integrated and coordinated centrally, through a single core agency, are likely to be more effective than dense cohesive networks integrated in a decentralised way' (1995, p. 24). Building on this work, Provan and Sebastian argue: 'If networks are to perform well... integration must occur, but at the clique or subnetwork level. To be most effective, clique integration must be intensive involving multiple and overlapping links both within and across organizations that compose the core network' (1998, p. 460). Confirming their findings, Lemieux-Charles et al. conclude that 'centrality and multi-plexity seem to play the most significant roles in perceptions of network effectiveness' (2005, p. 463). Similarly Bazzoli et al. report that 'hospitals affiliated with centralized health networks had better financial performance when compared to hospitals in other types of networks' (2000, p. 247). But they warn that there were diminishing returns to 'centralization for system-affiliated hospitals' (Bazzoli et al. 2000, p. 248).

Considering similar issues under the heading of intensity, Nylen measures the extent 'to which cooperating parties are involved in each other's daily activities' (Nylen 2007, p. 146). On the basis of a study of seven human services collaborations in Sweden, Nylen reports that the benefits of intensity depend upon the nature of the collaborative endeavour. 'A low level of intensity might be quite sufficient when relatively simple sequential tasks are to be coordinated, whereas more complicated services for multi-problem clients require intense collaboration arrangements' (Nylen 2007, p. 164). Similarly, Hardy et al. found 'involvement among collaborators' to be the key to the acquisition of 'distinctive resources', while 'both involvement and embeddedness' was 'important for knowledge creation' (2003, pp. 337–9).

A number of studies have noted the benefits of formalization. Discussing the relative merits of incorporation, Weiner and Alexander (1998) point to a stronger identity, greater legitimacy, more autonomy in the receipt and distri-bution of funds, clarification of partner roles and responsibilities, and greater continuity. Nylen observes that the low levels of formalization are valuable in that 'input requirements are restrained', but that 'a certain degree of formal-ization is often necessary in order to implement collaboration practices across financial, professional and political boundaries' (2007, p. 164).

The question of 'who should be involved and how' is a key theme running through the partnership literature; Huxham and Vangen warn, however, that the meaning of membership is ambiguous, complex, and dynamic. It is often not clear who is in a partnership, who they represent, or how long they will be involved (Huxham and Vangen 2000*b*, p. 774–8). Nevertheless, it is frequently argued that the public, private, and voluntary sector agencies bring unique advantages to collaborative endeavour (Selsky and Parker 2005). Public sector partners may hold distinctive mandates or powers; private sector partners the ability to unlock finance or expertise; while non-profits are often credited with a greater capacity to communicate with excluded groups. In theory at least, cross-sectoral partnerships should enable public agencies to improve services by unlocking the comparative advantage of each sector.

Reviewing evidence from two case studies of public–private partnerships (PPPs), Grimshaw et al. question the promised performance gains of these arrangements pointing to imbalance of power between the public and private sector which put 'the private sector in the driving seat and enabled it to exploit the greater experience of working to contract and winning favourable terms' (Grimshaw et al. 2002 p. 499). Similarly, reflecting on a review of three Dutch PPPs, Klijn and Teisman conclude that 'PPP is an example of the right proposal at the wrong time. Real partnerships do not (yet?) fit in with the institutional rules, roles, and habits based on a public–private division at the beginning of the 21st century' (2003, p. 145). In a study of forty-six local authority services providers in Wales, Andrews and Entwistle found a positive association between respondents rating of public–public partnership and objective measures of service performance (Andrews and Entwistle, forthcoming). Public–Private partnership scores were negatively associated, and public–voluntary partnership showed no association with performance at all.

ENVIRONMENT

The final type of analysis reviewed in this chapter focuses on the environment of partnership activity. Environmental factors are distinctive in that they are beyond the control of partners in a network. Partnerships can adapt strategies and structures to their environment in a number of different ways, but they cannot expect to change the environment itself. This section is then concerned with the givens of partnership; Kenis and Provan describe them as exogenous (2008). Those considered here include the economic and institutional context, life-cycle, and policy context. A given for one partnership may, however, be negotiable for another. Mandated partnerships are, for example, often told how they should be structured, who their members should be, and indeed what they should do. In these cases, many of the factors considered in the previous sections could be regarded as exogenous to the partnership.

As perhaps would be anticipated, some of the work in this area confirms the importance of environmental variables identified by those looking at organizational environments (see Chapter 1). Provan and Milward confirm, for example, that 'adequate funding is critical for maintaining an effective system', but that 'high funding alone is insufficient to ensure favourable outcomes' (1995, p. 27). Similarly they find that 'instability brought on by attempts to make sweeping system wide changes in the funding and delivery of services can result in an ineffective system' (Provan and Milward 1995, p. 26). Johnston and Romzek describe instability prompted by contractual changes as imposing 'high organizational costs' on participating agencies and more importantly of 'undermining the progress of the child clients' (2008, p. 139).

Looking more broadly at the socio-economic profile of the local community, Chan et al. find that unemployment in the population served by the collaboration increases the costs and decreases the revenue per hospital admission. They note that these effects are much stronger, however, at the local hospital than at the aggregated consortium level (Chan et al. 1999). Bazzoli et al. found little by way of association between the 'munificence of local resources, underlying health conditions and partnership characteristics' (1997, p. 555). By operating at a higher level than many individual organizations, collaboration may serve to buffer from traditional socio-economic variables felt more keenly by small organizations.

One of the key rationales for partnership forms of governance is that of reaching out to previously marginalized or excluded groups. Studies focused on the inclusion agenda in partnership working have repeatedly found disappointing results (Lowndes and Sullivan 2004). Reflecting on the experiences of their case study partnership in East London, Perrons and Skyers argue that 'in the absence of transformative redistribution strategies', the formal mechanisms for inclusion used in these partnerships 'do little to redress the processes leading to the social disadvantage they are seeking to remedy' (2003, p. 282). Surveying a range of evidence, Jones questions whether 'we need to accept that participatory processes are therefore unlikely to alter social stratification within communities and may even reproduce it' (Jones 2003, p. 599). Studies of this kind seem to suggest that any attempts to use partnership-type vehicles as a way of engaging excluded groups are doomed by the structural power imbalances inherent in a capitalist economy.

The notion of a partnership life-cycle is one of the other staples of environment-type analysis. It has long been acknowledged in the general management literature that all attempts to organize go through a common life cycle of development (D'Aunno and Zuckerman 1987). Drawing on a large sample of private-sector alliances, Gulati suggests that 'cautious contracting gives way to looser practices as partner firms build confidence in each other'; 'familiarity', he concludes, does indeed 'breed trust' (1995, p. 105). Drawing on evidence from a sample of alliances between non-profit agencies, Isett and Provan argue however that 'contracts are necessary in a public sector context' and that formality therefore stays constant over time (2005, p. 162).

Lowndes and Skelcher similarly describe the delivery phase of partnership as highly formalized, relying on contracts to define the contributions of the different organizations (1998).

One of the consistent implications to emerge from life-cycle-type work is that the age of a collaboration matters. In their study of watershed partnerships Leach et al. report that 'one of the clearest findings is the positive relationship between each of the evaluation criteria and the age of the partnership' (p. 665). Partnerships cannot then be expected to achieve much in the early stages of their life-cycle, although given that almost all theorists suggest that there is a period where the basis of collaboration is reconsidered it seems unlikely that we can conclude simply that the older the collaboration the better the performance.

In a marked contrast to the alliance literature in private management, a great deal of work in public management has focused on the relationship between partnerships and higher levels of government. While governments have the authority to shape all organizational environments, they are particularly important in public management, because many partnerships are required or mandated by higher levels of government. In circumstances where networks are directed to a significant degree by higher levels of government, commentators talk of mandated collaboration (Rodriguez et al. 2007). There is then an additional dimension to collaboration in the public services as these higher levels of government try to persuade or direct partners to behave in particular ways. While the importance of government is uncontested, its effects are.

One perspective argues in simple terms, that while governments frequently use the rhetoric of a switch to new partnership forms of policy delivery, they continue in their choice of policy instruments to direct and regulate as if they were still operating hierarchically. As Taylor puts it: 'Despite the rhetoric, there is still too much evidence of top-down traditional control to create real optimism' (2000, p. 1033). Davies goes so far as to describe the partnerships to emerge from this landscape as little more than the 'bureaucratic conduits of government policy' (2002, p. 316). According to this line of analysis, partnerships fail to achieve their intended outcomes because hierarchical coordination from the centre crowds out trust and reciprocity on the ground (Entwistle et al. 2007; Hoggett 1996; Taylor 2000).

Diametrically opposed to this interpretation is one which sees networks or partnerships as benefiting from a strong lead from superior levels of government. Milward and Provan describe networks as 'inherently weaker forms of social action' (2000, p. 363); according to Rhodes, they 'resist government steering, develop their own policies and mould their environments' (Rhodes 1997, p. 46). Provan and Milward conclude from their 1995 study that 'systems in which external fiscal control by the state was direct, and to a lesser extent not fragmented, would be more effective than indirectly controlled systems in which allocation and control of state funding was delegated to a local funding authority' (Provan and Milward 1995, p. 25). As they explain, their findings contradict 'the prevailing wisdom that decentralized systems of fiscal control are best because they allow greater flexibility at the point of service delivery' (Provan and Milward 1995, p. 25).

Providing some support for these findings, Selden et al.'s study of collaboration in early childcare and education found that 'formalized performance standards and a national-level programmatic and professional support network' (2006, p. 416) had 'a positive and statistically significant impact on staff compensation, staff turnover and school readiness' (2006, p. 412). Selden et al.'s analysis seems to suggest that the more formally demanding the regulatory environment associated with the funding programmes, the better the outcomes.

Finally, those looking at the policy context of collaboration have questioned whether competitive institutional environments assist or hinder partnership. Bazzoli et al. did find that 'the presence and growth of HMOs [Health Maintenance Organizations in the United States] appears to be motivating partnerships to collaborate on identifying and reducing costly illnesses' reducing 'redundancies' and increasing 'efficiencies' (1997, p. 555). Competition may then act as a driver of collaboration. Entwistle et al. find however that 'rivalry between competing suppliers and the never-ending round of bidding for short-terms grants of small amounts of money are just as important as the dysfunctional effects of excessive bureaucracy' (2007, p. 76). Similarly, Johnston and Romzek describe the most unstable of the systems they studied as 'the most competitive and '"market-like"' (2008, p. 138).

Future prospects

The prominence of partnership forms of governance in public management is probably explained more by rhetorical appeal than concrete evidence of effectiveness. Partnership reforms are politically attractive because they promise new ways of dealing with old problems. There is nothing new about pursuing service improvement through reorganizing the scale and scope of service delivery; partnership just offers an apparently more palatable way of presenting these ambitions to key stakeholders. Although driven by considerations other than effectiveness, a large and rapidly growing literature has a lot to say about what makes partnerships tick. Of course, the literature has its limitations.

First and foremost of these is the shortage of studies which consider the outcomes of collaboration over time. Huge literatures consider the processes of collaboration, but there are still very few studies which establish whether collaborations deliver the public outcomes expected of them. Alongside the general paucity of studies of outcomes over time there is a dearth of studies which consider the effectiveness of partnership forms of organization relative to other forms of governance like hierarchical reorganization or contracting through competitive markets. Given the difficulty of conducting social experiments of this kind, it is not surprising that we know hardly anything about how partnership performs in comparison to its organizational alternatives.

Second, we need a more nuanced understanding of the determinants of effectiveness. Almost all of the theories of collaborative improvement emphasize variables which are likely to display a non-linear relationship to performance. Increased scale delivers reduced costs until diseconomies kick in. Trust is good until, as Klijn and Teisman point out, it leads to 'misrepresentation, asymmetric information, and opportunism' (2000, p. 92). The key question for collaboration research is not whether these things matter—clearly they do—but at what level and in what context are performance effects likely to be maximized?

An improved understanding of the individual ingredients of successful collaboration needs to go alongside an appreciation of how the different elements interact. There are already suggestions in the literature that the significance of the ingredients of partnership management depend upon the goals of collaboration. We know enough to conclude that a partnership focused on economies of scale can and should be very different from one focused on knowledge management and learning.

Gaps in our understanding of these issues lead to a confused prescription for good partnership governance. The behavioural or socio-psychological (Sarkar 2001) researchers point to the importance of equality, devolved authority, and trust. The structural-network researchers, however, underline the positive effects of a single coordinating agency. While these prescriptions are not necessarily contradictory, we need to be a lot clearer about the circumstances in which they hold true.

In doing this work, public management scholars need to reconsider the distinctiveness of their discipline. There are good reasons to think that much of the work on collaboration reads across the sectoral divide pretty well. There is no real reason why the two most distinctive benefits of collaboration—focused on learning through networks and economies of supervision—should manifest differently in public and private settings. There are, of course, areas of public sector distinctiveness. These are felt perhaps most strongly in multi-stakeholder perspectives of service improvement, the tendency for higher levels of government to require collaboration amongst its subsidiaries, and the suggestion that services will be improved through economies of scope or 'joining up' as the terminology has it. It is in these areas that public management researchers should focus their endeavours.

REFERENCES

6 Perry (2004). 'Joined up government in the western world in comparative perspective: A preliminary literature review and exploration'. *Journal of Public Administration Research and Theory* 14(1), 103–38.

Agranoff, R. (2008). 'Enhancing performance through public sector networks'. *Public Performance and Management Review* 31(3), 320–47.

—— McGuire, M. (2001). 'Big questions in public network management research'. *Journal of Public Administration Research and Theory* 11(3), 295–326.

—— —— (2003). *Collaborative Public Management: New Strategies for Local Governments*. Washington, DC: Georgetown University Press.

Andrews, R. and Entwistle, T. (forthcoming). 'Does Partnership Deliver? A Sectoral Assessment of Public Service Effectiveness, Efficiency and Equity'.

Andrews, R. and Entwistle, T. (2010). 'Does Cross-Sectoral Partnership Deliver? An Empirical Exploration of Public Service Effectiveness, Efficiency and Equity'. *Journal of Public Administraction Research and Theory*, forthcoming.

Bazzoli, G.J., Stein, R., Alexander, J.A., Douglas, A.C., Sofaer, S. and Shortell, S.M. (1997). 'Public private collaboration in health and human service delivery: Evidence from community partnerships'. *The Milbank Quarterly* 75(4), 533–61.

Bazzoli, G.J., Chan, B., Shortell, S.M. and D'Aunno, T. (2000). 'The financial performance of hospitals belonging to health networks and systems'. *Inquiry* 37(3), 234–52.

Chan, B., Feldman, R. and Manning, W.G. (1999). 'The effects of group size and group economic factors on collaboration: A study of the financial performance of rural hospitals in consortia'. *Health Services Research* 34(1), 9–31.

D'Aunno, T.A. and Zuckerman, H.S. (1987). 'A life-cycle model of organizational federations: The case of hospitals'. *Academy of Management Review* 12(3), 534–45.

Davies, J.S. (2002). 'The governance of urban regeneration: A critique of the "governing without government" thesis'. *Public Administration* 80(2), 301–22.

Dore, R. (1983). 'Goodwill and the spirit of market capitalism'. *British Journal of Sociology* 34(4), 459–842.

Edelenbos, J. and Klijn E-H. (2007). 'Trust in complex decision-making networks; a theoretical and empirical exploration'. *Administration and Society* 39(1), 25–50.

Eden, C. and Huxham, C. (2001). 'The negotiation of purpose in multi-organizational collaborative groups'. *Journal of Management Studies* 38(3), 372–91.

Entwistle, T., Bristow, G., Hines, F., Donaldson, S. and Martin, S. (2007). 'The dysfunctions of markets, hierarchies and networks in the meta-governance of partnership'. *Urban Studies* 44(1), 63–79.

Fung, A. (2006). 'Varieties of participation in complex governance'. *Public Administration Review* 66(1), 66–75.

Giddens, A. (1986). *The Constitution of Society*. Cambridge: Polity Press.

Grimshaw, D., Vincent, S. and Willmott, H. (2002). 'Going privately: Partnering and outsourcing in UK public services'. *Public Administration* 80(3), 475–502.

Gulati, R. (1995). 'Does familiarity breed trust? The implications of repeated ties for contractual choice in alliances'. *Academy of Management Journal* 38(1), 85–112.

Hardy, C., Phillips, N. and Lawrence, T.B. (2003). 'Resources, knowledge and influence: The organizational effects of interorganizational collaboration'. *Journal of Management Studies* 40(2), 321–47.

Hennart, J.F. (1988). 'A transaction cost theory of equity joint ventures'. *Strategic Management Journal* 9(4), 361–74.

Hicks, D., Larson, C., Nelson, C., Olds, D.L. and Johnston, E. (2008). 'The influence of collaboration on program outcomes'. *Evaluation Review* 32(5), 453–77.

Hjern, B. and Porter, D.O. (1981). Implementation structures: A new unit of administrative analysis. *Organization Studies* 2(3), 211–27.

Hoggett, P. (1996). 'New modes of control in the public service'. *Public Administration* 74(1), 9–32.

Huxham, C. (1993). 'Pursuing collaborative advantage'. *Journal of Operational Research Society* 44(6), 599–611.

——Vangen, S. (1996). 'Working together: Key themes in the management of relationships between public and non-profit organizations'. *International Journal of Public Sector Management* 9(7), 5–17.

—— —— (2000*a*). 'Leadership in the shaping and implementation of collaboration agendas: How things happen in a (not quite) joined up world'. *Academy of Management Journal*, 43(6), 1159–75.

—— —— (2000*b*). 'Ambiguity, complexity and dynamics in the membership of collaboration'. *Human Relations* 53(6), 771–806.

—— —— (2004). 'Doing things collaboratively: Realizing the advantage or succumbing to inertia?'. *Organizational Dynamics* 33(2), 190–201.

Isett, K.R. and Provan, K.G. (2005). 'The evolution of dyadic interorganizational relationships in a network of publicly funded nonprofit agencies'. *Journal of Public Administration Research and Theory* 15(1), 149–65.

Johnston, J.M. and Romzek, B.S. (2008). 'Social welfare contracts as networks: The impact of instability on management and performance'. *Administration and Society* 40(2), 115–46.

Jones, P. (2003). 'Urban regeneration's poisoned chalice: Is there an *Impasse* in (community) participation policy?'. *Urban Studies* 40(3), 581–601.

Keast, R., Mandell, M.P., Brown, K. and Woolcock, G. (2004). 'Network structures: Working differently and changing expectations'. *Public Administration Review* 64(3), 363–71.

Kenis, P. and Provan, K.G. (2009). 'Towards an exogenous theory of public network performance'. *Public Administration* 87(3), 440–456.

Klijn, E-H. (2001). 'Rules as institutional context for decision making in networks: The approach to postwar housing districts in two cities'. *Administration and Society* 33(2), 133–64.

——Skelcher, C. (2007). 'Democracy and governance networks: Compatible or Not?'. *Public Administration* 85(3), 587–608.

——Teisman, G.R. (2000). 'Governing public private partnerships', in S.P. Osborne (ed.), *Public Private Partnerships: Theory and Practice in International Perspective*. London: Routledge.

—— Teisman, G.R. (2003). 'Institutional and strategic barriers to public-private partnership: An analysis of Dutch cases'. *Public Money and Management* 23(3), 137–46.

Lasker, R.D., Weiss, E.S. and Miller, R. (2001). 'Partnership synergy: A practical framework for studying and strengthening collaborative advantage'. *The Milbank Quarterly* 79(2), 179–205.

Leach, W.D., Pelkey, N.W. and Sabatier, P.A. (2002). 'Stakeholder partnerships as collaborative policy making: Evaluation criteria applied to watershed management in California and Washington'. *Journal of Policy Analysis and Management* 21(4), 645–70.

Lemieux-Charles, L., Chambers, L.W., Cockerill, R., Jaglal, S., Brazil, K., Cohen, C., LeClair, K., Dalziel, B. and Schulman, B. (2005). 'Evaluating the effectiveness of community-based dementia care networks: The dementia care network's study'. *The Gerontologist* 45(4), 456–64.

Ling, T. (2002). 'Delivering joined-up government in the UK: Dimensions, issues and problems'. *Public Administration* 80(4), 615–42.

Lowndes, V. and Skelcher, C. (1998). 'The dynamics of multi-organizational partnerships: An analysis of changing modes of governance'. *Public Administration* 76(2), 313–33.

—— and Sullivan, H. (2004). 'Like a horse and carriage or a fish on a bicycle: How well do local partnerships and public participation go together?' *Local Government Studies* 30(1), 51–73.

Mathur, N. and Skelcher, C. (2007). 'Evaluating democratic performance: Methodologies for assessing the relationship between network governance and citizens'. *Public Administration Review* 67(2), 228–37.

McGuire, M. (2002). 'Managing networks: Propositions on what managers do and why they do it'. *Public Administration Review* 62(5), 599–609.

Milward, H.B. and Provan K.G. (2000). 'Governing the hollow state'. *Journal of Public Administration Research and Theory* 10(2), 359–79.

Mohr, J. and Spekman, R. (1994). 'Characteristics of partnership success: Partnership attributes, communication behaviour, and conflict resolution techniques'. *Strategic Management Journal* 15(2), 135–52.

Nylen, U. (2007). 'Interagency collaboration in human services: Impact of formalization and intensity on effectiveness'. *Public Administration* 85(1), 143–66.

O'Toole, J.R. and Meier, K.J. (2004). 'Public management in intergovernmental networks: Matching structural networks and managerial networking'. *Journal of Public Administration Research and Theory* 14(4), 469–94.

Perrons, D. and Skyers, S. (2003). 'Empowerment through participation? Conceptual explorations and a case study'. *International Journal of Urban and Regional Research* 27(2), 265–85.

Podolny, J.M. and Page, K.L. (1998). 'Network forms of organization'. *Annual Review of Sociology* 24(1), 57–76.

Prager, J. (1994). 'Contracting out government services: Lessons from the private sector'. *Public Administration Review* 54(2), 176–84.

Provan, K.G. and Milward H.B. (1995). 'A preliminary theory of network effectiveness: A comparative study of four community mental health systems'. *Administrative Science Quarterly* 40(1), 1–23.

—— —— (2001). 'Do networks really work? A framework for evaluating public-sector organizational networks'. *Public Administration Review* 61(4), 414–23.

—— Sebastian, J.G. (1998). 'Networks within networks: Service link overlap, organizational cliques and network effectiveness'. *Academy of Management Journal* 41(4), 453–63.

Rhodes, R.A.W. (1997). 'From marketisation to diplomacy: It's the mix that matters'. *Australian Journal of Public Administration* 56(2), 40–53.

Rodriguez, C., Langley, A., Beland, F., and Denis, J-L. (2007). 'Governance, power and mandated collaboration in an interorganization network'. *Administration and Society* 39(2), 150–93.

Sarkar, M.B., Echambadi, R., Cavusgil, S.T. and Aulakh, P.S. (2001). 'The Influence of Complementarity, Compatibility, and Relationship Capital on Alliance Performance'. *Journal of the Academy of Marketing Science*, 29(4), 358–373.

Selden, S.C., Sowa, J. and Sandfort, J. (2006). 'The impact of nonprofit collaboration in early childcare and education on management and program outcomes'. *Public Administration Review* 66(3), 412–25.

Selsky, J.W. and Barbara Parker, B. (2005). 'Cross-sector partnerships to address social issues: Challenges to theory and practice'. *Journal of Management* 31(6), 849–73.

Shortell, S.M., Zukoski, A.P., Alexander, J.A., Bazzoli, G.J., Conrad, D.A., Hasnain-Wynia, R., Sofaer, S., Chan, B., Casey, E. and Margolin. F.S. (2002). 'Evaluating partnerships for community health involvement'. *Journal of Health Politics, Policy and Law*, 27(1), 49–91.

Taylor, M. (2000). 'Communities in the lead: Power organizational capacity and social capital'. *Urban Studies* 37(5–6), 1019–35.

Thompson, G. (2003). *Between Hierarchies and Markets: The Logic and Limits of Network Forms of Organization.* Oxford: Oxford University Press.

Van Buuren, A. and Klijn, E-H. (2006). 'Trajectories of institutional design in policy networks: European interventions in the Dutch fishery networks as an example'. *International Review of Administrative Sciences* 72(3), 395–415.

Vangen, S. and Huxham, C. (2003a). 'Nurturing collaborative relations'. *Journal of Applied Behavioral Science* 39(1), 5–31.

—— —— (2003b). 'Enacting leadership for collaborative advantage: Dilemmas of ideology and pragmatism in the activities of partnership managers'. *British Journal of Management* 14(S), 61–76.

Warner, M.E. (2006). 'Inter-municipal cooperation in the U.S.: A regional governance solution?'. *Urban Public Economics Review* 6, 221–36.

Weiner, B.J. and Alexander, J.A. (1998). 'The challenge of governing public private community health partnerships'. *Health Care Management Review* 23(2), 39–55.

10 Organizational Learning

James Downe

Introduction

Theory from the private sector suggests that organizations need to be flexible, have the capacity for change, and learn what works and what does not if they are to remain competitive. Organizational learning is one approach which organizations can use to improve competitiveness and innovativeness. The concept was introduced in the early 1960s (Cyert and March 1963) as a response in Western countries to technological advancement and alternative forms of industrial organization (also especially in Japan) (Dodgson 1993), and a failure of organizations to improve services by implementing new practices.

There has been a focus predominantly on organizational learning in the private sector (on individual organizations and units within organizations) rather than the public sector. Private sector literature on organizational learning is wide and varied, from the case studies of two breweries in Mexico (Vera-Cruz 2006) to six European nuclear reactor sites (Jones et al. 2006). What these unusual examples show is that context is important. Organizations (and individuals within them) can learn in many different ways in different places. While there are differences between the private and public sector, some researchers suggest that public sector organizations are not qualitatively different from private sector organizations but are slower to change (Finger and Brand 1999). This slowness may be why public sector organizations need to make more use of the concept of organizational learning.

Various governments have introduced schemes to encourage the spread of good practice and learning across the public sector. In the United States, the Innovations in American Government programme has been recognizing and promoting excellence and creativity in the public sector for more than twenty years. In the United Kingdom, the government has introduced a number of mechanisms of inter-organizational learning such as peer review (Jones 2004, 2005), capacity-building programmes (Nunn 2007), and the Beacon Scheme (Downe et al. 2004; Rashman and Hartley 2002; Rashman et al. 2005). All of these initiatives aim to improve services through organizational learning.

This chapter begins by defining organizational learning and discussing the main themes of previous research on the concept. We then consider the implicit links between organizational learning and improvement in both the private and the public sectors. Organizational learning theory is discussed next, with a particular focus on enablers and barriers. Finally, the evidence on the links between organizational learning and improvement is analysed before the chapter concludes by assessing areas for future academic research.

Defining organizational learning

There has been a massive growth in the number of articles on organizational learning (OL) in the last couple of decades (see reviews by Crossan and Guatto [1996]; Easterby-Smith et al. [2000]) and there have been a number of journal 'special issues' on the subject (Easterby-Smith et al. 2000, 2004, 2008). But despite this extensive literature, there is no definition of OL which is universally agreed upon or consensus on how it occurs. In its simplest form, 'organisational learning involves the detection and correction of error' (Argyris and Schon 1996). Huber takes this definition wider by suggesting that 'an organisation learns if any of its units acquires knowledge that it recognises as potentially useful for the organisation' (1991, p. 126), and that OL is a combination of four processes: knowledge acquisition, information distribution, information interpretation, and organizational memory. It is these four factors which should have an impact on performance.

Research on organizational learning has covered a wide range of areas. Some papers have focused upon debates around definitions and areas of analysis (e.g. 'organizational learning' and the 'learning organization'). While organizational learning can be defined as the way organizations build, and organize knowledge and routines, and use the skills of their work-force to improve organizational efficiency, a learning organization is one that purposefully constructs structures and strategies to enhance and maximize organizational learning (Dodgson 1993). In other words, organizational learning is a process or a set of actions that an organization *does*, whereas a learning organization is something the organization *is* (Denton 1998). Some authors (e.g. Easterby-Smith and Araujo [1999]) have suggested that research on learning organizations is represented by consultants who focus on the design of models and methodologies for creating change in the direction of improved learning processes, while academics study the nature and processes of learning within organizations. This chapter focuses on organizational learning rather than the learning organization.

Knowledge management is an important aspect of organizational learning, and can be defined as 'any process or practice of creating, acquiring, capturing, sharing and using knowledge, wherever it resides, to enhance organisational learning and performance in organisations' (Scarbrough et al. 1999).

The majority of early literature on knowledge management focused on knowledge as an object and how it could be stored electronically. There is relatively little research on knowledge management in the public sector (Syed-Ikhasan and Rowland 2004) and this will not be the main focus of this chapter.

Other debates in the organizational learning field have concerned types of learning such as 'single-loop learning' (or adaptive learning) which is where errors are detected and corrected, and organizations continue with their present policies and goals; and 'double-loop learning' (or generative learning) which is more radical and may include a critical examination and change in an organization's norms, procedures, policies, and objectives. A number of papers have examined the nature of knowledge and whether it is tacit (which is personal, contextual, and often embedded in practice which makes it difficult to articulate, i.e. 'know how') or explicit (which concerns rules and facts that can be articulated and codified, i.e. 'know what'). The nature of knowledge is important, as it is the intersection between tacit knowledge and explicit knowledge that creates learning (Nonaka 1994). Literature has also focused upon the mechanisms by which learning is transferred. One such mechanism is a network where individuals come together in a collaborative arrangement to share knowledge and 'best practice'. Learning may also take place in a community of practice, which is a process of social learning that occurs when people who have a common interest interact regularly and share ideas and knowledge which lead to improvement (Lave and Wenger 1998).

Debates on the level of analysis have taken place for a number of years. While some argue that organizational learning is simply the sum of what individuals learn within organizations, others say that this is a mistake (Fiol and Lyles 1985). Hedberg (1981), for example, argues that organizations have memories which store certain behaviours, norms, and values, so that individual learning is captured in organizational policies, standard operating procedures, cultural norms, and organizational stories.

What seems to be clear from the literature is that there are three levels where learning takes place as knowledge spirals upwards from individuals, to groups, and then to the organization (Nonaka 1994). At each level there are different learning processes: intuiting at the individual level (where you question existing ways of working and present your own ideas), interpreting at the group level (involving feedback and discussion), and institutionalizing at the organizational level (when learning is imbedded in structures and routines) (Vera and Crossan 2004). The thinking here is that individual learning promotes organizational learning through knowledge being made explicit and shared with others.

This chapter will touch on a number of these debates in the organizational learning field (in particular the nature of knowledge being tacit or explicit and the level of analysis), but will concentrate upon the enablers and barriers to learning, as these are most important in determining whether learning leads to improvement. The next section moves on to examine organizational learning in the public sector, and then considers the links between organizational learning and improvement.

Organizational learning in the public sector

A wide range of initiatives have been introduced to improve the performance of organizations in the public sector. While there has been a particular focus on externally driven performance assessment such as regulation and inspection (see Chapter 2 in this edition), the last ten years have also seen the introduction of benchmarking and networks which assumes that organizations can learn from each other, on a voluntary rather than coerced basis, by examining their own performance and that of others. This recognition of learning as an approach to improvement in the public sector has, though, been dwarfed by the top-down approach to improvement adopted by some governments (Hartley et al. 2005).

In the UK public sector, the Beacon Scheme was introduced in local government in 1998 as a mechanism for organizations to learn from each other through the sharing of good practice and the provision of awards. In the health sector, collaborations (using a community of practice approach) have been introduced which aim to provide a bottom-up learning-based improvement process. Here, horizontal networks are set up which 'enable a wide range of professionals in a large number of organizations to come together to learn and "harvest" good practice from each other' (Bate and Robert 2002, p. 645). These collaboratives were adapted from the Institute of Healthcare Improvement's 'Breakthrough Series' in the United States.

There are important differences to note in terms of learning within health and local government. For example, in health, Currie et al. (2008) note the importance of cultures which cohere around professional boundaries rather than the organizational unit. This silo working and the often difficult relationship between professionals and managers can act as a barrier to learning. This seems to be more prevalent in health than in local government, and is supported by research carried out by Dopson (2006) which concluded from the health sector that it is difficult to transfer knowledge across professional boundaries that have grown up over time.

Research suggests that organizational learning can result from setting aside time for productive and purposive exchanges, allowing people the time to reflect (Senge 1999). The schemes adopted in local government and health suggest that this learning will lead to change in the organization and ultimately practical and measurable improvements in service delivery. This chapter continues by exploring the assumed link between organizational learning and improvement in the public sector.

Organizational learning and improvement

Organizational learning is a multistage process. First, individuals from organizations need to interact in a network (or similar) and be exposed to new ideas. The second stage is where knowledge is acquired by the individual and then taken back to their organization. The next stage is applying this new knowledge to the organization so that it leads to action or changes behaviour. The final stage is service improvement if the actions or changes in behaviour are superior to the original behaviour. In theory, this new knowledge brought into an organization can help to make better decisions, streamline processes, and improve collaboration which may lead to increased efficiency, innovation, productivity, and quality of service. In the private sector, this knowledge can provide a competitive advantage. Garvin concurs by suggesting that 'continuous improvement requires a commitment to learning' (2000, p. 78).

The literature on the link between organizational learning and service improvement is 'negligible' (Bate and Robert 2002). Ingram concluded that 'there are severe problems associated with the fact that we know little about the actual organizational practices that result in inter-organizational learning' (2002, p. 660). There are many reasons to explain why there is a lack of research on OL and improvement. For example, OL and tacit knowledge are difficult to measure and collecting appropriate measures is a complex and costly enterprise (Spector and Davidsen 2006). Larrson et al. suggest that 'it is much easier to develop and argue for a multi-dimensional, interactive, dynamic, and contextual framework conceptually than it is to test it empirically' (1998, p. 301). The link between learning and improvement is either assumed, implicit, or taken for granted. Part of the problem may be that organizational learning is both a process (learning at different levels, etc.) and an outcome (what have you learnt), and therefore it is difficult to determine the impact. Where there is research evidence, there has been an overemphasis on individual learning which means that analysis of learning and changes at the organizational level has been mostly ignored (Vince 2000). What seems to be important for some authors is the belief that organizational learning, in itself, is a good thing, regardless of whether there is evidence of actual improvement as a result.

While the concept of OL is difficult to define, it is even harder to determine whether it has taken place. It is said that organizational learning has taken place when organizations perform better (Dodgson 1993); these changes may include increased employee loyalty or reduced staff turnover. If learning takes place between individuals, groups, or organizations, the assumption is often that it will lead to action and improvement. Generally, where OL is examined, theory and practice focus on the positive aspects of learning. However, a culture of continuous change is not necessarily a positive thing, and just because a network is in place does not mean that learning has taken place. There can also be negative effects of learning such as the idea of 'unlearning', where the inability to forget acts as a barrier to learning (Hedberg 1981) and OL can be dysfunctional (Shipston 2006). Individuals may also learn and improve themselves, but this may not benefit the organization and lead to service improvement. The chapter continues by examining the theories which suggest why organizational learning should lead to increased performance in the public sector.

Theories of organizational learning and improvement

Organizational learning theory revolves around understanding the nature and processes of learning in organizations. What enables organizational learning to occur, and what factors act as barriers? There is no distinctive theory of OL, as there are different approaches from different disciplines (Easterby-Smith et al. 2000). One theoretical perspective is a socio-cultural or social constructionist approach to organizational learning where people learn through engagement and interaction with others and the resulting knowledge is tacit (Brown and Duguid 1991). Here, individuals do not learn alone, because learning is the product of a group experience. The context is important, as it shapes what is learnt and how it is learnt. The way to promote organizational learning according to this perspective is to recognize its tacit dimension and to support communities as they develop the mechanisms for sharing knowledge. Easterby-Smith et al. suggest that 'the most significant contribution of this new school was the emphasis—and legitimation—it gave to ethnographic and other research methods for investigating learning processes' (2004, p. 374), although, of course, generalizations from this type of research are difficult.

Literature on organizational learning and improvement suggests that there are a number of conditions that need to exist within an organization and between learning partners for the transfer of learning to occur (Child and Faulkner 1998; Finger and Brand 1999; Nahapiet and Ghoshal 1998). In order to understand organizational learning in both the private and the public sector, it is not simply the quality of the new knowledge that is important, but also the source of learning, the recipient of the learning, and the context (Rashman and Hartley 2002; Szulanski 1996).

A number of theoretical models have been designed which outline the relationship between the sender and the receiver of learning, and the processes and actions which lead to organizational learning and improvement. One such model shown below (Fig 10.1) suggests that both the donor and the recipient need absorptive capacity to recognize the value of new knowledge and use it (Easterby-Smith et al. 2008). Absorptive capacity is the preparedness of an organization to absorb external knowledge which is largely dependent upon prior knowledge and skills, including shared language, technical knowledge, and team functioning (Cohen and Levinthal 1990). The donor organization needs intra-organizational transfer capability so that it can disseminate the knowledge to the recipient in an effective way. The final factor which influences inter-organizational knowledge transfer is both the motivation to teach and learn from the respective partners. The nature of knowledge is also important, as various studies have shown that how the knowledge is stored (its tacitness), its ambiguity, and its complexity can all determine the success of organizational learning.

The inter-organizational dynamics are the factors which enable learning to be transferred. Easterby-Smith et al. (2008) suggest four main factors: power relations, trust and risk, structures and mechanisms, and social ties. These inter-organizational factors come from private sector research and not all are relevant for the public sector. We have already mentioned that power relations and trust between organizations are perhaps less of an issue in the public sector than in the private sector, although regardless of sectors, people are more likely to absorb knowledge from those they trust (Gambetta 1988). In

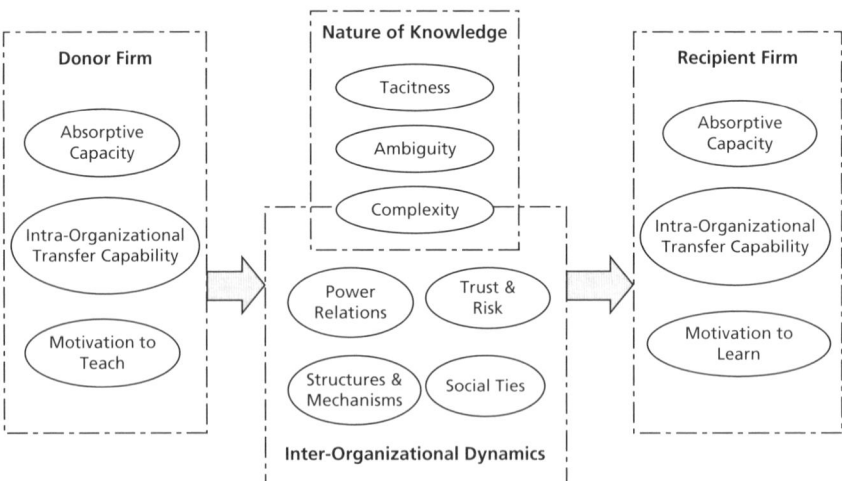

Figure 10.1 Factors influencing inter-organizational knowledge transfer (From Easterby-Smith et al. 2008)

Table 10.1 Summary of empirical evidence

Study	Dimension of learning	Country and sector	Sample and time period	Measure of performance	Finding
Currie, Waring and Finn (2008)	Nature and management of knowledge; power relations	England, National Health Service	Case study of a single university teaching hospital between 2000 and 2003	Impact of the introduction of a knowledge management system; Managers' perceptions of organizational learning and improvement	The knowledge management system is inappropriate for organizational learning. There are cultural and political problems in transferring learning
Denton (1998)	Structures and mechanisms; leadership and culture	England, private sector	Survey of 400 medium and large firms in England in the mid-1990s; Case studies of five companies	Managers' and author's perceptions of organizational learning and improvement	Organizational learning should be part of the toolbox for successful organizations as it represents an important route to competitive advantage
Downe, Hartley and Rashman (2004)	Nature of knowledge; structures and mechanisms; role of donor and recipient	England, local government	Survey of 386 local authorities and 12 case studies in 2001	Managers' perceptions of organizational learning and improvement	Beacon learning events are a successful means of sharing good practice and encouraging organizational learning in local government
Finger and Brand (1999)	Structures and mechanisms; levels of learning; role of context; leadership and culture	Switzerland, Swiss postal service	Case study of a single organization in 1992; Survey of the top 100 managers	Managers' perceptions of organizational learning and improvement	There are various indicators which can be used to measure progress towards being a learning organization
Hartley and Allison (2002)	Nature of knowledge; structures and mechanisms; levels of learning	England, local government	Survey and interviews within a network of 23 local authorities	Managers' perceptions of organizational learning and improvement	Participants in the network valued the exchange and transfer of tacit knowledge. Outputs from the networks are largely abstract and difficult to measure

(continued)

Table 10.1 Continued

Study	Dimension of learning	Country and sector	Sample and time period	Measure of performance	Finding
Naot, Lipshitz and Popper (2004)	Leadership; culture; role of context	Israel, Israel Defence Force	Case study of a single organization; Survey of 69 officers	Managers' perceptions of organizational learning and improvement	The outcomes of high quality organizational learning are effective lessons learned that are assimilated into the organization's mode of operation
Orthner, Cook, Sabah, and Rosenfeld (2006)	Structures and mechanisms; culture; leadership	US and Israel, education	19 after school programmes in two countries visited twice in an 18-month period in 2002–3	Used the Organizational Learning Assessment Scale—an instrument designed for this study	Organizational learning had a significant positive impact on performance in one of the two countries
Rashman, Downe and Hartley (2005)	Nature of knowledge; structures and mechanisms; role of donor and recipient	England, local government	Survey of 386 local authorities in 2001 and 2004; 12 case studies in 2001 and revisits to 5 cases in 2003	Managers' perceptions of organizational learning and improvement	Learning through Beacons is effective but is more modest than its potential
van Wijk, Jansen and Lyles (2008)	Nature of knowledge; inter-organizational dynamics	Meta-analytic review	Papers published on organizational knowledge transfer between 1991 and 2005	Antecedents of transfer grouped into knowledge, organizational, and network characteristics	Knowledge transfer increases both performance and innovativeness

addition, organizational learning is more likely to occur in an arena where there is trust, a willingness to take risks, and an acceptance that mistakes can be made. The remaining parts of this section assess these inter-organizational factors and others which enable organizational learning to take place in the public sector.

FACTORS WHICH INFLUENCE ORGANIZATIONAL LEARNING

The structure within which learning takes place is an important enabler. In the private sector the most common kind of structure or mechanism is an alliance (Inkpen 2005). Research has shown not only the growth of alliances as platforms for organizational learning as they provide access for imbedded knowledge in organizations, but also that differences in partners' skills and knowledge provide the catalyst for learning (Inkpen 2000; Zollo et al. 2002). Lane and Lubatkin (1998) conclude from their research on pharmaceutical alliances that a firm's ability to learn from another firm is dependent upon the similarity of both firms' knowledge bases, organizational structures, and dominant logics. Research in public services has come to the same conclusions, as there was also a preference for learning from similarly sized organizations facing similar issues (Downe et al. 2004).

In the public sector the focus is more on informal constructs such as networks (or similar), rather than alliances, to facilitate the transfer of knowledge from one organization to another. Networks (such as collaboratives in health) can be a good place where managers can come together to share knowledge, and there is some evidence to suggest that people learn more effectively in informal settings. The process of transfer is not easy, as there needs to be careful consideration of the most appropriate method of learning to transfer different types of knowledge (e.g. the increased use of site visits, mentoring, or shadowing to share tacit knowledge) (Dixon, 2000). In the public sector, where organizational learning occurs in networks, the focus is often on the donor organization offering the best practice for the recipients to learn. This means that there needs to be either altruism or an incentive for the donor unless they are also able to learn from others (Hartley and Downe 2007).

Although leadership is not specified as an enabler in its own right in Figure 10.1, strategic leadership is regularly cited as being an important variable in implementing organizational learning in firms (Vera and Crossan 2004) and in the public sector, leadership and leadership styles have also been found to be significant (Bate and Robert 2002; Finger and Brand 1999). Case-study research has shown that introducing change was often dependent upon an individual or a small number of individuals working together (Downe et al. 2004). These political or managerial champions are those tasked with coordinating knowledge transfer and generally making the learning happen. It does not matter who the champion is; what is important is whether the individual is able to influence, shape, and create the climate for change.

Social ties are another factor which enable learning to be transferred, and are likely to be important in all types of organization. Successful inter-organizational learning is more likely to happen where it is embedded in a collaborative relationship (Child and Faulkner 1998) and this relationship relies upon good social ties between participants. Where knowledge is tacit, learning can only take place where people are willing to share, and this is aided if there are good relationships between participants. Dopson found from the health sector that 'tacit and experiential knowledge is perceived by clinicians to be a persuasive form of knowledge' (2006, p. 85).

Research in the private sector has produced a wide range of enablers of organizational learning, including organizational culture. The culture of an organization is an important influence on its capacity to generate innovation and implement learning (Nonaka 1994), and needs to be supportive of knowledge management and transfer. Models of organizational learning also tend to stress the need to focus on the structure of the organization (Dixon 2000), resources and capacity, and team-working (Nonaka 1994). Technology is also viewed as an important enabler, but it is not the easy solution to organizational learning problems—'it makes connection possible, but it does not make it happen' (O'Dell and Grayson 1998). What makes organizational learning happen are the people creating, acquiring, and utilizing knowledge within the organization. Finally, the context is the key as it 'is an important and interacting element of the diffusion process' (Dopson 2006, p. 85). All of these private-sector enablers seem to be equally valid for the public sector too.

It is important to acknowledge that the enablers outlined above can of course be barriers. Where there is no trust between disparate members in a poorly designed learning structure, this will militate against organizational learning taking place. Is the public sector special? We mentioned above that culture is an important enabler for organizational learning, and some suggest that the bureaucratic characteristics and strong departmental cultures of the public sector mean that it can be resistant to learning (Common 2004). Bundred believes that the barriers to organizational learning in the public sector can be summarized as 'organizational and professional boundaries, lack of trust between professions, cultural tensions, and lack of awareness of the best practice from other parts of the public (and private) sector' (2006, p. 129).

A range of authors have considered the barriers to organizational learning. O'Dell and Grayson (1998), for example, outline four potential barriers to learning and change. They suggest that ignorance (e.g. individuals with knowledge, not realizing that others may find it useful); capacity (in terms of money and time); relationships (between people, and needing a critical mass of people); and motivation (no 'real' reason to transfer information) can act as barriers. These barriers and others can exist at different levels—at the individual level (getting the right people involved and ensuring that those who have the knowledge share it but recognizing that this requires time and effort) to the organizational level (where sharing learning needs to be part of an organization's culture).

Barriers can also include the attitudes of those involved in the learning. For example, Huxham and Hibbert (2004) suggest that there is a spectrum of sharing, from selfishly acquiring knowledge exclusively for the participant's own organization, thus *exploiting* a partner, to sharing knowledge with specific partners in a controlled pattern, thus *exchanging* with a partner, sharing knowledge in a broad open manner amongst a range of partners, thus *exploring* innovative solutions to problems in a collaborative way, and finally, sidelining any consideration of learning, thus *excluding* a partner. They found all four types of attitudes to learning in their research and each attitude will have a different effect on learning outcomes.

This discussion has shown that the key to understanding the success of organizational learning, and the impact on improvement is to consider the importance of the various enablers and barriers of learning. For successful knowledge transfer to take place there needs to be a focus not only upon the originating organization, but also the recipient organization. However, Figure 10.1 did not include an explicit link to improvement. Thus, we now need to consider literature which has further explored this relationship between organizational learning and service improvement.

One would have expected numerous studies to have analysed these factors which influence organizational learning to see their impact on improvement, but the literature has generally focused on a few factors and described their significance without testing them empirically. For example, Vera and Crossan (2004) developed a theoretical model which suggested that different types of leadership (both transactional and transformational) have a positive impact on organizational learning, and Skerlavaj et al. (2007) found a positive direct impact between organizational learning and non-financial performance. There seems to be no equivalent study examining the performance of public-sector organizations.

One paper, though, has examined the impact of various factors on organizational knowledge transfer using a meta-analysis of existing empirical research in the private sector (van Wijk et al. 2008). The authors found that knowledge ambiguity impacted negatively on organizational knowledge transfer; that is, the more tacit, specific, and complex the knowledge, the harder it is to transfer. They also found a positive relationship between absorptive capacity and knowledge transfer, so the amount of prior knowledge and skills in an organization helps in transferring learning between organizations.

Denton's large-scale survey (1998) of UK companies as well as in-depth case studies provides the most comprehensive account of the effectiveness of organizational learning. His research concluded that there are a large number of enablers of organizational learning which include having a flexible structure, leadership, commitment, or desire by top management, team-working, a blame-free culture, and a supportive atmosphere (all included in Figure 10.1 above). An index of enablers was constructed, and managers were asked in each case study to rate their performance on each variable. The research concluded by suggesting that there is a link between organizational learning and improvement, as the three most successful case studies best fit the ideal of the learning organization.

Evidence on organizational learning and improvement in the public sector

This section focuses solely on evidence from the public sector which principally comes from the United Kingdom and the United States. The most popular source of evidence on organizational learning comes from managers' perceptions using surveys (Table 10.1). Hartley and Allison (2002) used open-ended survey responses from an informal network to explore the extent of inter-organizational learning. They concluded that respondents could identify gains that they had achieved personally from attending the network such as new knowledge and having the opportunity to challenge current thinking. However, they could not easily identify how their organizations benefited from the network beyond reporting findings of the event back to colleagues. While there were reported intentions to introduce changes after attending the network, the paper, based on a small sample, leaves the crucial question of whether improvement occurred as a result of organizational learning largely as a topic for future research.

Two papers have attempted to assess the extent of organizational learning and change in public services by evaluating the effectiveness of the Beacon Scheme in UK local government (Downe et al. 2004; Rashman et al. 2005). The first paper (Downe et al. 2004) used a national survey of public managers (in 2000/1) to explore involvement in the Scheme, learning from events and the extent of change as a result of attending events. While the survey provided representative views of all local authorities, twelve in-depth case studies of local authorities provided further details on any changes implemented. The results suggest that learning has taken place but managers had not learnt as much as they had expected. Seventy-seven per cent of respondents expected to learn 'a fair amount' or 'a great deal' about 'developing new solutions to problems', but actual learning was lower, with most respondents (41%) learning only 'a little'.

More than a quarter of managers (26%) expected to learn a great deal about 'practical details on how to implement improvements', but only 5 per cent suggested that they learnt this much. Overall, more than half (55%) of attendees at learning events stated that they had made, or intended to make, changes to procedures after learning 'best practice' from other authorities.

The amount of learning and the impact on performance through the Beacon Scheme may have improved over time. The second paper by Rashman et al. (2005) showed that by 2004, the vast majority of respondents who had attended a learning event reported that they had made a change in their council which was attributable wholly or mainly to attending the network. Fifty-two per cent of managers have made 'improvements to working practices', and 38 per cent have 'introduced new working practices'. The case studies revealed numerous examples of service improvement. For example, in one authority, learning was brought back from an event and disseminated to staff using a variety of methods including a short report to senior managers and training sessions. As a result, new working practices were introduced which led to the clearing of a backlog of housing benefit claims, and the time taken to process the claims reduced. A government department has recently used this authority as an example of how to clear a backlog, so that the *recipient* of the learning from the award winner is now acting as the *donor* of learning for others to learn from.

Another organization saw a reduction of 25 per cent in youth annoyance after the introduction of a temporary building for local youth to use for activities—an idea copied from a nearby organization. In addition to these quantifiable improvements, the case studies also revealed qualitative changes such as shifts in organizational culture. Rashman et al. (2005) concluded that organizational learning is more effective where the culture of the organization is receptive, and where key 'champions' work well together. While confirming that learning has taken place and service improvement resulted, there are still numerous barriers to learning, such as work-load pressures (personal and organizational) and financial constraints to overcome. The paper concluded, in a similar way as Downe et al. (2004), that the service improvements are more modest than its potential.

In addition to using perceptual data from surveys, another popular research method in organizational learning is case studies—often a single organization case using interviews and observation. While there are some potential difficulties with single case studies, it does depend upon the quality of the academic analysis. Currie et al. (2008) have conducted an exhaustive methodological study focusing on the 'patient safety' policy agenda in the National Health Service (NHS) in England to see whether sharing knowledge (and the management of this knowledge) across organizational boundaries leads to improved services (e.g. reducing death by clinical error). They evaluated a new knowledge management system which gathered information about actual and potential threats to safety, and then analysed this information to identify the opportunities for organizational change. Their findings show that there are many difficulties in using a knowledge management system. First, the development of knowledge needs active, direct communication between people through networks or communities of practice (i.e. which could be categorized as being 'social ties' in Figure 10.1). Second, the system only captured explicit knowledge so that important tacit knowledge remains in the heads of the professional staff (i.e. structure/mechanism is important). Third, there was a perception from doctors that the process of incident reporting made little difference to improving performance within the hospital (i.e. lack of motivation). Fourth, sharing learning through the system was not successful because of wider cultural (e.g. level of trust between types of staff inhibiting knowledge sharing) and political (e.g. differential power relations between clinicians and managers) factors.

Outside the United Kingdom there are other notable papers which explore the relationship between organizational learning and improvement in the public sector. Naot et al. (2004) examined the quality of learning in the Israeli Defence Forces by assessing the conditions where organizations succeed or fail to learn from their experience (e.g. the death of a soldier during a training exercise). They used a questionnaire and in-depth interviews to explore episodes of post-accident reviews, and concluded that there are twenty-two indicators of high-quality organizational learning. Analysis of this framework suggests that organizational learning leads to improvement (measured by observed behaviour), where effective lessons learned are assimilated into the organization's mode of operation. Second, the key to getting commitment to the implementation and assimilation of the lessons learned is to gain the hearts and minds of the organization's members. Third, they found that leadership was the most important factor in determining the quality of OL. The usefulness of this research is the development of a framework, albeit from a unique military organization, that can be tested in other parts of the public sector.

Orthner et al. (2006) examined the impact of organizational learning on after-school programmes involving children classified as being 'at risk' in two countries—Israel and the United States. The researchers used a quasi-experimental design with control groups in both countries. Staff were trained in the treatment sites on the principles of organizational learning, and it was hypothesized that this training would lead to lower rates of behavioural problems. Staff were surveyed on structural (the amount of sharing and ability to test new ideas) and cultural (whether staff meet to learn from each other and set measurable outcomes to achieve) dimensions of organizational learning. Their results showed that there were fewer behavioural problems with children in programmes with trained staff in the United States but not in Israel (although the relationship was in the same direction). Staff who had received training in OL in both countries reported higher levels of staff satisfaction and empowerment than those in the control groups. This was a small exploratory study with only a subset of an organization as its unit of analysis, so it would be interesting if the research could be scaled up to the organizational level and whether it produces the same results.

As mentioned in the introduction to this chapter, attempts to use organizational learning to improve performance are not necessarily positive. Finger and Brand (1999) used training and seminars focused on internal and cultural transformation to assess the extent of organizational learning. They surveyed the top 100 managers of the Swiss Postal Service to critically evaluate any cultural obstacles to learning. The staff then worked in small groups with the authors to consider how these impediments could be removed. They concluded that while individual and collective learning took place, this was not connected to any organizational change or transformation. They conclude from their work that 'it is not possible to transform a bureaucratic organization by such learning initiatives alone' (1999, p. 146).

In another article, Betts and Holdern (2003) also found a failure to connect the individual, social, and organizational learning together in their case study of organizational learning. In this example, the organization failed to understand how individual learning might be made to work for their organization. This finding is similar to the experiences of Hartley and Allison (2002) discussed above. More research is needed, therefore, in defining indicators of individual and collective learning, and then seeing how this learning can be institutionalized at the organizational level.

Future research issues

This chapter has shown that there is now some agreement on the factors which influence organizational learning, but, to date, there has been little empirical research to investigate which measures are more important than others and lead to improvement. Too much time and effort has been spent on designing frameworks which are not linked to action. According to Garvin, the focus has been on 'high philosophy and grand themes, sweeping metaphors rather than gritty details of practice.... We need better tools for assessing an organization's rate and level of learning to ensure that gains have in fact been made' (2000, p. 79). Future research needs to ensure that key terms are clearly defined and operationalized and could also explore, not simply the degree of organizational learning, but also the speed and quality of knowledge transfer (van Wijk et al. 2008).

There has been reliance upon managers' perceptions of both organizational learning and improvement. For instance, the measures used to evaluate if the

Beacon Scheme had contributed to improvement included questions about whether it has increased confidence in being innovative and increased participation in joint action in partnerships, not how or whether it had impacted on service or organizational improvement. While surveys can offer some conclusions about the extent of *individual* learning in the public sector, it does not necessarily enable us to come to firm conclusions about *organizational* learning. What is needed, therefore, is a mix of quantitative and qualitative research methods. Longitudinal studies are also needed, as what may be effective in the short term may be ineffective in the longer term (Whitelaw et al. 2004).

Future research needs to test whether the models of learning developed and tested in the private sector have resonance in the public sector (Hartley and Benington 2006). There also needs to be further exploration on whether the 'best practice' being transferred is in fact the *best* the sector can offer or whether the winners of awards are simply better at completing the application process (Brannan et al. 2008; Hartley and Downe 2007). In the United States, the Malcolm Baldridge National Quality Award requires winning organizations to prove that their processes have positively affected the quality of outputs (Milakovich 2004), but this is not the case for all award schemes. More attention needs to be placed on providing the best support for both the provider of the learning and the recipients. For example, the provider may have excellent performance in a service, but it does not mean that they will be excellent at transferring this knowledge. For the receiver, research needs to consider which enablers of learning have the best chance of making an impact on performance.

Conclusions

Evidence on the impact of organizational learning on improvement seems to be more advanced in the private sector than in the public sector. We can infer from this that public service organizations have some catching up to do, and this is recognized by some authors. Bundred, for example, suggests that 'the failure to share knowledge and information has been the cause of serious public service failures' (2006, p. 125), and as a result of a blame culture in the public sector, organizational learning is impaired (Vince 2000).

Earlier in the chapter we explained that organizational learning is a multi-stage process. There is a significant amount of evidence on the earlier stages of this process where individuals from organizations interact in a network and take this new knowledge back to their organization. Researchers have also considered the ways in which this new knowledge is applied, but there has been little empirical analysis on whether this learning leads to service improvement, and this is particularly the case in the public sector. It seems that, following Huber's earlier definition (1991) of organizational learning, knowledge is often acquired, distributed, and possibly interpreted but it is not embedded by organizations, and for learning to occur it also needs to be transformed into action.

To understand whether organizational learning leads to improvement, we need to assess the nature of the knowledge, the characteristics of the source of learning, the recipient of the learning, and the context and the method of transfer. When the link between the organizational learning and improvement has been explored, the evidence is largely positive but often inconclusive. For example, Downe et al. (2004) and Rashman et al. (2005) have shown that the amount of learning and the impact on performance through an inter-organizational network has improved over time but its impacts are more modest than its potential. Similarly, Denton concluded from his research that 'it is difficult to attribute specific benefits to organizational learning but that it is probable that benefits do exist' (1998, p. 12). These are not very forceful conclusions, and clearly indicate that further research is needed to explicitly determine the link between organizational learning and public service improvement.

REFERENCES

Argyris, C. and Schön, D. (1996). *Organizational Learning II: Theory, Method and Practice.* Reading, MA: Addison-Wesley.

Bate, S. P. and Robert, G. (2002). Knowledge Management and Communities of Practice in the Private Sector: Lessons for Modernizing the National Health Service in England and Wales. *Public Administration* 80(4), 643–63.

Betts, J. and Holden, R. (2003). Organisational Learning in a public sector Organisation: A Case Study In Muddled Thinking. *Journal of Workplace Learning* 15(6), 280–7.

Brannan, T., Durose, C., John, P. and Wolman, H. (2008). Assessing Best Practice as a Means of Innovation. *Local Government Studies* 34(1), 23–38.

Brown, J. S. and Duguid, P. (1991). Organizational Learning and Communities of Practice: Towards a Unified View of Working, Learning and Innovation. *Organization Science* 2(1), 40–57.

Bundred, S. (2006). Solutions to Silos: Joining Up Knowledge. *Public Money & Management* 26(2), 125–30.

Child, J. and Faulkner, D. (1998). *Strategies of Co-operation: Managing Alliances, Networks and Joint Ventures.* Oxford: Oxford University Press.

Cohen, W. and Levinthal, D. (1990). Absorptive Capacity: A New Perspective on Learning and Innovation. *Administrative Science Quarterly* 25, 353–65.

Common, R. (2004). Organisational Learning in a Political Environment. *Policy Studies* 25(1), 35–49.

Crossan, M. and Guatto, T. (1996). Organisational Learning Research Profile. *Journal of Organizational Change Management* 9(1), 107–12.

Currie, G., Waring, J. and Finn, R. (2008). The Limits of Knowledge Management for UK Public Services Modernization: The Case of Patient Safety and Service Quality. *Public Administration* 86(2), 363–85.

Cyert, R. M. and March, J. G. (1963). *A Behavioural Theory of the Firm*. Englewood Cliffs, NJ: Prentice-Hall.

Denton, J. (1998). *Organisational Learning and Effectiveness*. London: Routledge.

Dixon, N. (2000). *Common Knowledge: How Companies Thrive by Sharing What They Know*. Boston, MA: Harvard Business Press.

Dodgson, M. (1993). Organisational Learning: A Review of Some Literatures. *Organization Studies* 14(3), 375–94.

Dopson, S. (2006). Why Does Knowledge Stick? What We Can Learn from the Case of Evidence-Based Health Care. *Public Money & Management* 26, 85–86.

Downe, J., Hartley, J. and Rashman, L. (2004). Evaluating the Extent of Inter-organisational Learning and Change Through the Beacon Council Scheme. *Public Management Review* 6(4), 531–53.

Easterby-Smith, M. and Araujo, L. (1999). 'Organizational Learning: Current Debates and Opportunities', in M. Easterby-Smith, J. Burgoyne, and L. Araujo (eds.), *Organizational Learning and the Learning Organization: Developments in Theory and Practice*. London: Sage.

—— Crossan, M. and Nicolini, D. (2000). Organizational Learning: Debates Past, Present and Future. *Journal of Management Studies* 37(6), 783–96.

—— Antonacopoulou, E., Simm, D. and Lyles, M. (2004). Constructing Contributions to Organizational Learning: Argyris and the Next Generation. *Management Learning* 35(4), 371–80.

—— Lyles, M. and Tsang, E. (2008). Inter-Organizational Knowledge Transfer: Current Themes and Future Prospects. *Journal of Management Studies* 45(4), 677–90.

Fiol, C. M. and Lyles, M. A. (1985). Organizational Learning. *Academy of Management Review* 10(4), pp. 808–13.

Finger, M. and Brand, S. (1999). 'The Learning Organization in the Public Sector', in M. Easterby-Smith, J. Burgoyne, and L. Araujo (eds.), *Organizational Learning and the Learning Organization: Developments in Theory and Practice*. London: Sage.

Gambetta, D. G. (ed.) (1988). *Trust: Making and Breaking Cooperative Relations*. New York: Basil Blackwell.

Garvin, D. A. (2000). Building a Learning Organization. *Harvard Business Review* 71(4), 78–91.

Hartley, J. and Allison, M. (2002). Good, Better, Best. *Public Management Review* 4(1), pp. 101–18.

—— and Benington, J. (2006). Copy and Paste, or Graft and Transplant? Knowledge Sharing Through Inter-Organizational Networks. *Public Money & Management* 26(2), 101–8.

—— and Downe, J. (2007). The Shining Lights? Public Service Awards as an Approach to Service Improvement. *Public Administration* 85(2), 329–53.

—— Rashman, L., Radnor, Z., and Morrell, K. (2005). 'Rich aunts and poor cousins: A comparison of service improvement through audit and inspection and through sharing good practice'. Paper presented at the International Research Symposium on Public Management, Bocconi University, Italy, April 2005.

Hedberg, B. (1981). 'How Organisations Learn and Unlearn', in P. C. Nystrom and W.H. Starbuck (eds.), *Handbook of Organizational Design*. London: Oxford University Press, pp. 3–23.

Huber, G. P. (1991). Organizational Learning: The Contributing Process and the Literatures. *Organization Science* 2(1), 88–115.

Huxham, C. and Hibbert, P. (2004). *Collaborating to Know: Interorganizational Engagement and Learning*. London: Advanced Institute of Management Research.

Ingram, P. (2002). 'Inter-organizational Learning', in J.A.C. Baum (ed.), *Companion to Organizations*. Oxford: Blackwell.

Inkpen, A. C. (2005). Learning Through Alliances: General Motors and NUMMI. *California Management Review* 47(4), 114–36.

Inkpen, A. C. (2000). Learning Through Joint Ventures: a Framework of Knowledge Acquisition. *Journal of Management Studies* 37(7), 1019–43.

Jones, B., Cox, S., Wahlström, B., Kettunen, J., Reiman, T. and Rollenhagen, C. (2006). A comparison of organisational learning practices at nuclear sector sites in Finland, Sweden and the UK. In C. G. Soares and E. Zio (eds.), *Safety and Reliability for Managing Risk*, pp. 341–46. London: Taylor and Francis.

Jones, S. (2004). Improving Local Government Performance: One Step Forward Not Two Steps Back. *Public Money & Management* 24(1), 47–55.

——— (2005). Five Faults and a Submission: The Case for the Local Government Improvement Programme. *Local Government Studies* 31(5), 655–76.

Lane, P. J. and Lubatkin, M. (1998). Relative Absorptive Capacity and Inter-organisational Learning. *Strategic Management Journal* 19, 461–77.

Larrson, R., Bengtsson, L., Henriksson, K. and Sparks, J. (1998). The Interorganizational Learning Dilemma: Collective Knowledge Development in Strategic Alliances. *Organization Science* 9(3), 285–305.

Lave, J. and Wenger, E. (1998). *Communities of Practice: Learning, Meaning and Identity*. Cambridge: Cambridge University Press.

Milakovich, M. E. (2004). Rewarding Quality and Innovation: Awards, Charters, and International Standards as Catalysts for Change. *Lecture Notes in Artificial Intelligence [subseries of Lecture Notes in Computer Science]* 3055, pp. 67–74.

Nahapiet, J. and Ghoshal, S. (1998). Social Capital, Intellectual Capital, and the Organizational Advantage. *Academy of Management Review* 23(2), 242–66.

Naot, Y. B-H., Lipshitz, R. and Popper, M. (2004). Discerning the Quality of Organizational Learning. *Management Learning* 35(4), 451–72.

Nonaka, I. (1994). A Dynamic Theory of Organizational Knowledge Creation. *Organization Science* 5(1), pp. 14–37.

Nunn, A. (2007). The Capacity Building Programme for English Local Government: Evaluating Mechanisms for Delivering Improvement Support to Local Authorities. *Local Government Studies* 33(3), 465–84.

O'Dell, C. S. and Grayson, C. J. (1998). *If Only We Knew What We Know: The Transfer of Internal Knowledge and Best Practice*. New York: Free Press.

Orthner, D. K., Cook, P., Sabah, Y. and Rosenfeld, J. (2006). Organizational learning: a cross-sectional pilot-test of effectiveness in children's services. *Evaluation and Program Planning* 29, 70–78.

Rashman, L. and Hartley, J. (2002). Leading and Learning? Knowledge Transfer in the Beacon Council Scheme. *Public Administration* 80(3), 523–42.

—— Downe, J. and Hartley, J. (2005). Knowledge Creation and Transfer in the Beacon Scheme: Improving Services Through Sharing Good Practice. *Local Government Studies* 31(5), 683–700.

Scarbrough, H., Swan, J. and Preston, J. (1999). *Knowledge Management: A Literature Review.* London: Institute of Personnel and Development.

Senge, P. (1999). *The Fifth Discipline: The Art and Practice of the Learning Organization.* New York: Doubleday.

Shipston, H. (2006). Cohesion or Confusion? Towards a Typology for Organisational Learning Research. *International Journal of Management Reviews* 8(4), 233–52.

Skerlavaj, M., Stemberger, M. I., Skrinjar, R. and Dimovski, V. (2007). Organisational Learning Culture: The Missing Link Between Business Process Change and Organisational Performance. *International Journal of Production Economics* 106, 346–67.

Spector, J. M. and Davidsen, P. I. (2006). How Can Organisational Learning Be Modelled and Measured? *Evaluation and Program Planning* 29, 63–9.

Syed-Ikhasan, S. O. S. and Rowland, F. (2004). Knowledge Management in a Public Organisation: A Study on the Relationship Between Organizational Elements and the Performance of Knowledge Transfer. *Journal of Knowledge Management* 8(2), 95–111.

Szulanski, G. (1996). Exploring Internal Stickiness: Impediments to the Transfer of Best Practice Within the Firm. *Strategic Management Journal* 17, 27–43.

van Wijk, R., Jansen, J. J. P. and Lyles, M. A. (2008). Inter- and Intra-Organizational Knowledge Transfer: A Meta-Analytic Review and Assessment of its Antecedents and Consequences. *Journal of Management Studies* 45(4), 830–53.

Vera, D. and Crossan, M. (2004). Strategic Leadership and Organisational Learning. *Academy of Management Review* 29(2), 222–40.

Vera-Cruz, A. O. (2006). Firms' Culture and Technological Behaviour: The Case of Two Breweries in Mexico. *International Journal of Technology Management* 36(1–3), 148–65.

Vince, R. (2000). Learning in Public Organizations. *Public Money & Management* 20, 39–44.

Whitelaw, S., Watson, J. and Hennessy, S. (2004). Promoting Health in Hospitals: The Role of Beacons. *Health Education* 104(5), 272–80.

Zollo, M., Reuer, J. J. and Singh, H. (2002). *Interorganizational Routines and Performance in Strategic Alliances.*

11 Reflections on Theories of Public Service Improvement

Rachel Ashworth, George Boyne, and Tom Entwistle

Introduction

This collection has presented the first assessment of the theoretical and empirical validity of a variety of mechanisms that have been used in attempts to generate improvements in public services over the past twenty years. We have provided a series of chapters which have undertaken systematic and critical literature reviews in order to unpack the underlying theoretical basis of each strategy for improvement, and ascertain whether predictions of improvement logically flow from these theoretical assumptions. As many of the mechanisms of public service improvement originate from the private sector, a key test of these theoretical assumptions has been whether their subsequent application to a public service context can be considered to be appropriate. In addition, the chapters have all considered a critically important question: whether there is any empirical evidence to support the theoretical prediction of relationships between this series of mechanisms and improvements in public services. Finally, each chapter has offered an outline of a future research agenda for exploring the validity of each theory.

This closing chapter has three main aims. Firstly, it draws together and summarizes the main findings and conclusions from across the collection in order to identify which mechanisms can be linked theoretically to service improvement and, on the basis of the evidence, are linked to better performance. Secondly, the chapter seeks to highlight the key features of research conducted to date on public service improvement, such as, for example, what methods have been predominantly employed, which sectors and countries were studied, and the theories that have been most researched in recent years. Finally, the chapter reflects upon the state of knowledge on public service improvement and outlines a future research agenda for public management scholars.

Mechanisms of public service improvement: theories and evidence

In Chapter 1 of this collection we defined service improvement as 'a closer correspondence between perceptions of actual and desired standards of public services' (Boyne 2003, p. 223). However, we acknowledged that this definition raised a series of questions around perceptions of improvement and standards of public services. We argued that we need to consider which criteria different groups of stakeholders use in order to make a judgement on service performance, how these criteria are determined, and how they vary across groups (according to gender, ethnicity, income etc.), and how closely performance improvements, as defined by central governments in the form of movement against performance indicators and targets, relate to stakeholder perceptions of improvement, such as levels of public satisfaction with services. We then outlined the characteristics of a good theory of public service improvement which should

- be able to explain variations in service standards, and elaborate on why some organizations perform to a higher degree than others;
- be clear about both why and how a particular mechanism or strategy drives improvement, and whether additional variables moderate its effect;
- be able to be further assessed and tested on the grounds of correspondence with empirical evidence.

A lack of theoretical specificity, doubts surrounding underlying theoretical assumptions, issues of causal direction, and a lack of supporting empirical evidence, while not of themselves grounds for invalidation, could shed doubt on several established theories of public service improvement. Therefore, it is important that we further review the theoretical perspectives explored within each chapter in order to evaluate (*a*) the plausibility of underlying theoretical assumptions and (*b*) the extent of supporting empirical evidence.

THE PLAUSIBILITY OF UNDERLYING THEORETICAL ASSUMPTIONS

The chapters in this book reveal variations in the clarity and logic of the theoretical underpinnings of different approaches to public service improvement. Nevertheless, for the most part, there are clear and plausible assumptions about the theoretical relationships between the series of mechanisms identified in this collection and the improvement of public services. For example, Chapters 2–4 demonstrate that the nature of an organization's environment, the degree of regulation to which it is subject, and the extent of strategic planning can all be plausibly linked to improvement. In other instances, theoretical connections between the mechanisms and improvement were a little more problematic. This was most evident in Chapter 6 on culture, which revealed that the key assumption underpinning the culture–performance link—the argument that organizational culture is something an organization 'has' which can be manipulated and managed in order to improve performance—remains under debate.

Closer reading of the chapters revealed a number of important theoretical issues which merit further discussion. The first concerns the degree of fit between theory and public sector context. Many of the theoretical perspectives reviewed for this collection had been originally developed and modelled on the behaviour and performance of private firms, and have only been applied to a public service context relatively recently. Clearly some of these perspectives, and their associated assumptions, have transferred more easily to the public sector than others. There have been instances where policy and practice have moved way in advance of academic work, and consequently there has been little explicit specification of theoretical effects relevant to public sector circumstances.

For example, some chapters revealed concerns around the operationalization of key concepts and the development of typologies, arguing that these have not always been appropriate for a public sector context (see Chapter 6 on culture and Chapter 9 on collaboration, for example). Indeed, several authors felt the need to elaborate specifically public sector theories improvement. Gould Williams, for example, in Chapter 7 offers us a Public Service HR Model which incorporates the service need priorities of public organizations, the specific organizational context and climate associated with the public sector, and employee and managerial perceptions. A similar model is presented in Chapter 8 on innovation where Walker presents initial thoughts on the relationships between internal and external organizational determinants, and the diffusion and adoption of innovation in the public sector.

Entwistle's analysis of collaboration in Chapter 9 suggests that while parts of the management literature read across the sectoral divide pretty well—the benefits of common goals, trust, and communications, for example—the private management literature has little to say about the theory of joining-up or mandated partnership. In these areas, at least, public management researchers cannot assume that the benefits of alliances documented in private management will necessarily be realised in public management. There is indeed a need for distinctive theories of public service improvement in these areas. Taken together the evidence considered here suggests that public management scholars need to give careful attention to the theoretical models of service improvement underlying particular interventions. More work is needed to ensure that theoretical models are applied carefully, and adapted where necessary, to ensure a better fit to the public service context.

A second issue concerned the nature of causality. In cases, such as HRM, innovation and leadership, the relationship between mechanism and improvement was found to be a little fuzzy, raising issues of causal direction. Here there were doubts as to whether more innovation, strong leadership, and particular bundles of HR practices lead to improvements in services or whether high-performing organizations tend towards being innovative, adopt HR practices, and are characterised by a particular leadership style. For example, Gould Williams cites evidence on reverse causality which reveals that organizational success leads to an increase in job satisfaction. Walker also presents reverse causality as a key unresolved issue which he argues acts as a significant impediment to the development of better theory and insightful policy advice on innovation in the public sector. Chapter 10 on organizational learning is characterized by similar concerns. In the absence of an explicit theoretical model of organizational learning and service improvement, Downe proceeded to isolate various conditions believed to facilitate organizational learning. Whether these conditions are mere associations or causes of learning, change, and improvement is at this stage unclear.

Future studies need to develop research designs that deal with the issue of reverse causality, at a minimum by including a lag between the measurement of the explanatory and dependent variables. Beyond this, a simple but useful strategy is to include an autoregressive term in statistical models, so that the performance baseline is taken into account when assessing the impact of mechanisms such as innovation and HRM.

The third issue relates to the unintended theoretical effects highlighted within a number of chapters. For example, Boyne reviewed the contradictory nature of the theoretical arguments around planning which include the potential 'decoupling' of planning from real organizational decision-making, the effects of planning on organizational commitment, and possible displacement of activity resulting from the excessive pursuit of targets. Martin discusses similar effects in terms of regulatory systems in the public sector which might provide 'false reassurance and introduce perverse incentives'. It is clearly possible to imagine scenarios where a greater emphasis might result in poorer performance, as Downe demonstrates in Chapter 10, where he considers the negative consequences of organizational learning. These issues are considered further in the next section on supporting empirical evidence which considers whether any of these effects are observed in practice, and draws tentative conclusions on whether performance has worsened as a result.

THE EXTENT OF SUPPORTING EMPIRICAL EVIDENCE

There were clear variations in terms of the strength of conclusions on whether various theoretical mechanisms had an effect on public service improvement.

The evidence indicates that a number of mechanisms (or aspects of them), lead to better public services. For example, Andrews firmly indicates that the nature of the organizational environment has an impact on whether public services improve, although he does add that this judgement is based largely on the analysis of long-term rather than short-term (e.g. annual) changes in environmental circumstances. Similarly, Chapter 7 reports that HRM is likely to be positively related to organizational performance measures. Judgements on the impact of strategic planning, organizational learning, and regulation are all positive too. For example, Boyne suggests 'that planning is likely to have a positive rather than negative impact on public service effectiveness', whilst Downe finds some support for a link between organizational learning and improvement.

Martin concludes that the impact of regulation and inspection is positive in that it leads to improvements in internal structures and processes, although he emphasises that whether these changes lead to improved services is 'far from guaranteed' (p. 54). The same judgement is reached in relation to leadership. Entwistle is more tentative, pointing to positive evidence of improvement in some dimensions of partnership, but doubts and concerns in others. Walker concludes that 'the extent to, and the way in which, it (innovation) impacts on performance remains opaque', while Ashworth finds that, overall, evidence on the link between culture and service improvement in the public sector is mixed.

It is possible to identify a number of common themes emerging from the evidence reviewed in the collection which have important implications for future work on public service improvement. The first concerns the import-ance of external constraints. The evidence indicates that the organizational environment is especially significant for service improvement in the public sector. Theoretical specification is clear and convincing, and the empirical evidence is overwhelmingly supportive of a connection, much more so than in relation to any other mechanism. This would seem to suggest that it is the characteristics of the external environment—the aspects that are at the great-est distance from the organization—that can determine whether services improve or not. In contrast, those variables over which the organization can exercise greater control, such as leadership, innovation, even strategy, do not demonstrate the same consistent impact on service improvement. There could be a number of explanations for this. For example, it may be more straightforward to measure the impact of environmental characteristics as, unlike leadership and culture, measurement relies less heavily on employee perceptions. Nevertheless, the importance of the environment is clear, and as Andrews argues in Chapter 2, it should be acknowledged and incorporated within any theory of public service improvement. However, a key question concerns the role of managers in interpreting and 'enacting' the environment they face. As Andrews intimates, this might involve developing strategies to proactively engage with certain stakeholders or to shape central government policies. This is an area which remains considerably under-researched in terms of public services, and the evidence presented here suggests there is an urgent need to examine how organizations and their managers might shape and enact environments that are more likely to deliver improvements to services.

Secondly, many chapters highlight the importance of contextual and contingent variables, with most focusing on the importance of internal contingencies, such as leadership, management, organizational culture, and so on. For example, Martin cites 'clear evidence' associating effective inspection with an ability to respond, determined by leadership and management capacity, whilst Boyne recommends that we need to learn more about the links between corporate capacity, employee engagement, and the effects of the planning process.

The chapters reflect a concern to emphasize the importance of *external* contingencies—most notably the organizational task environment and the extent of its moderating influence.

Furthermore, the nature of the institutional environment is also important here—in particular the question of whether organizations are developing, adopting, and implementing certain processes that are regarded as appropriate in order to gain wider legitimacy within their institutional field. For example, one of the most consistent themes of the UK partnership literature—as Entwistle explains in Chapter 9—is the claim that local collaborative activity is frustrated by the coercive attentions of higher levels of government. Further work on service improvement informed by institutional theory might help us gain a greater understanding of the extent to which these processes and practices are firmly embedded within public organizations.

Finally, as highlighted above, several chapters were at pains to point to potential unintended consequences which might disrupt organizational activities and slow down service improvement. Although there was some evidence reporting perceived negative effects (see Chapter 3 on regulation, for example) there was no empirical evidence to suggest that aspects such as regulation, planning, innovation, and HRM contributed to lower levels of performance. In other cases, such as collaboration and organizational learning, there was too little evidence to draw any firm conclusions on this. Overall, we must conclude at this stage that there is little evidence to support the view that any unintended consequences have proved to be so significant that they have actually outweighed efforts to improve services.

To summarize, the evidence demonstrates that, of the nine mechanisms applied by policy-makers and politicians to secure improvement, five—an organization's environment, HRM, strategic planning, collaboration, and regulation—can be linked to service improvement. A further four—innovation, organizational learning, culture, and leadership—have some positive impact on service improvement, but the evidence is either limited or mixed. Thus a 'best guess' on the basis of the current empirical evidence is that the most promising strategies for public service improvement are to alter organizational environments, develop HRM strategies and practices, adopt a planning process, engage in collaborative ventures with other organizations, and design a regulatory regime that is responsive to the characteristics of service providers. By contrast, an emphasis on leadership, innovation, more organizational learning, and changes in organizational culture appear to be more risky strategies that have uncertain prospects for public service performance, despite their current appeal to policy-makers in various nations. However, it is vitally important that these conclusions are placed in context, as the nature of the empirical evidence base itself might undermine the certainty of any conclusions drawn on the validity of theories of public service improvement. Therefore, the next section of the chapter discusses the nature of the existing empirical evidence.

Characteristics of the evidence on public service improvement

There are variations in the extent of available empirical evidence across the theories of public service performance. It is worth noting a number of features of the empirical work published to date at this stage. The first point to note is that, compared to equivalent work based on private firms, empirical evidence tends to be thin on the ground. The chapters reveal that there have been few comprehensive studies of leadership, strategic planning, organizational culture, innovation, organizational learning, and so on, conducted within a public sector context, and even fewer studies that make a connection between these mechanisms and improved public services. Despite the application of fairly generous search criteria (specified in Chapter 1), studies of improvement identified within chapters ranged from twenty-six on partnership governance, to just seven on organizational learning, and a mere four for innovation—evidence of what is described by Walker as a 'glaring gap in our knowledge'.

A further point of observation is that the range of evidence available is further limited by the context under study; for example, the vast majority of empirical studies based their research within the United States, United Kingdom, or another Western country. Furthermore, much of the evidence in relation to each mechanism is sector-specific. The majority of evidence on the impact of the organizational environment is drawn from a batch of Cardiff studies and is therefore based on UK local government, whilst a large volume of the work on the culture–performance link has been conducted on health-care organizations in the United States and United Kingdom. Similarly, the review of evidence on the effects of strategic planning is based almost exclusively on UK/US studies of local/state government. The chapters identified very little work on key areas of the public sector, such as social services and the police service, whilst work on education and health is piecemeal. Thus, we have to acknowledge that the existing evidence on mechanisms of public service improvement is limited but also partial, as it presents data from a narrow selection of public service organizations within a small range of countries.

An additional point to remark upon is the considerable degree of uniformity in terms of the methodological approach applied within studies of improvement. Whilst there were many qualitative studies based within a public service context, overall, much of the work linking mechanisms to improvement was quantitative in nature. Typically, these studies reported multivariate analyses of the impact of mechanisms on the performance of public service organizations over a fairly short time period. Dimensions of each mechanism of improvement have been operationalized and measured, mainly through large-scale questionnaire surveys, and tested against measures of organizational performance.

This kind of study has produced large-scale and representative analyses of the relationship between various improvement mechanisms and subsequent performance, and some have also included mediating variables. However, in almost every chapter the author has raised concerns about the ways in which both explanatory variables and service performance improvement have been operationalized in many of these studies. Chapters 5, 6, and 10 go further to highlight the view that questionnaire surveys are not necessarily the best way to capture data on the nature of leadership, learning, and culture, due to the nature of the phenomenon under investigation. However, given those criticisms, the lack of qualitative evidence on service improvement is striking. As stated earlier, there are many studies of organizational culture, leadership, organizational learning, and so on, that have been conducted in the public sector and draw on qualitative data. However, these pieces tend to be process-oriented, and there is little explicit, or even implicit, reference to any likely improvement outcomes or effects; often it is left to the reader to speculate. As Martin indicates, often these studies focus on the perceptions of key actors (such as those working in public services subject to regulation) and not other stakeholders such as service users or the regulators themselves.

Each of the chapters demonstrates that existing studies only offer a partial interpretation and examination of the mechanism in question. It seems the evidence cannot be used to underpin a definitive judgement, because it is incomplete in various ways. For example, it is argued in Chapter 8 that the study of innovation to date has privileged the early stages of the innovation process—that is, adoption—whereas any assessment of the impact of innovation on performance is more likely to be accurately understood through an examination of the subsequent management and implementation of innovation. Downe in Chapter 10 makes a similar point in relation to the early stages of the organizational learning process. Other chapters revealed that studies often prioritize a particular dimension of a theory, thereby ignoring others. So work on strategic planning, for example, has tended to focus on two dimensions: goal clarity and performance targets, with Boyne reminding us that his conclusions can only be considered in relation to the two dimensions most frequently studied, and calling for more evidence on the impact of other dimensions, such as environmental scanning and action plans. Andrews in Chapter 2 identifies a lack of systematic attempts to explore the relative malleability of the environment, arguing that 'the extent to which environments are susceptible to the proactive influence of organizations would reveal much about the nature of public service improvement'. Entwistle suggests most studies offer just a snapshot of processes of collaboration when longitudinal outcome-related analyses could be more useful.

Finally, the chapters in this book identified the lack of public service-specific interpretations and measures of mechanisms of improvement. This was the case in Chapter 6, where Ashworth makes the case for typologies that accurately reflect the sub-cultural and occupational divisions prevalent within public service organizations, rather than those based upon private firms. In some cases, models of improvement, specific to the public sector, have been proposed and developed within this collection. For example, Gould Williams (Chapter 7) offers a public service HR model of which contains 'bundles' of HR practices, and incorporates both managerial and employee perspectives, whilst Walker develops his conceptualization of the combined influences on the diffusion of innovation, and subsequent impacts on performance in Chapter 8. The conclusions of these chapters suggest that a good theory of public service improvement is different from a private sector theory of improvement.

Finally, we need to further reflect on the different ways in which studies have interpreted public service improvement. Chapter 1 contained a lengthy discussion which highlighted alternative definitions and conceptualizations of service improvement and performance based on a combination of final outcomes, service outputs, processes, and practices. It is no surprise, then, that each of the chapters revealed that there are huge variations in the ways in which performance and service improvement have been conceptualised and measured. The model of public service improvement outlined in Chapter 1 incorporates the performance perceptions of many stakeholder groups—such as users and partner organizations—along with a variety of 'objective' measures of performance such as equity, efficiency, and quality. The studies reviewed for this collection include measures of performance that are based on perceptions, but they tend to be predominantly managerial views of performance, although it should be noted that the Cardiff studies of local government, along with those of Texas school districts, prove an exception, as they also incorporate other measures of performance. This is due to the availability of a wide range of longitudinal performance data produced for government in the United Kingdom and collected and verified by audit bodies. However, the objective performance measures used are efficiency or effectiveness indicators in the main. Quality is rarely addressed, and there are very few studies which assess impacts on equity.

This section has highlighted the fact that existing evidence on public service improvement is a little sparse, partial, and predominantly quantitative. However, it should be remembered that research on public service performance and improvement is fairly recent, and so it is unsurprising that the academic work conducted to date has not been extensive. The gaps in our knowledge of what improves public services, how and when, are important, and the next section on future research explores how these might be addressed.

Improving public services: a shared research agenda?

The lack of extensive research on the empirical validity of theories of service improvement presents two major causes for concern. The first centres on the core purpose of public management research, whilst the second relates to policy. The final section of this chapter addresses these two concerns by outlining an agenda for future research on public service improvement.

Each chapter in this collection reports research findings derived from a systematic review of empirical evidence on a particular theory of public service performance. The search terms for the review were extremely wide-ranging and included all aspects of effectiveness, public service performance, and improvement. Nevertheless, each chapter has commented on the lack of empirical evidence. Scholars of public management must surely hope that their work will lead to better policy-making, practice, or management which will in turn improve public services. Why is it, then, that so few studies are able to offer any evidence on public service improvement?

Andrews and Boyne (forthcoming) argue that public management research has a 'moral purpose', with academics entitled to use whatever data is available in order to shed light on determinants of improved public services and subsequent evidence derived from their studies acting as a 'check' on government reform programmes. If this is the case though, how can we ensure that future studies of the management of public service organizations make a firmer contribution to the debate on public service improvement? Every chapter in this collection has made a plea for additional research on aspects of public service improvement; more specifically, research that is longitudinal, cross-sectoral, and multi-methodological. However, there are a number of broader questions around organizational change and improvement which public management researchers might seek to address in the coming years.

The first is which internal organizational characteristics (culture, leadership, strategic planning) have the smallest and largest impact on performance, and which are more likely to change over time? Repeated attempts to change organizational culture may be futile, while focusing on strategic planning might prove to be more worthwhile. Secondly, it will be important to consider the determinants of organizational change in the public sector in order to ascertain whether central government reforms, institutional forces, or internal management actually drive change at all. Equally, it will be important to consider the positive (adaptive) versus negative (disruptive) impacts of change and reform. For example, cultural change programmes could be divisive and disruptive with little positive effect, whilst leadership might have a more positive impact. These all underline the need for longitudinal studies of improvement. A final question concerns the nature of contingencies that affects types of change. Is regulation more likely to lead to change if an organization's environment is stable, and is culture change more likely if a certain type of leader is in charge of an organization? Overall, it seems research that is likely to make a contribution to public service improvement needs to extend and elaborate on our understanding of whether, why and how public organizations change, and whether this has any subsequent impact on performance.

This collection also presents a challenge for policy-makers. Given the distinct lack of positive evidence supporting theories of public service improvement, why are practitioners and politicians investing considerable resources attempting to improve public services through cultural change, strong leadership, regulation, more partnership working, and continuous innovation? That leads us to question the nature and efficacy of the dialogue between academics and policy-makers engaged in driving public service reform. It may be that policy-makers are simply unaware of academic work on public service improvement or that they do not find it accessible, but it is vitally important that those designing and implementing public service change programmes are enlightened through a wider dissemination of research findings on what does and does not drive improvement. However, it seems that our observations provide an all too common illustration of the disjunct between academe and practice. The 'messy' nature of this relationship is well-documented (Davies et al. 2008), but we would lend our support to recent calls for a greater understanding of the factors that shape responses to, and uptake of, academic research (Meagher et al. 2008), and would argue that greater efforts need to be made to ensure that the government's attempts to improve public services are better informed by the growing body of academic work in this area.

Conclusion

This collection has examined the theoretical and empirical validity of a variety of mechanisms currently being used to generate improvements in public services. The extent of theoretical validity is generally strong, but varies across the improvement mechanisms. Strategic planning and the nature of an organization's environment can be logically and plausibly linked to improvement. However, for some mechanisms (collaboration and organizational learning) there was an absence of a clearly specified theoretical connection, and for others, such as innovation, leadership and HRM, greater adaptation is required in the transfer from private to public sector. In terms of empirical validity, our reviews of the evidence reveal that a munificent, simple, and stable organizational environment has a clear and positive impact on the improvement of public services, and that strategic planning, regulation, collaboration, and organizational learning are associated with public service improvement.

We have acknowledged that the existing work on public service improvement suffers from a series of limitations. However, this collection marks the first comprehensive attempt to evaluate the theoretical and empirical validity of theories of service improvement. Our conclusions demonstrate an urgent need for additional research which is cross-sectoral, comprehensive, multi-methodological, and longitudinal. Such work should seek to further investigate the various determinants of public service improvement. The results should then be effectively disseminated to those responsible for delivering improved performance across public services. The lack of empirical evidence is disappointing, but we need to remember that this is a new and developing field of academic research. However, the lack of firm evidence linking the various theories to public service improvement is more of a cause for concern, given that policy-makers across the world have spent over twenty years pushing and pulling these numerous mechanisms through successive reform programmes. On that basis, this collection challenges the international community of public management researchers to ensure that our future work makes a more comprehensive and robust contribution to this critical theoretical debate, and informs current and future public service reform programmes.

REFERENCES

Andrews, R. and Boyne, G. A. (forthcoming). Better public services: the moral purpose of public management research. *Public Management Review.*
Boyne, G.A. (2003). Sources of public service improvement: a critical review and research agenda. *Journal of Public Administration Research and Theory* 13(3), 367–394.

Davies, H., Nutley, S. and Walter, I. (2008). Why Knowledge Transfer is Misconceived for Applied Social Science Research. *Journal of Health Services Research and Policy* 13(3), 188–90.

Meagher, L., Lyall, C. and Nutley, S. (2008). Flows of Knowledge, expertise and influence: a method for assessing policy and practice impacts from social science research. *Research Evaluation* 17(3), 163–173.

⌑ INDEX

Figures, notes and tables are indexed in bold.

reverse causality 208
Reuer, J. J. 193
Rhodes, R. 65
Rhodes, R. A. W. 1
Riccucci, N. M. 83, 104
Rice, T. W. 28
Richards, C. 100
Richardson, R. 120, 129, 135, 138, 139
risk regulation 40
risk-taking 44, 89
Robert, G. 187, 188, 193
Roberts, P. W. 146
Robinson, Sir G. 82
Rodriguez, C. 177
Roering, W. 63
Rogers, E. 144, 145, 151, 156
Rogers, R. C. 83
Rollenhagen, C. 184
Romero-Fernandez, P. M. 125
Romzek, B. S. 176, 178
Rondeau, K. V. 129, 135
Rosenfeld, J. 198
Rost, J. C. 79, 80
Rothstein, H. 40
Rousseau, D. 111
Rowan, B. 17
Rowland, F. 186
Rowlands, R. O. 144, 146, 147, 152, 157
Rudd, P. 45, 50
Ruet, M. 146
rule of law 82
rural areas 21, 27
Rutt, S. 45, 50
Ryu, J. F. 149, 150, 151

Sabah, Y. 198
Sabatier, P. 165, 177
Saffold, G. 101
Salancik, G. R. 16, 83
Salvaggio, A. 125, 138
Sanchez-Gardey, G. 125
Sandelands, L. 21
Sanderson, I. 51
Sandfort, J. 178
Sanguk, K. 102
Sartori, G. 79

Savoie, D. J. 82
scale diseconomies 27
scale economies 19
scale rationale 164, 165
Scarbrough, H. 185
Schein, E. 99, 113
Schilling, M. A. 147
Schneider, B. 125, 138
Scholes, K. 16
Schön, D. 185
schools:
    Colombia 88–9
    culture 114
    England (inspection) 45, 50
    formal plans 70–1
    inspection 44, 45
    missions 68
    secondary 84, 91
    USA 16, 27, 30, 88, 91, 162, 214
Schuler, R. 123
Schulman, B. 174
Schultz, J. 65
scope diseconomies 27
scope rationale 165
Scotland 52
Scott, C. 36, 38, 41, 44, 53
Scott, T. 99, 100, 101, 103, 110, 111, 113, 114
Scott, W. R. 17
Scully, J. 129, 135, 139
Sebastian, J. G. 174
Selden, C. 103, 105, 106, 110, 113
Selden, S. C. 178
Selsky, J. W. 175
Selznick, P. 79, 80, 93
Senge, P. 187
service innovations 146–8, 155
service management 1, 7
service quality 22, 38, 41, 68, 72, 90, 115
Shah, S. M. 22
Sharkansky, I. 65
Shaw, I. 50
Shaw, M. 44
Shipston, S. 189
Shortell, S. M. 111, 163, 165, 170, 171, 173, 174, 176, 178